Deborah Cooper is a highly qualified naturopath and herbalist with a thriving practice in Sydney, and the mother of two. Co-author with Sandra Cabot of *The Body Shaping Diet*, she has many years of clinical experience helping and healing women. During her Australia-wide lecture tours and on her ABC radio program, Deborah has spoken to thousands of women about the use of traditional natural medicine.

Deborah Cooper has always been interested in issues that affect women and she sees her role as both a healer and an educator. Through this book and her lecture tours, she welcomes the opportunity to share her knowledge of women's health from her perspective as a natural therapist.

Women's
Health
in
Women's
Hands

DEBORAH COOPER

RANDOM HOUSE

AUSTRALIA

The information provided in this book is intended for general information and guidance only, and should not be used as a substitute for consulting a qualified health practitioner. Neither Deborah Cooper nor Random House Australia Pty Ltd can accept responsibility for your health or any side-effects of treatments described in this book.

Random House Australia Pty Ltd
20 Alfred Street, Milsons Point, NSW 2061

Sydney   New York   Toronto
London   Auckland   Johannesburg
and agencies throughout the world

First published in 1995
Copyright © Deborah Cooper 1995

National Library of Australia
Cataloguing-in-Publication Data

Cooper, Deborah, 1956– .
  Women's health in women's hands.

  Includes index.
  ISBN 0 09 183064 8.

  1. Women—Health and hygiene. 2. Self-care, Health.
  3. Naturopathy. 4. Herbs—Therapeutic use. I. Title.

613.04244

Designed by Catherine Martin
Illustrations by Amanda Upton
Cover photograph by Jenny van Sommers
Typeset by Midland Typesetters, Maryborough
Printed by Australian Print Group, Maryborough
Production by Vantage Graphics, Sydney

Contents

Acknowledgments

I
T IS the sharing of stories, experiences and information that makes a book like this possible. Thanks to all those women who have contributed to my gathering of knowledge.

My sincere thanks to my parents, Gwen and Derrick, for allowing me to follow my own destiny and for always believing in my ability. A special thank you to my sisters, Barbara, Dianne and Joanne, who are all strong and beautiful women. You have been a great source of encouragement while writing this book.

To Paul, for your ongoing support, love and friendship. Thank you for giving me the space to create and for all the times when you selflessly took on more than your share in caring for our family. You provided the type of support only a loving partner can give. To my son Daniel, thank you. All your patience, understanding and help is deeply appreciated. To my daughter Ki, thank you for your sense of humour.

A special thank you to Nancy Evelyn, for whom I have deep regard and admiration. You always managed to open a window to let in some light when my writing lost its purpose or direction.

I would also like to acknowledge the following people: Dr Oscar Horky and Caroline Riley for checking the manuscript. Thank you so much for your kindness. The staff at the Albion Street Clinic for providing me with useful information on HIV and AIDS as it relates to women. Bernadette Foley, my editor, for her inspiration, direction and expertise. Margaret Sullivan, my commissioning editor, for providing me with the opportunity to share information with other women.

Introduction

WOMEN'S *Health in Women's Hands* is a practical and positive guide to women's health. It provides useful information about what women can do to help themselves and offers a variety of options for achieving and maintaining good health. Through this book, women can gain access to knowledge about their bodies that is often difficult to acquire. They will learn to use food as medicine and discover that there are various simple self-help treatments for common ailments that are highly effective.

I have outlined many health options and combined traditional medicine with modern concepts in an attempt to bridge the gap between traditional and orthodox medicine and to give a balanced perspective. The traditional systems of medicine are those that have been handed down from generation to generation for centuries, while orthodox medicine is the more commonly accepted, Western medical model.

For a number of years I have worked in women's health clinics that use both systems. This has given me the opportunity to develop a sound understanding of the modern medical approach to women's health, which complements my role as a traditional therapist.

In this book I present current information that incorporates traditional medicine as it relates to women, dietary advice and practical self-help solutions to health problems. I have also included information on female anatomy and physiology in order to help women understand how their bodies function physically. I hope the book will assist you in developing the confidence required to engage in discussions with your health practitioner, enable you to make informed decisions regarding your health and to be comfortable with your choices.

Much of the traditional healing information I have provided has been shared with me by many women who have influenced the direction of my life and my work. *Women's Health in Women's Hands* is the medium through which I can pass on this knowledge to others.

I have had discussions with, and listened to, thousands of women and I understand the issues that affect them. My own experiences have taught me many lessons about life as a woman, and have no doubt influenced my commitment to helping others.

On lecture tours to parts of rural Australia I have talked with women who live in isolated areas, who are very interested in the practical self-help and preventative approach that traditional medicine has to offer. Many of these women continue to write to me and ring me for advice.

I understand the frustration and despair they often feel at the lack of health services for women living in country areas. They know there are alternatives to the orthodox medical model but they do not have easy access to this information. When I first started working as a natural therapist, in a country town in northern New South Wales, 90 per cent of the people who came to see me were women. They were seeking women's health information with a view toward self-help and prevention of illness. Many were very interested in effective alternatives to drug therapy and surgical intervention, and they preferred that it came from another woman.

Like many rural areas of Australia, there was no women's health centre, no women's health nurse, and at that time, only one female doctor working full time. In hindsight, we were lucky to have her. In a recent phone conversation with a friend who still lives in that area, I was told that this woman was the first doctor who had asked to examine her breasts, so that my friend had her first breast examination at age 35.

While there are some good general practitioners, it is often difficult to find one who has a thorough understanding of all the options available to women. Slowly, women are changing a system that has been dominated by male doctors who did not have a passionate or committed interest in women's health. This was supported by an education system and community attitudes that encouraged privileged boys to become doctors and lawyers, while girls could set their sights on becoming school teachers, nurses and housewives. We are now moving towards a more balanced system where women are once again taking control of their own health care.

It is time to put women's health back into women's hands.

Your Choices in Health Care

WOMEN supported each other in pregnancy and childbirth for centuries, until modern obstetric procedures took over. When this occurred, many women relinquished their power or they had it taken away from them. Midwives were replaced with male doctors and obstetricians, and anaesthetics, stirrups and forceps deliveries became routine.

Today more women are studying health sciences and we have access to information and services from many different systems of medicine. For too long we have been led to believe that orthodox Western medicine is the only effective system available to us. In fact, it is only one system of medicine among many others.

There are numerous treatment options available that can restore and maintain health for women, and it is possible to achieve a harmony and balance within the body using non-invasive methods. Women can choose from acupuncture, herbalism, homoeopathy, massage therapy and other bodywork techniques, ayurveda (an ancient healing system from India), aromatherapy, nutrition, Bach Flower remedies, colour therapy, crystal therapy, naturopathy, emotional release work and reflexology. These are all natural systems of medicine that have been shown to be effective therapies for many health imbalances experienced by women.

It is possible to work in a complementary way and combine different systems of medicine. For instance, if surgery has been necessary, women will benefit from the assistance of their natural therapist who will provide a treatment program to speed healing processes and hasten recovery.

A fundamental difference between most traditional therapies and orthodox medicine is that the traditional therapist's aim is to restore a person's vital energy using natural methods to assist the body's ability to overcome disease. They have a general philosophy of treating the whole person and work to assist your body's natural healing power, rather than against it.

The orthodox medical approach is to treat the symptoms of disease and hope that the vitality will return. In doing so, there is a danger of keeping patients in a sickness mode by failing to address the underlying cause. Orthodox medicine achieves its best results in the treatment of acute, life-threatening disorders, bacterial infections and serious injuries. I acknowledge that drug therapy or surgical intervention is necessary at times, and may even save your life. It is important however, to only use these forms of therapy when they are really needed. Women should be aware of the processes involved and any harmful outcomes, such as the long-term side effects of drug therapy.

Your body generally lets you know when things aren't right and if you pay attention and act swiftly, you will be able to restore your health with minimal intervention. If your body needs added help to regain balance, and some form of medicine is required, it is beneficial to consult with an accredited natural therapist who has the expertise to diagnose the cause of the imbalance and provide an effective treatment program.

Traditional therapy has withstood the test of time and it has an important role in women's health care today.

Women as healers

Women have had to fight hard for all their achievements in their own health care and it must be acknowledged that the feminist movement has been responsible for initiating many positive health reforms. In the provision of services and policy making, women have been able to initiate some valuable changes such as education reforms, cancer screening, developing women's health centres and rape crisis centres, but we still have a long way to go.

While we still have a majority of doctors, gynaecologists and obstetricians who are men, it is not surprising that many women feel embarrassed, vulnerable and humiliated during routine medical procedures that involve the handling and penetration of intimate parts of their bodies. Most routine examinations are uncomfortable, invasive and often unnecessary, and because sexism within the orthodox medical system has kept women ignorant about their bodies, they often feel powerless to question the need for such procedures.

Many cities and towns do not have women's health centres and so there is a danger that a large number of women avoid having annual Pap smears and breast examinations because of this lack of services and previous negative experiences.

It should come as no surprise that women prefer to deal with women when discussing personal aspects of their health. They are more likely to feel safe and comfortable in the company of another woman, especially as some are survivors of domestic violence, rape and sexual abuse.

Traditionally, women from many different cultural and religious backgrounds have gathered together in small groups to exchange experiences and share information with one another. These gatherings gave women an opportunity to talk freely among themselves. Women generally communicate well together and part of this exchange involved the sharing of health information.

It is so important to continue this tradition and establish more women's health clinics where women can openly discuss intimate aspects of their health with other women. We have a long and proud history as healers and by sharing information we not only improve our health, we also guarantee the survival of traditional health practices for women.

The natural therapist today

The term natural therapist refers to those health practitioners who use natural, drugless systems of medicine, and there are many women today who benefit from their advice. It is an umbrella term that encompasses a range of traditional and modern healing techniques. In choosing a therapist, it is important to enquire as to whether they are an accredited member of a professional body. For instance, the Australian Traditional Medicine Society or the National Herbalists Association have registers of members who are well-trained health professionals. They work by a strict code of ethics and have undertaken lengthy studies in both natural therapies and compulsory science subjects that often include anatomy and physiology, biochemistry, differential diagnosis, nutrition and pharmacognosy. They know how to take a thorough medical history and are trained in many modern and traditional diagnostic techniques and procedures.

It is illegal for a natural therapist to call themselves a doctor, however it is not illegal for a doctor to call themselves a natural therapist. Be wary of

3

doctors who refer to themselves as 'naturopathic' because there are only a few who have taken the time to complete the necessary studies required to advise people about such things as nutritional therapy or herbal medicines. Ask them where they trained, for how long and to what association they belong. You can always check by ringing the association yourself and you can find out if there are any other good therapists in your area.

A naturopath is trained in a variety of health sciences that often include nutritional therapy, massage therapy, herbal medicine and homoeopathy. While the other therapies are self-explanatory, I should explain that homoeopathy is a non-toxic form of medicine based on the concept that 'like cures like'. For instance, homoeopaths would use a remedy made from onions to treat hayfever symptoms of streaming eyes and a runny nose. In other words, that which would cause a set of symptoms to occur in its crude form is given in a medicinal form to treat those same symptoms. These are safe remedies and it is possible to use them for self-help, although best results will be achieved by consulting with a homoeopath.

Nutritional therapy involves working with food and nutrients as medicine. Nutritionists and naturopaths are trained in this field. Doctors only study nutrition briefly as part of their medical degree and often have very limited knowledge of nutritional medicine.

Keep in mind that a lot of time and money can be wasted by self-medicating with over-the-counter preparations, and if you do purchase vitamin and mineral supplements, do not exceed the recommended dosage provided by the manufacturer. It is provided for your safety. Many minerals and fat-soluble vitamins are stored in your body and can build up to a toxic level if dosages are not strictly adhered to. Nutrients interact in the body and if any one nutrient is taken in extremely high levels, it may lead to a deficiency of another. For example, high zinc levels can deplete iron stores in women. Also, some nutrients are absorbed better when they are provided in very small amounts. When it comes to vitamin and mineral therapy, more is not always better. Seek professional advice before commencing nutritional supplements.

With the exception of herbal teas, I do not recommend that people self-medicate with herbs. They are medicines after all, and some plants can be poisonous. They should only be prescribed by qualified and accredited herbalists who are well trained in prescribing traditional medicines with accuracy and safety.

In this book I have listed some herbal remedies that are effective in treating women's health imbalances. I included them in order to demonstrate the role of traditional herbal medicine as it relates to women's health. You will not be able to purchase many of these medicines, however you can consult with a practitioner of herbal medicine who can dispense them in combination to meet your individual requirements.

PART 1

CYCLES, RHYTHMS and BALANCE

A Healthy
Menstrual Cycle

DEVELOPING an awareness of your menstrual cycle is a fundamental step towards maintaining harmony and balance within your body.

So many negative attitudes have surrounded menstruation in the past and much of the literature on women's health available today still focuses on the downside of being a woman. We are led to believe that it is normal to experience the discomfort of period pain, clotting, vaginal dryness and premenstrual tension. They are all part of a woman's lot! While it is no surprise that some women experience these symptoms, it is distressing that they suffer without knowing that these disorders can be remedied so easily without harmful chemicals or surgical intervention.

In this section I will share what I have learned about women's health and I will explain how traditional therapy and diet can help to correct menstrual imbalances. It is also important to understand that in order to correct and prevent menstrual irregularities we may need to deal with any negative attitudes we have about ourselves as women and begin to feel positive and comfortable with our menstruation. Bear in mind that poor self-image influences not only our emotional health but also our physical health.

How can we feel positive about our sexuality and reproductive function when so many of us have been made to feel unclean when we are menstruating? In some cultures women are barred from entry into places of worship and from preparing food for others during menstruation.

Young girls should not have to feel punished during menstruation by being discouraged from swimming or playing sport. Many women still feel the need to hide napkins and tampons or dispose of them secretly so no-one can see. Hopefully, with education, negative attitudes and myths about menstruation will change or disappear, and women must take the lead in bringing about this change.

While it is understandable to feel inconvenienced if menstruation coincides with travel arrangements, or disappointment if we desired a pregnancy, women should not feel embarrassed or uncomfortable about this very natural female function. In many cultures the onset of menstruation is a time for celebration. It is a symbol of fertility and a distinguishing feature of womanhood.

Ultimately, menstruation is a very personal aspect of femininity. If we begin to think in a positive way about menstruation we will find that there are many women who enjoy their period and actually look forward to it. They explain that they like the way their breasts become firmer, they feel more creative or they become more in touch with their inner selves.

When we are able to accept and flow with the rhythm of our cycle, we allow ourselves to experience the wonderful sense of release that occurs on many levels which can be incredibly satisfying.

Creating balance

Experiencing a regular menstrual cycle without any discomfort is an indication of a healthy body that is in tune with nature and, like everything in nature, it is intended to be balanced.

When women experience irregularities in their menstrual cycle it is usually attributed to some type of imbalance that may be dietary, emotional or physiological. In the quest to regulate or improve your menstrual cycle, you may discover that you need to rebalance other aspects of yourself. For instance, if you lead a busy, stressful life, you will need to balance that with some form of relaxation. Otherwise your period may become erratic due to ongoing high stress levels.

Your reproductive system is interrelated to many other body systems and these are all sensitive to your emotional state. Try not to dwell entirely on your physical self but look at yourself as a whole person. The naturopathic approach to healing acknowledges the importance of the mind–body connection and this is what we are referring to in the term wholistic health. Adopting a wholistic approach to your health is the most effective way to discover what really alters your body's homoeostasis or equilibrium.

Before you can restore your body's delicate balance you will need to become aware of yourself both emotionally and physically. Your emotional state will influence your physical condition and equally, changes in your body will influence your emotional state. Take the time to tune in and observe your emotional and physical patterns and develop a greater understanding of your body and its intricate cycles and rhythms. It helps to keep a diary in which you can chart your menstrual pattern and record your feelings.

Try not to dwell completely on the negative aspects of menstruation, even though they can feel overwhelming at times. Instead, maintain a balanced approach by placing equal importance on the positive and negative changes throughout your cycle. After a few months you will have a greater knowledge of yourself and your cycle. It will reveal your times of strength and confidence, as well as those times when you may feel more sensitive or vulnerable. This knowledge will help you to utilise your positive and creative energies and show you when you should try to avoid confrontation and stressful situations.

Menstrual rhythms

The menstruation process is sensitive to many emotional and physical influences. Although it is in a constant state of change, it still flows with a definite base rhythm. A woman's natural menstrual cycle will often correspond with the phases of the moon and average around 28 days. In nature, as the moon is waxing (becoming full), the tides become higher and the nutrients in plants rise to the leaves and flowers, making them ideal for harvesting. Many women around the world are also influenced by the moon's phases and, just like the tides and the plants, their body fluids and secretions are very much affected by lunar changes. This is understandable given that the term menstrual is derived from the Latin word *mensis* which means moon or month.

Not every woman, however, will experience a regular 28-day cycle. Many women have shorter cycles of around 21 days and others bleed every 32 days. When a long or short cycle occurs regularly, it is considered to be a normal pattern and what is normal for one woman can be totally different for another.

The delicate balance of menstruation is strongly influenced by hormonal changes, but our bodies can be sensitive to many other influences too. For example, it is not unusual to find women who work or live together whose cycles may eventually become synchronised and they bleed at the same time. Air travel can alter your cycle as can excessive exercise, dietary changes and emotional stress.

Taking an oral contraceptive pill or undergoing hormone therapy interferes with your natural rhythms because these types of therapy take over from your own hormone secretions. The body detects these chemicals in the bloodstream and is tricked into thinking it is manufacturing the hormones itself. When this happens the ovaries receive no stimulation and cease to function. They will not function normally again until the synthetic hormones are completely out of your system. When you take synthetic hormones your body can be adversely affected, sometimes permanently, so it is important to think carefully about whether you really need them and what the possible side effects will be.

Occasionally synthetic hormones are required and may be tolerated by some women. This, of course, will depend on the type of hormone given, how it is administered (injection, tablet, patch or implant), the dosage and the individual's ability to break it down. It will usually take about three to six weeks for your body to regulate itself once you cease taking synthetic hormones.

One of the main causes of fluctuations in menstrual patterns is positive or negative stress that tends to make your period late. If the stress is severe the cycle may stop altogether but once the stress is alleviated it usually returns to normal. There are times when it is very natural and healthy for menstruation to be absent, for example, during pregnancy, lactation and menopause. If a woman skips a period occasionally, there is no need for concern but if it is ongoing it may require further investigation.

From clinical experience I have found that women with shorter cycles often express a desire for a longer cycle. Just as one bleeding cycle finishes, another begins. If they have premenstrual tension in the week before their period, they may feel overwhelmed by menstruation. A 28-day cycle gives them more space between periods and often helps to reduce emotional distress.

Women with a long cycle can experience a build-up of tension and feel more bloated and congested before menstruation. They usually feel better once their period arrives because it provides a release. In these instances, traditional herbal medicine and dietary changes can be used to balance and regulate menstruation. After five or six weeks any unpleasant aspects of menstruation have usually been corrected.

Naturally, if a woman is happy with her cycle there is no need to intervene. Although it is considered normal to have a cycle that varies from 21 to 35 days in duration, I feel it is desirable to have close to a 28-day cycle. It is often a good indication that your hormonal and reproductive functions are balanced. It also makes it easier to predict fertile times and I have observed that women with a regular monthly cycle generally have less menstrual distress.

Self-examination

Until recently, routine vaginal examinations had always been shrouded in mystery. I clearly remember the first time I was shown how to examine my own cervix. I was with a small group of women who were studying natural therapies and we were learning about gynaecology. We were a little nervous but nevertheless comfortable with each other and there was certainly no pressure to participate if we felt the need for privacy. I found it very interesting to see my cervix and I remember thinking how ridiculous it was that most women never had an opportunity to find out what this part of their body looked like.

The cervix is about 2 centimetres long and is located high inside your vagina. It is the entrance to the uterus and is actually part of the uterine muscle that surrounds your womb and extends into your vagina. If you feel inside your vagina with your finger it will feel like a firm, fleshy knob, a bit like the end of your nose, with a small dimple in its centre.

It has a small hole in the centre called the *os* and the passage from the os to the uterus is known as the *cervical canal*. The os remains fairly tight in women who are not pregnant but it has the capacity to stretch wide enough to allow a baby's head to pass through during childbirth. Despite its ability to stretch, there is no risk of a finger, penis or foreign object passing through it. The cervix has no nerve endings and you only feel pressure when it is touched or bumped during intercourse or a Pap smear. Mucus is produced in the cervical canal and this changes in texture according to hormonal secretions. During the fertile times of our cycle, the os dilates or widens a little to allow sperm to enter and swim through to the fallopian tubes. The os is also the outlet for our menstrual bleeding.

Not every woman will share my interest, enthusiasm or curiosity but if you are interested in looking at your cervix, ask to be shown during your next vaginal examination. Most practitioners or women's health workers are happy to show you. Alternatively, you can examine your own cervix easily using a disposable speculum from a chemist or women's health centre, a mirror and a torch. There is no danger of injuring yourself during self-examination because you have complete control over the entire process.

Lie back in a semi-seated position on the floor or bed with a cushion behind you to support your back. With your knees bent slightly and flopped sideways a little you can insert the closed speculum inside your vagina with the handle facing upwards or slide it in sideways and then turn it. You may need to moisten it a little with some lubricating jelly if you feel dry. When you open the speculum you will feel it click several times and then lock into place. This will not be painful and you will have full control. The speculum separates the vaginal walls and will hold them back enabling you to view your cervix, which usually looks pink and wet, by holding a mirror at the entrance and shining the torch into the mirror at the same time, for illumination. It is normal to see secretions that range from clear and slippery to creamy, white and thick. If you have thrush it will appear as small white lumps or curds. With practise it becomes easy to view your cervix and by doing this regularly you will soon learn what is normal for you. This also enables you to benefit from early detection should any abnormal changes occur that warrant further investigation by your health practitioner. You can remove the speculum in either an open or closed position. Never share your speculum and always wash it well and sterilise it with tea-tree oil, antiseptic or alcohol after use.

How hormones influence our bodies

Hormones are chemical messengers that are secreted into our body fluids by a cell or groups of cells. The basic function of all hormones is to maintain equilibrium in the body by changing the activities of cells. They may stimulate changes in the cells of an organ or a group of organs, an example being the growth of our uterine lining under the influence of oestrogen, or they may stimulate all the cells of the body, such as our thyroid hormones do. Their specific action is dependent on the nature of the hormone, and although they influence our body, they are controlled by other factors. Our hormonal system works in conjunction with our nervous system and both of these important control systems either stimulate or inhibit the flow of nerve impulses and hormonal secretions. In order for these systems to function well they must work together in harmony rather than pull in opposite directions. Once again we see how intricately balanced our body systems are and how important it is to take a wholistic approach to our health.

When hormones are secreted into our body fluids, they compete for receptor sites found on the surface of cells or inside cells. Once they lock into the receptor sites, they initiate a chain of specific reactions.

There are three main areas in the body that produce hormones to control reproduction. The first is the hypothalamus that is situated at the base of the brain. It acts as a collection centre for signals that it receives from various sources in the body. It is generally concerned with the body's wellbeing. It gathers information and uses it to control secretions in the pituitary gland, which is the second area to produce hormones. When it wants to stimulate the pituitary, it secretes the hormone GnRH (Gonadotrophin releasing hormone). The pituitary gland is less than 1 centimetre in diameter and it also lies at the base of the brain. It is sensitive to GnRH and under its influence, will release hormones to stimulate ovarian activity. The ovaries are the third area to produce reproductive hormones.

Let's take a look at the various ways our female sex hormones affect our bodies.

OESTROGEN

The hormone oestrogen develops and maintains our female reproductive structures, in particular the endometrial lining of the uterus and our breasts. It primarily causes the tissue growth and cell proliferation that occurs in specific areas of the body.

There are three main types of oestrogens produced in our bodies: oestradiol, oestrone and oestriol. The main oestrogen secreted by the ovaries is oestradiol and it is considered to have a more potent effect in the body than the others. Oestrone is secreted in smaller amounts from the adrenals, however it still has an important role, particularly during menopause when ovarian function decreases. Oestriol is a by-product of both oestrone and oestradiol that is produced primarily in the liver.

Oestrogen is responsible for our secondary sex characteristics including the fat distribution to our breasts, abdomen, pubic mound, labia, hips, buttocks and thighs, giving us our feminine curves. It is also stored within the fatty tissue in these areas. It causes our pelvis to widen, influences the pattern of our pubic hair, enlarges our fallopian tubes, uterus and vagina during puberty and influences the pitch of our voice, making it higher.

While it initiates the growth of our breasts and milk-producing ducts, oestrogen does not cause the breasts to produce milk. The hormones progesterone and prolactin are responsible for this function.

Oestrogen maintains the health of the vaginal lining and is responsible

15

for increased glucose production in vaginal tissue. It causes our cervix to soften, the os to dilate, or widen, and changes our cervical mucus, making it thin and stretchy, like the white of an egg. This prepares our internal environment for fertility, making the vagina sperm-friendly and opening the channels that allow the sperm to swim through for possible fertilisation of the released ovum.

Oestrogen helps to maintain our bone density by increasing osteoblast activity (osteoblasts deposit bone into our skeleton). It also affects our fluid and electrolyte balance and helps to retain the moisture in our skin and causes it to become more vascular. You may have noticed that women will often bleed more than men if they cut themselves.

PROGESTERONE

Progesterone is referred to as the hormone of maturation or development and it works with oestrogen to prepare the uterus for a possible pregnancy. It also prepares the inner lining of our fallopian tubes by promoting secretory changes to provide nutrition for the ovum as it travels to the uterus for implantation. Increased progesterone production during the secretory phase in the second half of our cycle creates changes in our breast tissue and tends to make our breasts slightly larger and firmer just before menstrual bleeding. This is because progesterone stimulates breast cells, causing them to enlarge and increase.

These changes occur in order to prepare our breasts for milk secretion. However breast milk will not be produced unless our breasts are further stimulated by another hormone called prolactin which, under normal circumstances, will only be released during pregnancy.

Progesterone can stimulate the appetite, causing us to feel increasingly hungry before our period and it can also raise our body temperature. It influences our kidneys to retain salt and water and this explains why we can weigh slightly more in the second half of our cycle and less after menstrual bleeding, when progesterone levels are low. It is natural for women to experience weight fluctuations of 1 to 2 kilograms due to hormonal ebbs and flows throughout the cycle. As progesterone levels increase in the second half of the cycle, it reduces the growth and glucose production in the vaginal lining and causes the os to tighten. The cervix itself changes in tone and becomes firmer. At the same time progesterone changes our cervical mucus to a thick and sticky consistency which plugs the cervix and makes it impenetrable to sperm. This seals the uterus to protect the possible embryo and is a natural contraceptive mechanism.

ANDROGENS

The word *androgen* is a collective term for sex hormones that are produced in large quantities by males. Both men and women have these hormones in their bodies but they are found in different amounts. Our adrenal glands secrete at least five different types of androgens, however the levels are very low and they do not normally cause masculine characteristics in women.

TESTOSTERONE

Testosterone is one of the androgenic hormones that is produced in small quantities through the adrenal glands and the ovaries in women. It has an important role in our sexuality as it helps with libido, although it is important to note that sexual desire is also increased by oestrogen, psychic stimulation and physical contact.

Excess testosterone that is not used in our bodies is broken down in the liver and excreted through the intestinal tract in bile or through the kidneys in our urine.

Androgenic hormones are produced in greater levels from about ten to thirteen years of age and rarely cause problems because oestrogens dampen their effects. After menopause when oestrogen levels drop, the androgenic hormones also start to slowly decline.

FOLLICLE STIMULATING HORMONE (FSH)

This hormone produced in the pituitary gland, stimulates the resting follicles in the ovaries to maturity during the first two weeks of the menstrual cycle. As the follicles mature they produce increased levels of oestrogen.

LUTEINISING HORMONE (LH)

This hormone is released from the pituitary gland just prior to ovulation under the influence of oestrogen. It triggers the release of the ovum from its follicle and stimulates the outer follicular cells to produce progesterone.

PROLACTIN

Prolactin is secreted by glands in the pituitary in response to a hormone called Prolactin Releasing Factor (PRF) and it is produced during pregnancy and also in quite large amounts during lactation. The main function of prolactin is to initiate and maintain milk secretion by our mammary glands.

Just before menstrual bleeding, when oestrogen and progesterone levels decline, our blood levels of prolactin rise slightly due to a fall in another hormone, Prolactin Inhibiting Factor (PIF), secreted by the hypothalamus, which inhibits prolactin release. This does not usually have any significant effect on the breasts because as soon as the cycle recommences and oestrogen levels start to rise again, PIF is released and prolactin levels drop.

PROSTAGLANDINS

Prostaglandins are made from fatty acids and are present in many of our body tissues. They are manufactured in small quantities in cell membranes and once they are secreted into the bloodstream they become highly potent substances. Prostaglandins mimic hormones, however they do not travel far in the blood. Instead they influence the surrounding tissues in their immediate area. They are stimulated by progesterone in the second half of the menstrual cycle. Prostaglandins have a number of important functions and have a variety of effects in our bodies. They are present in our menstrual blood and can either stimulate or prevent uterine contractions.

Some prostaglandins inflame tissue while others reduce inflammation. To keep the right balance of anti-inflammatory prostaglandins in our bodies we need to include the correct types of fatty acids in our diet. Sources include evening primrose oil, star flower oil, olive oil, fish oil and linseed oil.

How diet influences menstruation

Many studies have been undertaken that show the relationship between dietary intake and menstrual flow. There is no doubt that nutritional deficiencies affect menstruation and this can be demonstrated when women with severe iron deficiency fail to menstruate (amenorrhoea). Eating certain foods in excess has also been shown to create changes in the colour, odour and the amount of menstrual bleeding. The most common offending foods are overcooked meat, processed meats, eggs, cheese and some highly refined starches and sugars (white flour and white sugar products). Studies show that undigested proteins and chemicals from these foods can create a toxic overload in the blood that may contribute to pelvic congestion.

Another problem is created if you eat a large amount of highly processed food that is lacking in fibre. This overloads digestion and your system becomes sluggish, leading to constipation and the development of bowel pockets that can trap food and faeces. When the bowel becomes impacted and food is trapped, it tends to putrefy, allowing toxic matter to seep through the intestinal wall and affect the surrounding tissues and nearby organs. Due to the close proximity of the uterus, it is possible that toxins in the blood will seek an outlet through menstrual elimination. This can lead to greater inflammation and congestion in the uterus which may be felt as pain and spasm or heaviness and congestion. It has been suggested that women do not have adequate lymphatic channels in the uterus to deal with the removal of waste products and so we tend to store them within the endometrial tissue, resulting in possible inflammation or irritation.

To keep this problem in perspective, I would suggest that this is dependent on an individual's ability to breakdown and metabolise certain proteins in food. For example, some people do not produce adequate enzymes to digest dairy products and suffer gastrointestinal distress if they eat from this food group. Other people have highly efficient digestive systems and suffer no consequences from eating full-cream dairy products.

It has been observed that excessively high levels of protein in the diet can lead to a heavier bleed, while a vegetarian diet tends to produce a lighter flow. Decide for yourself whether you would benefit from following a vegetarian diet. If you suffer from painful periods it is certainly worth a try.

Recent studies reported in *New Scientist*, July 1994, have highlighted the benefits to women from the addition of soy products and foods that contain phyto-oestrogens (plant oestrogens) to their diet. These foods have the ability to correct hormonal imbalance and can influence our reproductive health.

A vegetarian diet will generally contain more foods that are naturally high in plant oestrogens, and these can help to reduce heavy bleeding in women who have very high oestrogen levels. They are weaker forms of oestrogen and they dilute the effects of the more powerful oestrogens by competing for receptor sites (*see* 'Menopause').

If you have no food allergies or intolerances you should be able to eat from a broad range of foods as long as you select those that are close to nature and free of harmful chemicals. By drinking plenty of fresh water, eating an abundance of fresh vegetables, cereals and grains and a moderate amount of fruit every day, it is unlikely that your diet will adversely affect your menstrual flow. Include with this a small amount of protein daily, selected from legumes, nuts and seeds, soy products, lean meats, fish or low-fat dairy products (if tolerated).

If you drink alcohol then do so in moderation because alcohol has been shown to increase inflammation generally in the body and may exacerbate pelvic congestion.

Restoring the balance with herbal medicine

From my own clinical experience I know how effective traditional herbal medicine is in the treatment of women's health irregularities. Many plants have been used by women for centuries to improve and balance their health. The herbs are generally given in a specific combination according to need and if they are taken regularly, positive results will be noticed fairly quickly. Some women find that lasting results occur after taking herbs for about three months, however this will differ according to the nature of the health problem. For instance, the treatment for endometriosis will tend to be slow because not only do we have to rebalance the hormones and assist ovarian function, we have to alleviate pain, inflammation and also breakdown adhesive tissue and cysts. This is quite a task but it can be done and obviously it is going to take some time.

Herbal medicine has a different effect on the body than synthetic hormones because herbs have a special affinity with certain areas of the body and tend to do their work at an organ level, restoring normal function and balance. The specific action of the herb is very dependent on the properties within the plant itself.

HERBS TO REGULATE THE CYCLE

The following herbs are available from qualified practitioners of herbal medicine only. Do not self-medicate. This information is provided to help you develop an understanding of how herbalists use these remedies as they relate to women's health.

CHASTE TREE, *Vitex agnus castus*: research shows that chaste tree will help to correct progesterone deficiencies that can lead to breakthrough bleeding, miscarriage or subfertility. When progesterone levels increase from taking this herb, women find their cycle may be longer and they can experience a reduction in premenstrual symptoms.

DAMIANA, *Turnera aphrodisiaca*: a reliable pituitary regulator that can reduce FSH levels during perimenopause. It has an aphrodisiac effect, as its botanical name suggests, and it acts as an antidepressant.

FALSE UNICORN ROOT, *Chamaelirium luteum*: this is referred to as a female corrective herb. It acts as a tonic to restore normal reproductive function. False unicorn is a bitter herb that contains plant oestrogens.

KELP, BLADDERWRACK, *Fucus vesiculosus*: has an affinity with the thyroid gland where it exerts a regulating action. It is a natural source of iodine.

PULSATILLA, PASQUE FLOWER, *Anemone pulsatilla*: good for correcting long cycles.

SHEPHERDS PURSE, *Capsella bursa*: will help to lengthen a short cycle of 21 to 23 days to 25 to 28 days. It regulates hormonal secretions and can correct a heavy menstrual flow or haemorrhage due to its vitamin K content and astringent action.

SOME HERBS THAT CONTAIN PROGESTERONES

CHASTE TREE, *Vitex agnus castus*: (*see above*).

LICORICE, *Glycyrrhiza glabra*: in high levels licorice has a progestogenic effect.

SARSAPARILLA, *Smilax officianalis*: the root of the sarsaparilla plant contains both progesterone and testosterone, which is why it has been traditionally used to treat sexual problems.

WILD YAM, *Dioscorea villosa*: contains a number of plant hormones.

SOME HERBS THAT CONTAIN OESTROGEN

ALFALFA, *Medicago sativa*: you can obtain oestrogens from eating the sprouted seeds of this herb.

BLACK COHOSH, *Cimicifuga racemosa*: high in oestrogen.

FALSE UNICORN ROOT, *Chamaelirium luteum*: (*see above*).

RED CLOVER, *Trifolium pratense*: contains plant oestrogens and is a very useful herb for many women's health problems.

ANDROGENIC (TESTOSTERONE) HERBS

DAMIANA, *Turnera aphrodisiaca*: (*see* page 20).

KOREAN GINSENG, *Panax ginseng*: a very powerful herb that contains steroid substances.

SARSAPARILLA, *Smilax officianalis*: (*see above*).

SAW PALMETTO, *Serenoa serrulata*: contains steroid substances that makes it a useful herb for hormonal disorders.

Menstrual bleeding is a very physical process, therefore if we desire to change an irregular cycle, we need to use very physical remedies such as plant remedies or nutritional supplements and dietary changes. Remedies that are not so physical are homoeopathic remedies and acupuncture, which can also be effective treatments but are best described as medicines of energy.

In my opinion, no other form of natural therapy will yield results as quickly as herbal medicines for the treatment of menstrual imbalance. Women are often amazed at how soon their cycle responds when they take traditional herbal medicines for this purpose.

Physiology of the menstrual cycle

By increasing your knowledge of your anatomy and physiology, you will improve your understanding of how your body functions at a physical level and this will enable you to take a more active role in consultations with your health practitioner. It will give you the confidence to make informed choices regarding your health and above all, to be comfortable with your decisions.

In nature we have the four elements of earth, fire, wind and water and throughout the year we have four seasons. During our menstrual cycle we experience the following four phases.

MENSTRUAL PHASE—SHEDDING OF THE ENDOMETRIAL LINING

On average, women begin a new cycle every 28 days and the start of menstrual bleeding is the beginning of each new cycle. We refer to the initial day of bleeding as Day 1 of the cycle and during the menstrual phase we will shed approximately two thirds of our endometrial (uterine) lining and one third will remain. In the absence of a pregnancy the lining collapses and is discharged from the uterus over a period of three to seven days. Some women will experience a shorter cycle and some may have a slightly longer one.

The flow may be light or heavy depending on hormonal secretions and how thick the endometrial lining has become. If ovulation has not occurred you may not produce enough progesterone in the second half of your cycle to control your bleeding, which can lead to a heavier flow. If oestrogen levels are low, you may only develop a very thin lining which will result in a light menstrual flow.

Usually the bleeding will be slow and dark in colour for the first few hours. The colour may range from brownish to dark red, then bright red for the next one to two days. The flow will usually slow down after this and become darker in colour again until the end of your menstrual bleed. It is not unusual for your menses (bleeding) to stop overnight and recommence during the day when you are more active.

The discharge during menstruation is made up of blood, vaginal and cervical secretions and the liquefied endometrial lining. This liquefied lining contains substances that prevent blood clotting. If your flow is very fast you may experience some clotting. You may notice pieces of tissue coming away that are often mistaken for blood clots, however this is part of a normal menstrual loss.

It is not unusual for women to have a looser bowel movement just before menstruation because the hormone relaxin is produced before bleeding and it can have a relaxing effect on the musculature of the bowel.

PRE-OVULATORY OR OESTROGEN PHASE

Once the menstrual lining has been shed, the cells lining the uterus increase rapidly and this causes the endometrial lining to thicken due to the influence of oestrogen, which is secreted in increased quantities by the follicles in the ovaries during the first two weeks of the new cycle.

The pre-ovulatory phase is when your body begins to become fertile again. During this phase, the follicles and ova start to ripen in the ovaries, prior to ovulation.

We are born with around 350,000 ovum or eggs in each of our ovaries and they remain in a resting state until sometime during our teenage years when we begin to ovulate. They are inactive during pregnancy and breast-feeding when women stop menstruating for long stretches of time.

Not all of the eggs are utilised in our bodies and from birth to menopause immature ova are constantly breaking down or disintegrating while others may be defective, and only one of the ten to twenty ova that begin to mature each month will survive. During our entire reproductive years we may only develop and expel about 450 of these ova.

Your pituitary gland releases Follicle Stimulating Hormone (FSH), which travels to the ovaries and stimulates one of the follicles to ripen and release an egg. The follicle that grows fastest is usually the one that will be successful because it will have more cells to attract the FSH when it is released from the pituitary.

During this phase the ovum enlarges and cells surrounding it multiply and produce fluid that separates them from each other. Ovarian cells outside the follicular membrane multiply and become packed together to form a capsule for the follicle, which will grow to about 1 to 2 centimetres in size. The cells in the inner layers of this capsule produce more oestrogen as the follicle matures. When the follicle has reached maturity it is full of fluid and bulges from the surface of the ovary. The complete development of the follicle takes about fourteen days and as it matures it produces higher levels of oestrogen. We call this the growth phase and it usually occurs from Day 6 to Day 14 of your cycle.

Stress can interfere with the release of FSH and this is why your period may stop or become irregular if you are experiencing emotional pressure. Physical stress, which includes excessive exercise, crash diets, eating disorders or illness, can also cause irregularities in your cycle.

OVULATORY PHASE

About 36 hours before ovulation takes place the anterior pituitary gland secretes an increased amount of Luteinising Hormone (LH) into the bloodstream. It is triggered by a high level of oestrogen in the blood and it surges into the bloodstream for a day. LH causes the taut, developed follicle to weaken and rupture so the egg can be released. Without the surge of LH the process of ovulation will not occur.

Once the egg is released, it is swept up by sensitive fringe-like projections called fimbria at the end of the fallopian tube and drawn down inside it. The unfertilised egg will then survive for approximately 24 hours.

After the follicle has released its egg, it collapses. The break in its wall is sealed and the inner layer of its capsule continues to produce oestrogen that causes the remaining one third of the endometrium to regrow. Increased levels of oestrogen are released to prepare the womb for fertility. The empty follicle that released the egg then changes to a gland called the corpus luteum. Under the influence of LH the outer cells of the corpus luteum then produce progesterone in high levels. Initially they also produce oestrogens but while progesterone levels stay high, oestrogen levels gradually start to decline and progesterone will dominate the menstrual cycle for the two weeks after ovulation and in doing so inhibits all future ovulation should a pregnancy occur.

Progesterone is often referred to as the pregnancy hormone because its production is necessary to enrich the lining of the fallopian tubes and the uterus in preparation for the implantation of a possible embryo. Changes in the endometrial lining provide nourishment for the dividing ovum as it moves through the fallopian tube and into the thickened, enriched uterus for implantation. During this phase, increased progesterone levels tighten the cervix and our cervical mucus thickens and forms an effective plug that will seal the entrance to the cervix, protecting the fertilised egg and preventing miscarriage. High progesterone levels also cause the endometrial blood vessels to thicken, coil and lengthen, and stimulate the glands to secrete fatty deposits, glycogen and various other substances.

PREMENSTRUAL PHASE

In the absence of pregnancy, a woman's body will change once again in order to shed the endometrial lining that has built up in the last thirteen to fifteen days. This is known as the premenstrual phase and if the cycle is regular, usually occurs between Day 25 and Day 28. Approximately two days before the menstrual bleeding begins, oestrogen and progesterone secretions from the ovaries decrease sharply to a very low level and reduce the stimulation to the endometrial cells in the uterus. In the 24 hours before menstruation, the coiled blood vessels in the walls of the uterus constrict and cut off the blood supply to the endometrium. Approximately 65 per cent of the surface tissue dies and gradually separates from the remaining endometrial tissue in the uterus. The dead tissue breaks down and combines with about 35 millilitres of blood to form the menstrual fluid, which is then released from the body with the aid of mild muscular contractions, down through the cervix and out of the vagina as our menstrual bleed.

Ellen's story

ELLEN first started having problems with her period during her final year at university. She was studying for long stretches of time and relying on stimulants such as chocolate, cola drinks and black coffee to keep her going.

Her menstrual cycle had always been short at around 23 to 25 days but for five months it had settled into a 21-day cycle. The duration of her bleeding was five or six days with some cramping on the first day. She felt premenstrual during the week before her period and her breasts felt lumpy and tender. In fact, she only felt good for about one week during the whole cycle.

Typically, Ellen came to see me about managing her stress not her menstrual cycle. She didn't realise that I could lengthen her cycle and reduce her discomfort. I took down her health details and then prescribed a mixture of herbs and Bach Flower remedies.

I dispensed several herbs together in one mixture that was to be taken in the dosage of twenty drops three times a day in a little water. The herbs I used were: golden seal and shepherds purse to lengthen her cycle; cramp bark for the pain and cramping; false unicorn root to improve her oestrogen; hypericum as a nerve nutrient and mild sedative; and oats because they are a tonic to the nervous system. The Bach Flowers I used were: walnut for change, because I had asked her to break some bad dietary habits; vervain for when you push yourself too hard; chestnut bud as a link breaker, I didn't want her to lapse into bad habits; wild oat to help her find her path; and Rescue Remedy because she needed it!

While there was no specific herb in the mixture for her breast tenderness, I was confident that when she stopped taking food and drinks that were high in caffeine they would improve. I also knew there was less likelihood of premenstrual symptoms once her cycle became more balanced.

Ellen's period was due about two weeks after the consultation, which gave the herbs enough time to have an effect on the immediate cycle. I asked to see her in three weeks and suggested a massage for the next visit. I felt it would help her to relax and ease the tension in her upper back and neck.

When I saw Ellen again, her cycle had lengthened to 24 days and her pain and premenstrual symptoms had reduced. I gave her a massage and decided to repeat the ingredients that I used in the first herbal mixture. She took away enough herbs to last for six weeks and her next period came after 26 days.

She took herbal medicine for the last five months of university, improved her diet, learned to manage her stress and passed her exams. Ellen still comes in for the occasional massage and reports that her period has remained regular, at around a 26 to 28-day cycle.

Moods and
the Mind

ALL women experience the natural flow and rhythm of their emotions, and through these emotions they are able to develop sensitivity and compassion to others. These are virtues associated with being a woman.

Moods are manifestations of emotions and inner feelings that seek a release. They can occur on both a conscious and subconscious level and by expressing emotions and communicating feelings in a healthy way, women will have a very positive influence on their emotional and physical wellbeing.

How emotions influence the body

Emotions can affect the physical body in ways that science cannot explain. For example, your neck will become tense and stiff if you are under stress, or you might feel 'butterflies' in your stomach when you are doing something new or exciting. Your lower back may give in when you are under financial pressure and your throat can close up or your voice will change when you have a need to express something of importance.

Sometimes we may not be aware that our emotions are affecting our physical body, yet in our everyday language we may reflect these emotional connections. For instance, we refer to people who are angry or irritable as being 'liverish', and the liver is recognised within many systems of medicine as being the seat of anger.

'Gall' is the term used to describe bitter feelings. This is a direct reference to the bitter substance stored in the gall bladder called bile. Gall

stones block the flow of bile and so they can be seen to be manifestations of bitterness. When we 'vent our spleen' we release our rage, and the emotion associated with the spleen is frustration. Churning in the stomach is often a result of anxiety and the emotion of worry is connected with this part of the body.

A 'broken heart' reflects a loss of love and, of course, the emotion of love is associated with the heart. Joy is expressed via the circulation or the blood and problems with circulation may reflect a lack of joy in your life.

Excessive fear can result in involuntary urination, and so kidney problems are often seen to be connected with it. Fear is not always obvious, like being afraid of the dark; it may be fear of expressing yourself or fear of letting others see the real you.

Too often, there is not enough importance placed upon a woman's emotional history and how it may be influencing her physical health. Women have been taught from an early age that it is not ladylike to express anger or rage, yet women are sometimes the victims of physical violence and sexual and emotional abuse. Many women are angry and filled with rage as a direct result of this abuse, and they don't know how to deal with these emotions. If these feelings are not released or expressed, they can lead to health problems that include depression, sexual health problems and cancers. This is why it is very important to work through them and in most situations people with ongoing emotional problems will need the support and assistance of a skilled practitioner.

Try to develop ways to release and express your feelings and emotions. Don't let them become bottled up. Talk about your feelings with someone you trust, write them down, laugh things off, breathe them away, sing them out or have a good cry.

Nerves and mood

Changes and sensations, both within and around your body are detected by your nervous system and information is sent by electrical impulses along nerve pathways to your brain. When the information reaches the brain, it can be interpreted and may or may not be acted upon.

Nerve impulses are transmitted with the assistance of chemical messengers that travel in your bloodstream called neurotransmitters, and they can also be referred to as brain chemicals. These neurotransmitters influence memory, learning, pain regulation, muscular response, sex drive, appetite, dreams, sleep patterns, and they also control your moods. They can be both excitory or inhibitory and they allow your brain to communicate with the rest of your body.

The inhibitory neurotransmitters can stop muscles from contracting and causing tension or they can help your mind to 'shut down' after a stressful day. These brain chemicals encourage good sleep patterns and alleviate anxiety and stress.

Excitory neurotransmitters allow impulses to move from one nerve to the next. Brain chemicals keep us switched on, which can be useful for improving memory or maintaining a clear head. These chemicals are made from amino acids that are found in protein foods, and some essential vitamins and minerals. This is why nutritional supplements and dietary changes can be effective in treating emotional disorders.

If you are considering treatment using amino acid and other nutritional supplements, I would recommend that you consult a good nutritional therapist who can monitor your treatment program. The manipulation of neurotransmitters using amino acid therapy can be highly effective in regulating mood and behaviour but it requires careful supervision. Our moods and emotions are very sensitive to either too much or too little of these brain chemicals and if nutrients are not used appropriately, instead of improving emotional health they can actually create problems such as irritability or depression.

How diet affects mood

It is not surprising that when a person is feeling depressed or anxious their diet will suffer as a consequence. It is also true that if a person continues to have a poor diet, this in turn can create alterations in mood and behaviour. Low levels of a neurotransmitter in the brain called seretonin will lead to insomnia, irritability and some types of depression. In order for your body to manufacture adequate levels of seretonin you will need to provide certain nutrients. One of these is an amino acid called tryptophan. It is naturally found in turkey, soy beans, lentils, rice, pumpkin seeds, sesame seeds and cottage cheese.

Glutamine is another amino acid which is found in rolled oats, cottage and ricotta cheese and most foods rich in protein. It is a major fuel source for the brain. When converted into Gamma aminobutyric acid (GABA) it helps to regulate mood and behaviour and is involved in improving your memory and IQ. It has the added benefit of blocking the appetite centre that craves sweets and alcohol. Conversion into GABA from natural food sources can be difficult and a diet high in salicylate foods can interfere with this conversion, so it is wise to eat a diet that keeps these foods in moderation. Some foods that are high in salicylates are tomatoes, eggplant, zucchinis, oranges, berries, dried fruits, green apples, rockmelon, grapes, pineapples, plums and almonds. L Glutamine is a synthetic form available as a supplement and it is absorbed very effectively.

Another essential nutrient for improving mood and behaviour is vitamin B6. Some good sources are avocado, egg, molasses, oranges, spinach, wheat germ and sunflower seeds. Deficiencies in vitamin B6 can be associated with depression, increased nervousness and irritability. Vitamin B3 is an important nerve nutrient that can help to regulate sleep patterns. Deficiencies can lead to irritability and depression. Foods high in vitamin B3 include salmon, sardines, legumes, eggs and sunflower seeds.

Carbohydrates are often craved when people are anxious or depressed. However, if your choices of carbohydrates are sugars rather than starches you may exacerbate the problem. Sugar will provide a quick energy boost but it will not last and you are likely to be tired, depressed and hungry after indulging in sugary foods. Instead, make a sandwich with a healthy filling or cook some pasta or rice or a jacket potato. These foods will be much more satisfying and nutritious. If you really must eat something sweet then have a muffin made with wholegrains and fresh fruit such as blueberries, apple or banana or a wholemeal fruit scone. Then you will satisfy your cravings in a more nutritious way.

Premenstrual syndrome is made worse by consuming large amounts of refined sugar, salt, animal fat and dairy products. Eat more starchy foods like rice, potato, pasta, bread, bananas and sunflower seeds. Even though you may crave sugar it is important to eat starchy foods. They will assist in controlling blood sugar levels which will help you to overcome hunger, mood swings and fatigue.

If you have depression it is essential to remove caffeine and all sugars, except fruit, from your diet. Foods and drinks rich in caffeine are coffee, tea, cola and chocolate. You can purchase caffeine-free tea or coffee or try herbal teas or dandelion beverage. Dandelion tastes very much like coffee and is actually a good tonic for the liver. Powdered cocoa and carob do not contain high levels of caffeine and can be good substitutes for blocks of chocolate which tend to be high in sugar.

People will often crave chocolate during times of stress and depression. While there are a few theories about this, it is probably due to a constituent in chocolate called theobromine, which is a stimulant that is rich in an amino acid, phenylalanine. This amino acid enhances natural endorphins in the brain that elevate the mood. It is also used as a reward food for children, so it is possible that we look for chocolate to boost our self-esteem or self-worth. If we are stressed and tired we may simply use it as a stimulant. Most people love the taste and texture of chocolate and they feel good while they are eating it. Chocolate has a history of use as an aphrodisiac and perhaps there is also some truth in the theory that it is a substitute for love.

Essential fatty acids (EFAs) should be included in your diet to keep your nervous system healthy. Try having LSA sprinkled on rolled oats or cereal in the mornings. LSA is made from three parts linseeds, two parts sunflower seeds and one part almonds. Grind all this together into a fine meal and store it in the refrigerator. Other ways of getting EFAs is to have a little olive oil in your salad dressing and to eat a small handful of nuts and seeds daily.

Many of the minerals are essential for a healthy nervous system. A good way of obtaining them is to have nutritious vegetable broths, stocks and soups regularly. Vegetable stocks are made by simmering the skins and tops of vegetables that you might normally discard, in a little water for twenty to thirty minutes. Strain, and keep the liquid as a base for sauces, stews, soups and casseroles. Alternatively you can add some chopped vegetables and barley or lentils to make a delicious mineral-rich soup. To avoid harmful chemicals or pesticides try to obtain organically-grown vegetables or rinse and scub your vegetables well to remove any chemical residues.

When we bring this information together it is not too difficult to eat well for your nervous and emotional health.

Premenstrual syndrome

There is no doubt that changes in hormonal patterns during our menstrual cycle contribute to fluctuations in our moods. Imbalances in the ratio of oestrogen to progesterone can contribute to mood swings and emotional outbursts.

In the past we referred to any emotional distress before our period as premenstrual tension or PMT. Today it is recognised as a condition or an illness, and it is called premenstrual syndrome.

Many women ask me to help balance their emotions in the week before menstruation. They are convinced that their hormones are completely responsible, and most literature on women's health supports this theory.

Some women feel remorseful about their behaviour and often worry that they have damaged their relationships with their partner or children. Accused of nagging or being unreasonable, they are often left feeling guilty and ashamed.

While hormonal changes can influence emotional behaviour, it is not unusual to discover that their behaviour is often understandable, given the stressful daily situations that women deal with. Women still do the majority of the housework, the cooking, the child care, the shopping and often have a job or career as well. They may have the added responsibility of mothering and holding their relationship together. Some common complaints from women are that they are tired of doing all the housework or they are fed up with being taken for granted.

Women are also good at compromise, although they shouldn't have to be. While compromise has its advantages for those who wish to avoid conflict and arguments, it can work against women, and it often does. It can contribute to a feeling of absolute powerlessness. As a consequence, a volatile cocktail of emotions including depression, frustration, resentment or anger may well up inside. These emotions seek a release and they often erupt premenstrually when women are more inclined to assert themselves as their power resurfaces.

There is no need for women to apologise for their emotions; it is healthy and natural to feel and express them. Negative mood swings and ongoing depression are more likely to occur as a result of suppressing feelings and emotions.

While I acknowledge that premenstrual tension exists for women, it is a concern of mine that in labelling this as a syndrome, we only acknowledge hormonal triggers, and trivialise the real issues for women. Many women experience an enormous amount of pressure and responsibility on a daily basis. It is understandable that premenstrually they might feel overwhelmed.

There is a danger in stereotyping women who speak out premenstrually as being irrational. By referring to this as a premenstrual syndrome, we risk contributing to and perpetuating negative attitudes toward women and menstruation. This becomes evident when women who do assert themselves premenstrually find they are dismissed with mutterings of 'that time of the month'.

There is no doubt that physical imbalances and changes in our bodies are closely linked to our emotional health. As well as the obvious hormonal changes that affect our emotions, it is also possible for women to contribute to premenstrual tension on yet another level. Women who regularly experience a difficult menstrual period, understandably, may look to it with fear and loathing. As their period gets closer, it is possible to develop negative emotions such as depression, due to anticipated pain and discomfort.

By correcting the physical problems associated with menstruation we often indirectly alleviate negative emotions that can contribute to premenstrual tension. In this chapter I outline some common physical and emotional patterns that have been observed in premenstrual tension. Although causes and symptoms will differ according to the individual, some women will certainly identify with a 'type' of PMS.

PMS TYPE A
Signs and symptoms of this type of PMS are increased nervous tension, anxiety and irritability. It is not unusual to feel weepy and have mood swings that are difficult to control. Your eyes may fill up with tears even though you are not really feeling sad (this can also be due to a B2 deficiency).

The period often begins quite suddenly and there is usually a very heavy flow, and because of this, it is possible to experience some clotting. Women with this type of bleeding pattern often have a gynaeoid, or pear shaped, body. This means there is a greater weight distribution around the buttocks and thighs.

This type of PMS is usually associated with a high oestrogen:low progesterone ratio.

Self-help

Supplement with vitamin B6, vitamin E, zinc, magnesium and essential fatty acids. Magnesium and B6 help the liver to break down excess oestrogen, and vitamin E is a mild antagonist to oestrogen.

Methionine reduces excess oestrogen and good natural sources are garlic and onions.

Avoid caffeine, which is contained in cola drinks, chocolate, tea and coffee. Drink dandelion beverage instead because it will help your liver to filter out excess hormone levels.

Generally avoid alcohol and foods that are high in yeast and animal fat.

If you are taking an oral contraceptive pill that contains high levels of oestrogen, it may worsen this type of PMS.

PMS TYPE B

The emotional changes with this type are often closely associated with increased stress. While both A and B can be irritable and moody, type B is definitely more aggressive and prone to depression, due to a higher progesterone:oestrogen ratio.

Physical changes include weight gain, with a greater weight distribution on the upper body. This can be described as android, or apple shaped and I have observed that women with this type of PMS often have this body shape. There can be swelling of the face, hands and feet, as well as breast tenderness due to hormonal changes or allergies.

Self-help

Supplement with vitamin B6, vitamin C with bioflavanoids, magnesium, zinc and essential fatty acids.

Reduce your salt and red meat intake because this does not suit your body type and may increase progesterone levels.

Some women will need a natural diuretic such as celery and juniper to help reduce fluid retention.

Drink dandelion beverage daily instead of tea and coffee.

PMS TYPE C

This type of PMS is often associated with fluctuations in blood sugar levels. The appetite is increased with a craving for sweet foods. There can be a hormonal headache and you may feel fatigued. If blood sugar levels drop there will be dizziness, fainting and your heart may be pounding. Moods will fluctuate with the blood sugar and irritability can be a consequence.

This type of PMS is associated with problems in insulin metabolism and can also be related to a magnesium deficiency. Insulin is the hormone that helps convert sugars and starches in our diet into glucose for energy. If you suspect you have fluctuations in blood sugar levels it may be worth having a glucose tolerance test.

Self-help

Supplement with vitamin B complex, zinc, manganese, magnesium and essential fatty acids.

This type of PMS will usually respond to dietary changes. Smaller meals must be eaten regularly and they should include starchy foods (rice, bread, potato, pasta, starchy fruits and vegetables) with some good quality protein (lean meat, poultry, fish, eggs, nuts and seeds, low-fat dairy). Avoid all sugar completely, including honey.

Drink fennel or nettle tea.

PMS TYPE D (DEPRESSION)

This type of PMS causes emotional changes that include depression, forgetfulness, confusion, insomnia and crying. It is often associated with thyroid hormone insufficiency and there is a low oestrogen:high progesterone ratio.

Self-help

Supplements that will be highly beneficial are kelp, spirulina and potassium iodide.

The diet should include foods that are easy to digest, such as fresh vegetables, lots of salads, fish (not fried), fresh fruit, rice and barley.

PMS TYPE H (HYPERHYDRATION)

Women with this type will have problems with fluid retention, weight gain, breast tenderness, swollen extremities and abdominal bloating. All of these symptoms can be directly related to increased sodium levels in the body and a high alcohol intake.

Self-help

Supplement with vitamin B6 to promote diuresis, B complex and vitamin E.

Do not have a diet that is high in sodium, so avoid adding salt to your food, and read packaging on prepared food to determine its sodium content. Your aim should be to keep sodium to between 300 and 600 mg each day. One slice of bread contains about 150 mg of sodium (unless it is salt reduced) and one level teaspoon of salt contains 2000 mg of sodium.

Taking nat mur as a cell salt can help to balance the fluid in your body.

GENERAL DIETARY GUIDELINES FOR PMS

Every woman has the capacity to improve her physical and emotional health by altering her dietary habits.

* Avoid alcohol, tea, coffee, chocolate.
* Don't smoke.
* Increase your dietary intake of fish products especially oily fish (cod, tuna, salmon) and seeds (sunflower, sesame, pumpkin, linseed).
* Maintain a diet that is low in animal fats (this includes the elimination of full-cream dairy products).
* Eat fresh fruit and vegetables every day.
* Use cold pressed linseed, olive or sunflower oil for salad dressings.
* Avoid refined sugary foods.
* Do not add salt to your cooking or your food and keep sodium levels to a minimum.

Stress and your moods

Emotional stress can be a direct result of either having too many demands placed upon you or a lack of stimulation in your life. If it is ongoing, it can have some serious effects on the body. These can include lethargy; listlessness; irritability; anxiety; nervous tension; crying for no reason; depression and social withdrawal.

It is very important to recognise the physical symptoms of stress because if they continue for too long, they can become life threatening. They include headaches; palpitations; over acidity of the stomach; trembling hands and a feeling of uneasiness; loss of concentration and loss of memory.

OVERCOMING STRESS

There are ways that you can help yourself overcome emotional stress.

* Stop smoking—it contributes to stress.
* Learn a relaxation technique and practise it regularly.
* Make sure you are getting enough sleep.
* Exercise for 30 to 40 minutes every day. Walking or swimming is great.
* Avoid alcohol.
* Check the side effects of any medicines you are taking with your doctor or pharmacist. Some pharmacies can provide you with a computer printout of information on medicines or alternatively you can check in the Mims Annual Drug Compendium at your local library.
* Avoid caffeine—it is found in cola drinks, tea, coffee and chocolate. Drink herbal teas such as chamomile and valerian instead.
* Maintain a healthy, balanced diet that includes lean meat, fish, legumes, fresh fruit and vegetables, wholegrains, nuts and seeds.
* Try to avoid exposure to environmental and chemical pollutants.

When your body's energies are building up it is important to rest. Be an observer of your stresses and limitations as if you were looking at a stranger. If you lead a busy life try to balance it with the right amount of relaxation, and if you are dying of boredom it is important to start doing something creative or stimulating.

Depression

Depression is not the feelings of sadness and frustration that we all experience occasionally. It is a lasting and distressing state that persists. It can come on as a result of social isolation, low self-esteem and poor self-image, pain and illness or loss and grief.

Emotional depression can be far worse than a physical illness. It often leaves women with a sense of hopelessness, loss of self-confidence and low energy. Women are vulnerable to depression after the birth of a baby, premenstrually or at menopause. While this can be attributed to changes in hormone levels, there are usually other influences. For example, a lack of physical or emotional support, nutritional deficiencies, broken sleep or ongoing conflict with a partner or other family members.

Many depressed women can get so low, they do not feel entitled to ask for help. They can be filled with guilt about appearing weak and letting people down. The idea of drug therapy, which involves taking tranquillisers or antidepressants, often fills them with fear. As a result, they don't always reveal their problems to their doctor. Sometimes relatives need to seek help on their behalf.

Suicidal thoughts and expressions are common and should always be taken seriously. They can turn depression into a fatal illness.

SYMPTOMS OF DEPRESSION

There are a variety of symptoms that can be associated with depression and some of these are:

* Persistent negative feelings of anger, sadness and sometimes guilt. These may vary from day to day.
* Negative thoughts about yourself, the world around you, the future or worry.
* Difficult concentration; you cannot finish anything that you start.
* Poor sleep patterns.
* Loss of appetite and weight or overeating for consolation which leads to weight gain.
* Increased use of alcohol, cigarettes and pain killers.
* Loss of interest in sex and other things you usually enjoy.

NUTRIENTS FOR DEPRESSION

There are a number of ways that you can help yourself when you are depressed and a good way to start is by improving your diet; poor nutrition can be a primary cause of mood swings and changes in behaviour.

When you are depressed it can be difficult to motivate yourself to prepare and eat healthy food. Fast, highly processed foods are often the preferred choice, and it is not uncommon to crave foods that are heavy, such as pizza, pastries, pies, chips and chocolate. These foods will not provide the necessary nutrients to keep the nervous system healthy.

There are some essential nutrients in food that influence our moods and behaviour in a beneficial way. You will obtain these by eating whole-grain bread and cereals, fresh vegetables, salad and fruit every day. Eliminate all sugar from your diet and avoid highly processed foods that are high in fat. Eat fish regularly and include olive oil in salad dressings to obtain essential fatty acids.

Oats are a wonderful tonic to the nervous system so eat them in the form of porridge or muesli. Also incorporate them in other foods such as breads, muffins and rissoles.

Green vegetables and wholegrains are a good source of B vitamins. Garlic, ginger and onions help to improve a vitamin B6 deficiency and can help to balance our brain chemicals. Try to include them in your diet every day.

Nutritional supplements that can help with depression are essential fatty acids such as fish oils or evening primrose oil, magnesium, B complex vitamins and vitamin C.

SELF-HELP

* Stop smoking because tobacco smoke destroys the important vitamins that fight depression.
* Avoid alcohol because it is a depressant.
* Avoid pain-killing drugs because they may make things worse.
* Improve your fitness because exercise leads to a natural release of endorphins which are 'happy' chemicals.
* Improve your social life and build your own support group of friends or join a self-help group.
* Resist becoming dependent by developing your own resources.
* Resist feeling powerless and turn your energy into action not reaction.
* Get out of a rut by discovering new possibilities for your life.
* Practise some form of relaxation such as yoga, tai chi or learn to meditate.
* Take time to play by going somewhere or doing something new just for the fun of it.
* Bring more joy into your life by going to a funny film or show and have a good laugh.

HERBS FOR DEPRESSION

DAMIANA, *Turnera aphrodisiaca*: has an antidepressant action but needs to be prescribed by a herbalist.

LEMON BALM, *Melissa officinalis*: easily grown in your garden or in a pot and it makes a refreshing tea.

ST JOHNS WORT, *Hypericum perforatum*: the common name for this herb is hypericum and it is useful for both anxiety and depression. It can be obtained from a herbalist and is also available from health food outlets in both a medicinal form and as a dried herb so it can be prepared as a tea.

It is important to remember that help is available for depression and you do not have to struggle with it. The first step to recovery is to stop ignoring the symptoms and seek help straightaway. Contact a women's health centre, your health practitioner or ring a women's help line listed in the front of your phone book. There are people in your area who can help.

Traditional medicine and moods

ESSENTIAL OILS

The ancient practice of aromatherapy is a safe therapy that will help you to relax and balance your emotional state. It is renowned for assisting relaxation that helps to alleviate stress and anxiety, and it can safely be used to complement other forms of therapy.

The distilled essences made from various parts of flowers, herbs, trees and plants can assist in restoring emotional balance. They work directly on the olfactory nerve cells located high inside the nose. As we breathe in aromas, we excite the olfactory cells. This stimulates impulses through nerve fibres in the central nervous system and sends signals to specific regions of the brain.

We know that aromas can trigger memories stored in our subconscious that will then influence our emotional behaviour. For instance, you may associate the smell of frangipani flowers with a park or garden where you played as a child. This can trigger memories of spring weather, warmth, happiness and a feeling of freedom. Perhaps the smell of lavender will trigger a memory of your grandmother's dressing table and bring about feelings of security and love.

Essential oils are readily available and easy to use. You can smell them directly from the bottle, apply them to your skin or use them in an oil burner or diffuser. Try soaking in a deep bath containing a few drops of essential oils, listening to some relaxing music by candlelight, and soothe away the tension of your day.

Indulge yourself by having an aromatherapy massage. By combining these two therapies you will benefit on both emotional and physical levels. Stress creates a build-up of muscular and nervous tension in the body that can manifest itself in many ways. Some common problems are headaches, neuralgia, neck and back pain, digestive disturbances, constipation or diarrhoea, frequency of urination, hypertension, teeth grinding and sleeplessness. Massage can help to correct these problems and by incorporating aromatherapy you will greatly enhance the benefits of the treatment.

Smelling good will often make you feel better about yourself and that in itself enhances your self-esteem. If you are feeling unworthy or unattractive it is important to pamper yourself and let your body know you love and care about it.

Some useful carrier oils are jojoba, almond, wheat germ and vitamin E. Use these as your base and add a few drops of the concentrated essences to them.

Some useful aromatherapy essences are:

BERGAMOT: a useful oil for relaxation and it is also good for treating nervous tension, depression and low energy.

CEDARWOOD: another oil for depression and it can also be used to calm fear.

CLARY SAGE: this oil balances your emotions and stimulates creativity.

JASMINE: helps to encourage happiness.

LAVENDER: good for alleviating stress and anxiety.

LEMON AND LIME: both of these citrus oils are recommended for depression.

MARJORAM: burning this oil may help you to be more confident.

NEROLI: use this oil to help manage anger.

ROSE: this beautiful fragrance may give you confidence and a feeling of happiness. It is good to use after a disappointment.

ROSEMARY: good for mental fatigue and depressive states.

SANDALWOOD: wearing this oil will stop you absorbing other people's negative energies. Use it if you feel overwhelmed.

YLANG YLANG: use this oil if you are feeling angry and frustrated.

BACH FLOWER REMEDIES

Bach Flower remedies were developed by Dr Edward Bach over 50 years ago and they help to improve your emotional health. Every remedy has a positive outcome.

Bach Flowers are excellent self-help remedies that you can choose according to your emotional needs. Read through the list and either select them individually or mix them together if you feel that more than one remedy is required. For instance, you may decide to mix honeysuckle, walnut and wild oat together because one remedy brings you out of the past, another will help you to cope with change and the last one helps you find your new direction. It is best not to use more than five remedies together at any given time.

All the flower remedies are available as over-the-counter preparations and are completely safe to use. They can be taken in a little water three or four times a day or they can be taken every fifteen minutes as needed during times of trauma or emotional distress.

There are 38 remedies and they are divided into seven categories.

Overcare

BEECH: for those who have a desire to change others; critical; judgemental; and intolerant.

CHICORY: for those who have a desire to possess; are fault finding; and martyrs to self-pity.

ROCKWATER: for those who want to be an example to others; strict; hard taskmasters.

VERVAIN: for those who have a desire to persuade; overenthusiastic; and unable to relax.

VINE: for those who have a desire to dominate; inflexible; and hard on others.

Oversensitivity

AGRIMONY: for those who hide their worries behind a brave face.

CENTAURY: for 'doormats'; overanxious to please others; and easily exploited.

HOLLY: for hatred, jealousy and suspicion; a good blockage-breaking remedy.

WALNUT: for times of change, such as adolescence and menopause; a good protective remedy.

Loneliness

HEATHER: for lonely people who are wrapped up in their own troubles.

IMPATIENS: for impatience and irritability.

WATER VIOLET: for those who like to be alone; proud, condescending and arrogant types.

Insufficient interest

CHESTNUT BUD: for those who repeat the same mistakes and fail to learn from experience.

CLEMATIS: for dreamy, inattentive types; a good grounding remedy.

HONEYSUCKLE: for those who are locked in memories of the past.

MUSTARD: for depression from an unknown cause.

OLIVE: for complete physical and mental exhaustion.

WHITE CHESTNUT: for persistent worrying thoughts.

WILD ROSE: for those who never try to improve things; apathetic; and lacking ambition.

Uncertainty

CERATO: for those who lack confidence in their own judgement; constantly seeking advice.

GENTIAN: for those who are easily discouraged, sceptical and pessimistic.

GORSE: for a lack of hope and a loss of interest in life; a good remedy for depression.

HORNBEAM: for a lack of strength and an inability to cope; that 'Monday morning' feeling.

SCLERANTHUS: for those who are indecisive and hesitant.

WILD OAT: for those who are unsure of their direction in life; helps you find your path.

Fear

ASPEN: for unknown fear, anxiety and apprehension.

CHERRY PLUM: for fear of the self; quiet desperation; and suicidal tendencies.

MIMULUS: for known fears, such as fear of heights or fear of the dark.

RED CHESTNUT: for excessive fear or worry for others, especially loved ones.

ROCK ROSE: for extreme fear or panic.

Despondency and despair

CRAB APPLE: for those who feel ashamed of their ailments; a cleansing remedy.

ELM: for temporary feelings of inadequacy; feeling overwhelmed.

LARCH: for those who feel inferior and have an expectation of failure.

OAK: for brave people who struggle on despite pressure or illness.

PINE: for feelings of guilt and self reproach; for those who are always apologising.

STAR OF BETHLEHEM: for shock and trauma.

SWEET CHESTNUT: for those who have reached the limits of their endurance; feeling isolated.

WILLOW: for when you feel sorry for yourself; feelings of bitterness and resentment.

Rescue Remedy

Rescue Remedy is made up of five remedies: impatiens, clematis, rock rose, cherry plum and star of Bethlehem. It is used for any emergency or in a traumatic situation to help people remain calm. It is a great remedy to carry in the glove box of your car in case of an accident or to keep in your medicine cabinet at home.

Women and tranquillisers

Many Australian women take tranquillisers and mood-altering drugs that have side effects and are habit forming. While there are legitimate situations where these drugs need to be prescribed, many women who take them do not really need them. When women try to give up these legal drugs of addiction they suffer withdrawal symptoms that are far worse than the symptoms that took them to their doctor in the first place. If they experience withdrawal, they often feel afraid to stop their medication because they worry that they will not cope. This is because the side effects can include anxiety, confusion, palpitation and dizziness.

With support, dependency on tranquillisers can be overcome. It is possible to control mood swings and emotional distress using natural therapies and I encourage women to believe in their own ability to maintain balance and control over their emotions through awareness, stress management, dietary changes, exercise and traditional medicines.

The Eastern theory of balance

Just as we need to balance emotional and physical aspects of ourselves, we also need to balance the feminine and masculine energies that exist in each of us. This is described in Eastern philosophy as the yin and the yang and you may be familiar with the symbol that depicts the harmony of these contrasting forces. In the symbol each half contains a spot of its opposing colour, which indicates that nothing exists in total isolation. The sign represents unity, harmony and balance.

Women and men have both yin and yang principles within themselves that are deeply connected. It is impossible for a woman to be without masculine characteristics just as it is equally impossible for a man to lack a feminine side.

We all originate from both male and female energies and we each carry the genes and characteristics of both our mothers and our fathers. Together they form our distinguishing features and they are reflected in our temperament, our personality, our hormones and our physical appearance. It is possible for a woman to be assertive and strong just as men can be receptive and sensitive.

So be creative. Acknowledge and use your male energies and be comfortable and receptive with your female energies. If we learn to recognise, accept and use both aspects of ourselves we will do much towards closing the gap between the sexes.

Let's look at some of the principles that these symbols stand for.

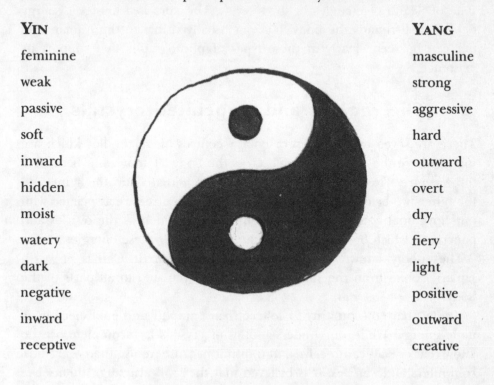

YIN	**Y**ANG
feminine	masculine
weak	strong
passive	aggressive
soft	hard
inward	outward
hidden	overt
moist	dry
watery	fiery
dark	light
negative	positive
inward	outward
receptive	creative

Your energy centres

Through physics we know that the Universe is composed of a sea of waves and energy. So too, our inner body consists of energy centres that are referred to in Eastern philosophy as the *chakras*, which correspond with body systems, glands and specific organs.

Eastern philosophy has always recognised the importance of the channels, or meridians, through which energy flows throughout the body in a particular pattern. Insufficient energy, energy blockages and excess energy can all create imbalances that result in health problems. Changes will take place in our energy levels before our physical body is affected. This explains why we often feel tired and run down before we get sick. Our bodies' energy fields will differ in intensity according to our state of health or disease. For example, if we have a cold coming on we will simply feel sluggish but if we have influenza, we will probably feel exhausted.

In recent years, research in the West has also revealed the existence of energy fields by monitoring the electromagnetic fields in the human body. These energy fields are illustrated in special pictures known as Kirlian photographs, which can show changes in a person's aura according to their state of health or changes in stress levels. The aura is a low-level energy field that surrounds the body. It is not usually visible to the human eye, but can be seen clearly in these types of photographs that support its existence.

The *chakras* and associated crystals

There are seven main *chakras* or energy centres in our bodies which are found where the energy channels cross the body 21 times and become a force centre. Five of these energy centres are situated up the spine and the other two belong to the head. All the main centres are associated with our hormonal system and our secreting glands (such as the ovaries and pancreas), which become the physical mediums for these energies.

The energy, known as *prana* (in India) or *chi/Qi* (in China) or *ki* (in Japan), comes from the sun. This energy is circulated to all parts of the body.

Crystals have the capacity to collect, focus, amplify and emit electomagnetic energy. While our understanding of crystals is incomplete, we do know that crystals can receive and transmit because we use them in radios, computers and watches. It is believed that they will also align themselves with each of the *chakras* or energy centres and can help to channel or focus energy in the body.

The base centre

This is situated at the base of the spine and it is related to the adrenal glands. We have two adrenal glands that are directly linked to the nervous system and they secrete several hormones, including adrenalin and noradrenaline, that stimulate our body into action by increasing the heart rate and constricting blood vessels. The physical health problems that can arise from this centre will tend to lead to problems with vitality and because the adrenals are situated above the kidneys, we may also develop problems with them, such as changes in fluid balance and blood pressure.

Smoky quartz can be used at the base centre to strengthen adrenal energy and to balance your sexual energy. It is a crystal that can enhance your dream awareness and is an excellent stone for meditation.

The sacral centre

This is slightly higher up the spine and relates to the reproductive system, more specifically, the ovaries in women and the testes in men. Energy problems here can cause increased or decreased sex drive, infertility,

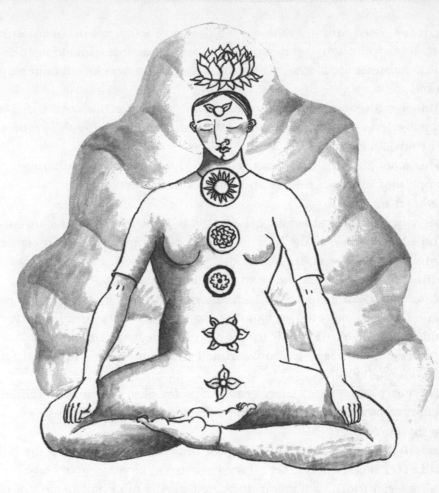

cystitis, growths such as tumours, cysts and fibroids and menstrual disorders.

A good stone for balancing this centre is carnelian, which ranges in colour from orange/red to deep gold. This stone has a calming and centring effect on the body and is especially useful in easing the trauma of sexual abuse. It can be placed directly over the centre or worn on the body. It is a stone that can help to ground those who have lost the focus in their life or feel scattered and confused. It is said to stimulate love, improve optimism and enable you to act with more spontaneity.

Both the base and sacral centres provide energies for our physical existence and activity.

The solar plexus
This is situated in line with the naval and is the gateway to our emotions and feelings. This centre relates specifically to self-centred desire. The

organ associated with this *chakra* is the pancreas, so energy problems with this *chakra* will often manifest as digestive disturbances including diarrhoea, constipation, ulcers, gall stones, diabetes or unexplained cramping around the naval.

Amber is a yellow stone that can be used to balance this *chakra*. If you feel powerless and out of control this stone may help to bring the joy back into your life.

The solar plexus is a very active centre responsible for gathering up energy from the lower centres and unblocking our emotions.

The heart *chakra*

This is between the shoulder blades and is associated with the thymus gland which is close to the heart. The flow of energy at the heart centre begins when we open ourselves to the needs of others. Energy problems at this centre manifest in the heart and the circulation.

Rose quartz is a good crystal to balance the heart *chakra* as it can heal internal wounds and enhances your ability to believe in yourself. This is a wonderful stone to use for clearing suppressed negative emotions such as anger, resentment, fear, jealousy and hate, but you must be prepared for the emotional release.

The heart *chakra* draws energy from the solar plexus creating a transfer of energy upwards from self to selfless development.

The throat *chakra*

This is in the throat as the name suggests and is associated with the thyroid gland. Too much energy here may lead to an increase in metabolism causing weight loss, palpitation, increased perspiration and nervousness. Underactivity of this gland can cause weight gain, sluggishness, dry skin and hair loss. Lung and throat problems may also relate to this *chakra*, which is your centre for creative expression.

To balance the throat energy use a blue crystal, such as the aquamarine, which will help to balance you on all levels. This stone protects the aura and will help with health problems affecting the kidneys, spleen, liver and thyroid gland.

The throat *chakra* channels energy that is first passed through the heart *chakra* and when these centres are balanced, we have creative energy expressed for the good of others.

The ajna *chakra*

This is also referred to as the third eye and it is situated directly between the eyes or at the eyebrow centre and it has a direct relationship with the pituitary gland. The pituitary gland receives instructions from the brain to stimulate other glands into production. Like the pituitary gland, the ajna *chakra* is affected by a higher centre called the crown *chakra*.

In the ajna centre, thoughts and ideas from our higher centre, the crown *chakra*, are worked over into a practical form and then distributed and expressed with the assistance of the throat *chakra*.

Health problems associated with an imbalance of the ajna *chakra* are eye problems and migraine headaches in a person who pushes themselves too hard.

When the ajna centre is balanced, it symbolises a highly creative and balanced personality and it is generally activated when you have control, harmony and direction in your life.

A useful crystal for balancing the ajna centre is the azurite which is a royal blue stone. This stone will help to increase your creativity and intuition as well as helping you to achieve mental clarity.

There is an interconnecting line of activity moving from the sacral *chakra*, the throat *chakra* and the ajna *chakra* which then relates to the highest centre, the crown *chakra*.

The crown *chakra*

This is our highest centre and relates to the pineal gland which is sensitive to light. The *chakra* is also sensitive to light but in a different way. Our highest *chakra* is sensitive to the inner light which is the light of the spirit or the soul and this is the area where we can achieve spiritual growth. Our bodies can be seen as temples for this inner light and when this *chakra* is activated through prayer or meditation, we can achieve greater clarity of thought and become more balanced in ourselves.

Imbalances manifest as tension headaches, having scattered thoughts, memory problems and anxiety.

The crystal for this centre is the alexandrite which is deep purple or red. This stone will help you to realign your mental and emotional body and it can enhance your spiritual growth.

The inner soul is the indestructible part of our nature and it expresses itself through our highest centre. Take the time to listen to this small voice that speaks with great wisdom.

BALANCING THE ENERGY CENTRES

Lesser energy centres are located in a number of places including the palms of the hands, behind the knees and the soles of the feet, and there are also many other smaller centres that are the traditional acupuncture points. The main *chakras* need to be balanced in order for the energy to flow freely to these other centres, ensuring optimum health and vitality. This can be achieved using many healing arts that include crystal therapy, kiniesiology (muscle testing), acupuncture, acupressure (without needles), reflexology, meditation and various forms of massage therapy. Even some forms of exercise and martial arts incorporate balancing and clearing energy flow exercises.

If you do not have access to these therapies and you simply wish to use crystals to realign your energy centres, choose one that is appropriate for your needs and keep it by your bed or on your desk at work. Alternatively you can carry it in your pocket or wear it as jewellery.

A SIMPLE SELF-HELP EXERCISE USING CRYSTALS

Quartz crystals will be either positive: masculine and clear, or negative: feminine and cloudy. To restore energy using crystals select four crystals, two feminine and two masculine, lie on the floor and arrange the crystals in the following way. Place a clear masculine crystal, point downward, a few inches from the top of the head or crown *chakra*. Place a milky female crystal between your feet with the tip directed inward. Place the remaining two crystals in each palm, the female in the left hand and the male in the right. The left point directed towards the heart and the right point towards the feet. Take your awareness to each crystal and generate positive feelings such as love or joy toward them. If you are good at visualisation you can imagine that these positive feelings are sent back to you in a burst of energy from crystal to crystal.

Sexual Desire

ENHANCING your libido and maintaining an active sex life requires a good diet, regular exercise and a healthy attitude to sex. Combining these factors with the information in this chapter will not only lead to good health, it will also enhance your sexual pleasure.

It is a myth that women have low libidos while men, due to higher testosterone levels, have very strong sexual urges. While it is true that testosterone can enhance libido, this does not automatically mean that women have a lesser sex drive. Women, however, are rarely encouraged to express their sexual desire, instead they are encouraged to be objects of desire. Well, it is time to liberate yourself and have some fun! Use your imagination and break the boredom of routine. Start by taking greater control over your own sexual experiences and try not to become dependent on your lover for sexual arousal. Make sex fun and exciting.

Communicate with your partner and be totally honest with each other about your desires and responses. Take turns in giving and receiving pleasure. In order to reawaken your libido you just might have to start pleasing yourself.

Substances that stimulate sexual responsiveness are referred to as aphrodisiacs, a term derived from the name of Aphrodite, the Greek goddess of love and beauty. By definition, an aphrodisiac is anything that arouses or increases your sexual desire.

Throughout history many substances have been used to enhance arousal, however some were extremely toxic and highly inflammatory. Most of these were chemicals or plants with powerful alkaloids and when they were taken internally, they were capable of causing violent inflammation of body tissues and sometimes death. Some irritants, such as stinging nettles or chillies, were rubbed directly onto the genitalia to increase blood supply and produce sexual excitation through stimulation. Don't be tempted to do this, it often creates congestion, burning and irritation.

When we feel a need to enhance our sexual health it is important only to use substances that are non-addictive, non-toxic, safe and natural. There are a number of traditional medicines that are very useful for boosting a flagging libido and aromatherapy can also excite the senses. I intend to disclose the secret ways aphrodisiacs can improve sexual arousal and I will provide you with a good understanding of how to use them.

By far, the most reliable and inexpensive aphrodisiac is good nutrition because having the correct balance of nutrients in your body will help you to be sexually responsive and energetic whenever an appropriate sexual response is desired. This is not limited to young people as our bodies can be sexually responsive at any age providing we keep them well nourished. For optimum sexual function we must feed our glandular system, which is referred to as the endocrine system. It is here that we produce the hormones responsible for our reproductive health and the stimulation of vaginal secretions necessary for lubrication.

The adrenal glands are situated above your kidneys and are part of your endocrine or glandular system. They secrete hormones such as adrenalin, which is essential for muscular contraction and increased blood supply to the muscles. It pours into your bloodstream during times of emotional excitement. The secretion of adrenalin improves your sexual stamina and responsiveness. Foods that balance and improve adrenal function are those that contain good levels of vitamins A, C, E, some of the B complex vitamins, zinc, magnesium and essential fatty acids.

Becoming orgasmic

During orgasm, the capillaries under the surface of the skin and genitalia become engorged with blood. This is sometimes referred to as the 'sexual flush'. Increased levels of histamine, which is transported in our blood and released in our body tissues, have been linked to this sexual flush. This is because histamine is an agent that can open blood capillaries, allowing them to fill with blood. It also accelerates the heart rate and causes muscular contraction. It is not the only substance in our body that has this function but research has shown that low blood levels of histamine may be associated with an inability to achieve orgasm.

NUTRIENTS THAT ASSIST ORGASM

To assist with the production of histamine you can include foods in your diet that are rich in the amino acid histidine. Good sources of histidine are cottage cheese, eggs and lentils.

Vitamin B5 and rutin, which are part of the bioflavanoid group of nutrients, are also required for the production of histamine.

Vitamin B3 causes the blood vessels just beneath the skin to dilate (open) and fill with blood. This will improve your sensitivity and responsiveness.

Vitamin B6 is directly involved in the production of our sex hormones so eating foods rich in this nutrient can re-awaken your sex glands.

Vitamin E has long been promoted as the 'sex' vitamin due to its beneficial effect on our reproductive health and hormone production.

Zinc is needed to assist with lubrication in the vagina and selenium is a mineral that can help to increase libido and regulate your hormones. Oysters are a good source of zinc and selenium; they are natural sexual arousers and have been considered an aphrodisiac for centuries.

The amino acid tyrosine has been shown to elevate mood and promote orgasm. It is required by the body in order to manufacture hormones and is found in almonds, beef, chicken, fish, soy beans and cheese.

Including foods that are rich in these nutrients in your diet will help you to reach your sexual potential. Good sources of these nutrients can be found in 'Understanding nutrients and their sources'.

Natural and safe aphrodisiacs

There are many plant substances reputed to be aphrodisiacs. All of the following substances are available from a herbalist or homoeopath.

BETH ROOT, *Trillium erectum*: most species of this plant are native to North America and have a long history of use by Indian women for treating a range of women's health irregularities. It is a powerful astringent tonic with a strong affinity with the female reproductive area. It has been traditionally used by women as an aphrodisiac and the white flowering species are considered to be the most effective.

DAMIANA, *Turnera aphrodisiaca*: as the name suggests, damiana has had a long history of use both as a tonic and aphrodisiac. It is a pituitary regulator and also has a stimulant effect on the mucosa of the genito-urinary tract.

FENUGREEK, *Trigonella foenum-graecum*: one of the oldest cultivated medicinal plants, it was found preserved, in King Tutankhamun's tomb and he died in 1323 BC. It is a highly nutritious plant that contains many essential minerals, vitamins and essential fatty acids; in particular vitamins A and D which help with hormone production. Fenugreek contains plant steroids and one of these, disogenin, is used for the synthesis of sex hormones. Many cultures have used fenugreek as an aphrodisiac.

KELP BLADDERWRACK, *Fucus vesiculosus*: considered to be an aphrodisiac due to its nutritive value. Kelp provides an abundance of vitamins, minerals and trace elements and it is the richest natural source of iodine. Iodine is essential for the health of our endocrine glands and in particular, the thyroid gland. When the thyroid gland becomes underactive, hormone production is reduced and the whole body becomes sluggish. This is because the thyroid gland controls our bodies' metabolic rate. Without healthy levels of thyroid hormones, women often experience diminished sexual vigour and libido. Bird's nest soup has been a famous Chinese aphrodisiac for thousands of years. The nest is made from seaweed (kelp) and fish spawn.

NUTMEG, *Myristica fragrans*: this common aromatic spice has an early history of culinary and medicinal uses. The oil is regarded as a rubefacient, which means it exerts local irritation to the skin, bringing blood to the surface and causing redness. Nutmeg is a narcotic herb and a stimulant to the gastro-intestinal tract. In small doses it will improve the appetite and assist digestion. It can be used in a couple of different ways. The oil may be rubbed directly on the clitoris or penis to achieve an irritant effect. This increases the blood supply to the surface tissue and enhances arousal. Secondly, its narcotic effect in low to moderate doses may bring about a feeling of intoxication enabling the user to let go of their inhibitions and prolong lovemaking. Nutmeg is considered safe to use as a spice.

Caution: oil of nutmeg must not be taken internally.

SAFFRON, *Crocus sativus*: has been used as an aphrodisiac for a long time. It is considered to be a sacred dye and it is used in cooking to flavour and colour food. Try using a little in your cooking.

VANILLA, *Vanilla planifolia*: is an orchid and the vanilla bean is a known aphrodisiac. It is mostly used today for its aroma and in cooking. The Aztecs used vanilla to flavour chocolate, which is also considered to be an aphrodisiac. When the English were introduced to chocolate they were very worried that it was dangerous for a woman's chastity. It wasn't until the end of the eighteenth century that women were allowed to drink it freely!

Essential oils

Modern perfumes are made in laboratories where chemical compounds are combined in the search for the ultimate aroma. Perhaps manufacturers should look no further than the heady aromas of the volatile essences in nature's garden.

One of history's most desirable women, Cleopatra, adorned her body with fragrant oils. She even soaked the sails of her ship in essential oils. Perfumes have long been used to inspire romance and some essential oils are highly erotic fragrances. They can arouse sexual desire and help you to seduce your lover in the same way that the fragrance of a blossom attracts the bees.

Essential oils can be used in an oil burner: place some water in the reservoir on the top of the burner, add a few drops of oil and light the candle below it. The oil will continue to give off its perfume until the water evaporates.

A few drops can be dropped onto a light globe. When it is on, the heat from the globe will burn the oil and release the aroma. You can buy clay rings for this purpose. For a more subtle aroma you can add a few drops to a porous clay pot. Once the oil soaks in it will continue to give off a mild perfume for some time. Add a few drops as needed to restore its fragrance.

Here are some essential oils you can use to enhance your sexual responses.

CEDARWOOD, *Cedrus atlantica*: the distilled oil from the wood of the cedar tree has a wonderful, dry, woody aroma that encourages sexual response. Cedarwood settles tension and will keep you centred.

CINNAMON, *Cinnamomum arromaticum*: the cinnamon tree is among the oldest aromatic plants that have been traditionally used as an aphrodisiac. This essential oil is used to flavour and scent food and perfumes. Cinnamon can also be used as a treatment for impotence in males.

CLARY SAGE, *Salvia sclarea*: belongs to the same family as the culinary sage but it has a more enticing aroma. If your mind is crowded with persistent

55

thoughts and you cannot relax and maintain your focus then this oil may suit you. Perhaps you would like to communicate better with your lover or would like them to communicate more freely with you. Sage has a strong affinity with the throat and can help to release blockages in the throat *chakra*. Clary sage opens channels of communication so it becomes easier to express your desires or let your heart energy flow.

GERANIUM, *Pelargonium*: geranium oil is distilled from the rose geranium. It is not listed as an aphrodisiac, however the oil from this plant is a stimulant to adrenal hormones. This action may improve stamina and sexual response.

JASMINE, *Jasminum grandiflorum*: is a very sweet and heady perfume that has a spellbinding aroma. Throughout history women have used this oil to induce ecstasy.

NEROLI, *Citrus aurantium*: made from the blossoms of the bitter orange tree and was an ingredient in eau de Cologne in the eighteenth century. It is slightly hypnotic and is calming in stressful situations. Neroli is listed as an aphrodisiac and is a treatment for low libido. It is important during foreplay or masturbation to feel relaxed enough to explore.

PATCHOULI, *Pogostemon patchouli*: comes from the leaves of a plant that originated in Malaysia. I first discovered patchouli oil during the early 1970s when it became a popular perfume. Its scent is exotic, hot and heavy and it has the capacity to encourage sexual response.

ROSE, *Rosa damascena*: legend has it that rose oil is the blood of the goddess Aphrodite. Its perfume is exquisite, stirring and speaks of love. It has a long lasting fragrance that influences the heart.

SANDALWOOD, *Santalum album*: this oil is extracted from the heartwood of an evergreen tree that has been sacred since the fifth century BC. The perfume excites the senses and has a soft, woody aroma that is very similar to the male pheromone or mating signal produced by the hormone androsterone.

YLANG YLANG, *Cananga odorata*: this oil is produced from the blossoms of an exotic tree grown in the tropics and it is known in the Philippines as the 'flower of flowers'. The blossoms are traditionally strewn across the beds of newlyweds to help them overcome nervousness and to heighten sexual pleasure. It has an intoxicating and exotic perfume.

Homoeopathic remedies for poor libido

Homoeopathic remedies are prescribed according to your individual needs. Here is a brief overview of how some remedies can be helpful to treat underlying problems that may be contributing to sexual debility.

Nat mur: for sexual debility associated with unresolved grief or suppressed emotions.

Phosphoric acid: a remedy for when you feel too exhausted to make love.

Sepia: for when you want to be left alone and feel indifferent to your lover.

Physical and emotional blockages

It is possible to inhibit sexual desire by blocking your sexual energy. Physical causes can be related to tension held in the lower back. Poor circulation and/or nerve damage to the lumbar vertebrae at the base of your spine can also affect your sex life. If your partner has problems with impotence or if either of you have pain or tension in your lower back, it is possible that structural or circulatory problems are the cause.

There are many avenues of treatment to consider. Some common and helpful measures include acupuncture, massage therapy, shiatsu, chiropractic, osteopathy and physiotherapy. Don't be afraid to try them as they can be highly effective forms of therapy.

The emotional factors that can block our sexual flow are many and varied. They can range from low self-esteem and poor body image to distressing memories of incest and sexual abuse. If possible, share any negative feelings you may have about yourself or your lovemaking with your partner, even though it may be difficult. Honest communication, understanding, reassurance and encouragement from them can help to heal sexual wounds and clear emotional blockages that may be inhibiting your desire.

Some women will benefit from the assistance of a professional counsellor who they can talk to in a confidential and safe environment; someone they can trust who will help to find the solution to their problems so they can enjoy a normal sex life in the future.

The Bach Flower essences are good self-help remedies that can assist with emotional blockages. Some worth considering are pine, gentian, hornbeam, red chestnut and willow. They are listed in detail in 'Moods and the mind' and are available as over-the-counter preparations.

Is it my hormones?

Many women who lose their sex drive often think they have a hormonal imbalance. While it is true that hormones can enhance or suppress your libido and virility, I think their influence is overstated. There are many other factors that can interfere with sex drive, such as back pain, anxiety, relationship problems, boredom, low self-esteem and poor body image.

Some doctors will recommend hormonal therapy using testosterone injections and implants. Think very carefully before you consider hormone therapy to correct problems with libido because it can be difficult to find the right balance. Low testosterone levels can lead to poor sexual function, diminished desire and reduced reaction time. However, high levels can also lead to a reduction of sexual function due to our bodies' sensitive feedback mechanisms. Make sure you are very clear about the side effects of these drugs before commencing therapy. They can affect your emotional and mental health, as well as the way you look. In some women they cause acne, increased body hair, deepening of the voice (which sometimes can be permanent), tension in the breasts and uterine bleeding.

Sensual massage for arousing desire

Massage can be a highly erotic way to improve your libido and responsiveness. I will share some thoughts and techniques on sensual massage to help you get started—the rest is up to you. Find your confidence and be guided by your intuition and your partner's responses. Let me assure you, formal massage training is not required.

Find a place where there are no distractions, take the phone off the hook and turn the lights down or light some candles. If you prefer background music, choose something quiet that will not distract you. Essential oils can be used to enhance the effect of arousal. Choose one from the list of aphrodisiacs provided and add a few drops to your massage oil. Use a light oil such as jojoba or almond oil and make sure it is warmed before you use it.

The partner who is receiving the massage should lie comfortably on the floor on a thin mattress or on the bed. If they are lying on their stomach, they may be more comfortable with a pillow under their chest, and/or under their hips. If they are lying on their back, place a pillow under their knees and under their neck, so they can relax their abdominal muscles.

For erotic massage, it is best to remove all clothing and keep the legs slightly apart but don't be tempted to head straight for the pleasure zones or your partner won't be able to relax.

Kneel beside your partner's body or between their legs, make sure you are in a balanced and comfortable position. Pause for a moment to centre yourself and regulate your breathing. Watch for the steady rise and fall of your partner's chest or back so that you can synchronise your breathing in rhythm with theirs.

When you are ready to begin, pour a small amount of oil in the palm of your hand and lightly rub both hands together. The oil should not be poured directly onto the skin but applied with the open palms in sweeping motions over the body. Start with a small amount of oil because if you use too much you reduce your ability to feel your partner's body.

Keep the contact firm but not too heavy, using the palm of your hands. This will initially help to relax both you and your partner. Beginning the massage using light, feathery movements with your fingers may put them on edge. Focus your awareness on their body and explore. Take turns with your partner and communicate your responses. Remember, you have lots of time. Always try to maintain contact with the body. Feel the sexual energy that flows between you and your partner's body. If you decide to make love feel the connections with your partner's body, your breath and the flow of sexual energy.

Fantasise, visualise your dream lover, unblock erotic thought channels to enhance your psychic stimulation while your body experiences the sensory stimulation.

Sexual desire is not totally dependent on hormones now is it?

Nutrition for your male sexual partner

Although this is a book primarily for women, I have included this section for those women who have a male partner who wants to improve his sexual performance. Refer to 'Understanding nutrients and their sources' for comprehensive lists of the various dietary sources of nutrients.

Good circulation and a healthy vascular system is crucial for male sexual health because during erection the penis contains eight times the amount of blood that is normally present.

Vitamin B6 is required by the tiny erectile muscles in the penis to maintain muscular rigidity and contraction so it can increase erection time.

A deficiency of B6 may contribute to a flaccid penis or a weak orgasm.

Vitamin E is essential for good circulation and oxygen transport to the cells and tissue. It is considered a good nutritional treatment for impotence.

Zinc is needed for the production of dihydrooxytestosterone, which is the biologically active form of testosterone. This male hormone is required to maintain a healthy libido. It increases sperm motility and sexual drive.

Manganese is a mineral that helps to prevent circulation problems caused by thickenings in the arteries. Poor circulation due to atherosclerosis can be a contributing factor of impotence in males. As a preventative measure eat foods that contain manganese.

Magnesium, calcium and phosphorous are all involved with muscular contraction and nerve transmission. Foods containing these minerals are essential for arousal and maintaining an erection.

Studies have shown that fenugreek, panax ginseng, damiana and saw palmetto can increase sperm activity and libido. They are available from a practitioner of herbal medicine.

Keep in mind that this information is only associated with the physical aspects of arousal and sexual stamina. Emotional factors and pressures on men can seriously affect sexual performance. Like us, they may need opportunities to communicate their feelings and their fears without judgement or criticism.

Common habits that dampen desire

Smoking has been linked with poor sexual health and reduced sperm count. If you want to improve your sexual health it is a good idea to stop smoking.

Some common medicines such as sedatives and tranquillisers can interfere with sexual response because they slow down muscular responses and dull the senses.

Keep alcohol levels to a minimum. While small amounts may be favourable to men who suffer premature ejaculation or anxiety, regular excessive intake of alcohol will gradually undermine sexual capacity. A drunk usually makes a very poor lover and alcohol can cause impotence and sterility.

Regular moderate exercise will be highly beneficial to sexual health, however excessive exercise can create adrenal fatigue that can negatively affect libido.

Sex and self-esteem

Most of us have experienced the pressures of our sexually-orientated culture at some time or another. A lack of interest in sex can be seen as a problem or a failure and your self-esteem can suffer.

It is not my intention to propose that we all require a powerful sex drive in order to achieve health and wellbeing, but sexual stimulation can enhance physical and emotional health. Keep in mind that problems with libido are often temporary. Try not to feel inadequate and seek professional help if necessary.

Anaphrodisiacs

As the name suggests, anaphrodisiacs act in the opposite way to aphrodisiacs. They are substances that dampen sexual desire. It should not come as a surprise that women might want to suppress desire and it is entirely up to the individual to determine if their sex drive is excessive.

There are many situations where anaphrodisiacs might be useful because there are times when women may find it is a burden to be preoccupied with sexual thoughts. Some women find themselves alone for long periods of time, for example, if you are widowed and not ready or willing to enter a sexual relationship. Perhaps you are separated from your lover and you are maintaining a monogamous relationship; you might find you need to reduce your sexual urges because of a desire to be faithful.

Strong sexual urges can prevent us from forming platonic friendships. They can be overwhelming at times and may affect the way we relate to others. There are also times when women need to recover from an illness or emotional trauma.

Maybe there is a need for some space or clarity of thought in order to make important decisions about your sexuality and intimate relationships. If you are practising natural fertility methods you may be having difficulty with your libido during the fertile phase of your cycle.

Some women choose a celibate existence for spiritual and other reasons. They choose not to pursue sexual relationships and are satisfied with this decision.

A large sexual appetite is not always easy to satisfy. Some women find they are very sexually demanding and may be in danger of making unreasonable demands on their partner. For all these reasons and more, women may find it helpful to know that anaphrodisiacs exist.

HERBAL ANAPHRODISIACS
HOPS, *Humulus lupulus*: has a mild sedative action and helps induce sleep. Hops have a reputation for controlling sexual desire and restlessness due to their high oestrogen content.
SKULLCAP, *Scutellaria lateriflora*: calms the nervous system and suppresses unwanted sexual desire.
WHITE POND LILY, *Nymphaea alba*: an aquatic herb that has a long history of use as an anaphrodisiac. As well as calming excessive sexual desire, it is also used to treat leucorrhoea.

ESSENTIAL OILS
LAVENDER, *Lavender angustifolia*: is distilled from the flower spikes of the plant. It has a cool, floral aroma and it is well-known for easing tension.
MARJORAM, *Origanum marjorana*: has a peppery scent and is a powerful relaxing oil that calms the mind and brings about relaxation.
MELISSA, *Melissa officinalis*: has a distinct lemon fragrance and can help calm an overstimulated body. It is a natural antidepressant.

HOMOEOPATHIC ANAPHRODISIACS
CANTHARIS: for when you feel a strong physical sexual urging.
HYOSCYAMUS: for those with excited desire and no concern for modesty.
PHOSPHORUS: for nymphomania with an aversion to intercourse.
PLANTINUM: to calm enormous sexual desire with voluptuous tingling.

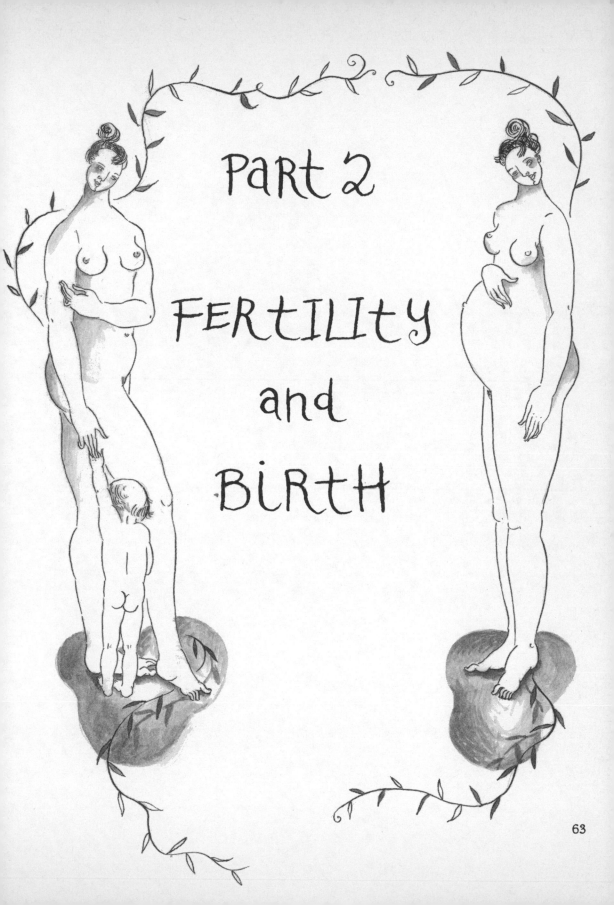

PART 2

FERTILITY and BIRTH

Conception

ALL women must be given a variety of contraceptive choices and the freedom to make their own decisions about reproduction so they can have greater control over their lives.

Family planning methods have given women the opportunity to choose whether or not they will have children. And if they decide to have them, they can plan how many children they will have and when they will have them. Also, by developing an understanding of the contraceptive options available and how to use them, women can improve their reproductive and sexual health. We know, for example, that it is preferable to have some space between pregnancies to allow women time to recover and to improve the survival rate of their infants.

It was not so long ago that we had very limited options for birth control and unplanned pregnancies were common. Family planning education and the availability of affordable contraception has certainly improved the health of many, however most methods of contraception have been far from ideal.

Women have been the main target for the contraceptive market. We have been encouraged and sometimes pressured into trying many different chemical combinations of oral contraceptive pills, hormonal implants and injectables. There have been many different intra-uterine devices (IUDs), spermicides and various surgical procedures used to bring about temporary and permanent sterilisation.

Many women today are moving away from this type of intervention to the more natural methods of family planning. This appears to be due to changes in sexual behaviour and a greater awareness of the risk of sexually transmitted diseases. A number of the women I have spoken with prefer to use natural methods because they are more comfortable with a minimum amount of intervention and they are quite prepared to go ahead with a pregnancy should it occur. Other women will consider using menstrual regulators or abortion as a backstop in the event that an unwanted pregnancy occurs.

Women have the right to choose to have a child or to remain childless regardless of their sexuality, religion, financial, social or marital position.

While decisions about contraception and fertility are deeply personal, they are strongly influenced by a mixture of cultural, moral, social, economic, physical, psychological and emotional influences. It is important to carefully consider all available contraceptive options in order to choose the method that will best meet your needs.

Conceiving—is it purely physical?

It is difficult to know how strongly our emotions and desires influence conception. The term 'birth control' implies that we can exercise complete authority over nature using only physical methods. Do we really have total power to delay or create life?

There is no birth control method that is 100 per cent effective and women can and do fall pregnant with an IUD fitted or while regularly taking the pill. Although there are often reasons why contraception fails, there are many instances that cannot be explained. Perhaps it is possible for us to assist or delay conception in an emotional or spiritual way. Certainly we know that a high level of emotional stress can prevent pregnancy occurring. By focusing only on conception in physical terms we may be underestimating the power of our inner desires. Is it possible that a secret desire for a child can influence our ability to conceive? It is sometimes very clear to women who have an unplanned pregnancy, in hindsight, that they were ready to accept a child on an emotional or spiritual level.

We know that our deeper thought patterns are closely connected to our physical body. Thoughts and ideas come from the higher centres of the brain which have a strong influence over our pituitary gland; the gland that controls the secretions of the reproductive hormones required for successful ovulation and fertility. When a woman desires a child, positive thoughts and desires can be very powerful catalysts for conception.

Experiences of conception differ immensely according to our level of awareness and the situation we are in at the time. While there are some women who do not know when it happened or how it happened, there are many others who distinctly recall a strong emotional sensation of 'knowing' that the creation of their child had taken place. Others experience a powerful 'sense' of a child waiting. When women speak about these intuitive feelings, they present a different perspective on conception, strongly connected but extremely different to the physical side. Women sometimes convey that they simply 'had a feeling' at the time. While this can appear vague perhaps it reflects the difficulty we have in communicating these intuitive feelings.

Where does this sense of 'knowing' that some women experience come from? Perhaps it is simply enough to acknowledge that it exists.

Physical conception

The physical role of our male sexual partner in the conception of a child is a very active and important one. Most literature available on fertility focuses on the need for men to produce strong, healthy sperm and for women simply to provide the access for it, free of blockages and obstructions. This indicates however, that the role of women in the creation of child is a very passive one, and this is not the case.

Information has become available that provides us with a new insight into conception. Women can and do make an active physical contribution in assisting the passage of sperm to their ovum. This is achieved by rhythmically contracting the muscles of the pelvic floor and orgasm is nature's exquisite way of aiding this process. When the female orgasm was captured on camera it revealed an unexpected physical aspect of conception.

A small camera was placed high inside a woman's vagina. The male sexual partner achieved orgasm before the woman, which meant there was a small pool of semen lying in her vagina, just beneath her cervix. During the woman's orgasm, her cervix rhythmically dipped down into the sperm pool with each muscular contraction. Every time it dipped, the opening in the cervix widened, as if it was drinking from the pool. When it pulled back, it tightened and appeared to suck the sperm up into the cervical canal. As it repeatedly dipped with every muscular spasm, it became more evident that the rhythmical pulsing associated with female orgasm, quite apart from pleasure, definitely has a beneficial role in assisting conception. This of course is dependent on your male partner achieving orgasm before you do!

Many women successfully become pregnant without orgasm of course, and couples don't have to simulate orgasm to achieve conception. If orgasm can help though, what a bonus.

Natural birth control methods

The following methods of contraception are generally considered to be natural family planning techniques. They do not require the use of drugs, barriers, spermicides or herbs to prevent pregnancy; instead they rely on hormonal changes, observation and self-control.

LACTATION

Regular breastfeeding is a natural form of birth control because it delays the return of fertility. After childbirth, the levels of oestrogen and progesterone in the mother's blood decrease. This, combined with the sucking action of an infant on the mother's nipple, stimulates the release of the hormones oxytocin and prolactin, which in turn promote milk secretion or lactation. Lactation is a natural family planning method because it usually represses the female sexual cycle by inhibiting the release of Follicle Stimulating Hormone (FSH) and Luteinising Hormone (LH), and without these two hormones, ovulation cannot occur. Remember, ovulation must occur before you can become pregnant because without it, no egg is released for fertilisation.

The success of breastfeeding as a contraceptive method is highly dependent on your baby's feeding habits. During the first six months your baby tends to feed well, around five or six times a day, and most women have a good milk supply to meet their baby's demands. So if this is the case and your baby is completely breastfed, you would only have a very slight risk of pregnancy. However, if your baby has small, irregular feeds that are supplemented with a formula or solids, I would recommend that a barrier method of contraception, such as a diaphragm, or condoms, be used.

If the baby is feeding well but your period has returned, you would definitely need to use a barrier method for adequate contraceptive protection.

I do not recommend the minipill for breastfeeding mothers. There are some women who seem to experience problems with their milk supply when they take oral contraceptives. Given the variety of contraception available and the importance of breastfeeding, I feel it is an unnecessary risk.

Sex without intercourse

When a woman is comfortable with her body and her sexuality she may decide to express and receive love without penetration. Many women achieve sexual fulfilment without the need for intercourse. Techniques can involve stroking, touching and oral sex, and as long as semen is kept away from the vagina pregnancy will not occur. Lovemaking can still be imaginative, interesting, stimulating and very physical.

Withdrawal

This is a simple contraceptive measure, often underrated, that is used by many people around the world. Withdrawal method is also referred to as *coitus interruptus* or 'spilling seed'. Its success relies completely on the male partner withdrawing his penis from the vagina before ejaculation takes place, to ensure that no sperm is released either at the entrance or inside the vagina. This presents a problem as the woman has no control and has to rely on her male partner to have perfect timing.

Withdrawal can be an effective method of contraception in circumstances where it is used by couples who know their bodies well and are able to maintain good control over the timing of ejaculation. Under these circumstances it is considered to have a success rate of 80 to 95 per cent, although its overall success is very difficult to determine. The belief that sperm leaks out in pre-orgasmic fluid is now considered unfounded.

Withdrawal is obviously a poor method of contraception for inexperienced couples and men who experience difficulty in controlling ejaculation. This method does not protect against any STDs so it is best used by couples in monogamous relationships.

Abstinence or celibacy

This means not having intercourse at all. Some women for religious, moral or other reasons of personal preference choose to avoid intercourse. A woman may decide to become celibate at any time in her life and her decision should be respected. This method is also known as continence.

Periodic abstinence

Periodic abstinence describes the avoidance of intercourse during the fertile times of the menstrual cycle. It is an integral part of other natural family planning methods such as the Billings and Rhythm methods. If women want to use periodic abstinence as part of a natural method of contraception they will need to have a very regular menstrual cycle. Ideally

69

the cycle should be observed and charted for six to twelve months before women can safely rely on these techniques for birth control. In order for these methods to be successful it is best to learn about them from your health practitioner or a qualified teacher in natural fertility management.

BILLINGS METHOD

The Billings method is used to assess a woman's fertile times by observing and recording changes in vaginal mucus that indicate ovulation (*see* 'Mucous method'). Women often find this method very interesting and helpful because it can teach them a great deal about their bodies.

RHYTHM OR CALENDAR METHOD

The Rhythm method involves avoiding intercourse near the time of ovulation and is known to be the acceptable form of natural birth control by the Catholic Church. Unfortunately, the Rhythm method has a reputation of having a high failure rate because it can be difficult to predict the exact time of ovulation unless you have a regular 28-day cycle.

We know that thirteen to fifteen days will elapse from ovulation to menstruation regardless of the length of your cycle. So if your cycle is 28-days long you will ovulate within one day of Day 14. However, if your cycle becomes irregular and one is 40 days long, you are likely to ovulate within one day of Day 26. Day 26 would normally be outside the calculated days of abstinence.

To calculate your fertile time you must first observe and record your cycle for six to twelve months. You then subtract twenty days from your shortest cycle, which indicates the first day of your fertile phase. This makes an allowance of approximately six days for sperm survival time and roughly fourteen days to elapse after ovulation. Next you subtract eleven days from your longest cycle to calculate the last day of your fertile phase. Therefore, if over twelve months your cycle varies from 25 to 31 days you will abstain from intercourse from Day 5 to Day 20. Menstruation is likely to occur from Day 1 to Day 5 so most couples will not engage in sexual penetration with a penis for a great deal of the woman's cycle. They may however, still engage in other satisfying sexual activities.

If you have a regular cycle and this method is used correctly it can have a success rate of 83 to 93 per cent. This method alone offers no protection against STDs.

MUCOUS METHOD

By observing changes in cervical mucus, women are able to predict when they are likely to be fertile. On examination, they will notice that the texture, amount and appearance of the mucus changes regularly throughout the cycle in synergy with their hormones. Intercourse is 'safe' when there is no mucus or sticky mucus present and 'unsafe' when fertile mucus is produced during ovulation. The second 'safe' phase begins three days after the mucus becomes thick, sticky and opaque again. This is an accurate and successful method for those couples who adhere to it conscientiously.

Observing mucus

Sit comfortably in a relaxed position and gently insert one or two fingers into your vagina. Reach back into your vagina and gently pull down some of the mucus. While you are doing this you can take the opportunity to feel your cervix. When you are fertile, it feels soft and plump. During your infertile phase it becomes more rigid and the os (opening) is tight and unyielding.

When you withdraw your fingers you will have a sample of mucus for examination. Feel its texture between your thumb and first finger. Immediately after your menstrual bleeding you will tend to have no mucus present and the entrance to your vagina may feel quite dry. In the next few days, as your oestrogen level begins to rise, you will start to produce a sticky mucus that often appears cloudy or opaque. As ovulation gets closer and the follicle becomes ripe, fertile mucus is produced in copious quantities. This is clear mucus, long and stringy, resembling the white of an egg. It has strands that are able to be stretched between your fingers without breaking. The sperm can survive in this mucus and it is the medium through which they can swim. Fertile mucus is produced for about four days and it reaches its peak on the day of ovulation. During the time of ovulation you will notice a thick plug of mucus that comes away from the cervix. It can range from being clear and jelly-like to yellow, thick and creamy. Fertile mucus is produced for a few days after ovulation and then it becomes thick and sticky again. Prior to menstruation when the hormone levels drop, the vagina becomes quite dry once more until bleeding commences.

Observing mucous patterns is a useful indicator of vaginal health, even if you do not require contraception. Many women worry that they have an abnormal discharge while often they are experiencing normal, healthy mucus. By observing changes in vaginal fluids, you will be alerted promptly

71

to any abnormal changes that may indicate an infection.

If you rely on a mucous method for contraception observe the following precautions:

Try to have intercourse in the evenings during the first 'safe' phase in case infertile mucus changes to fertile overnight. Having spontaneous sex in the morning without first observing your mucus may lead to pregnancy.

The presence of semen or a lubricant in the vagina can lead to confusion and anxiety if a woman thinks it is fertile mucus. You may find it is helpful to have intercourse every second day until you feel you know your pattern well.

Keep in mind that inflammation of the vagina and abnormal discharges can make it difficult to assess mucus correctly.

TEMPERATURE METHOD

Women can accurately detect when ovulation occurs by taking and recording their basal body temperature daily. During ovulation progesterone is released and your basal body temperature rises. It is only a slight rise of 0.2 to 0.6 degrees centigrade and if it is sustained for three days, it is a strong indication that you have ovulated. During these three days you are in a fertile phase and intercourse should definitely be avoided if you do not desire a pregnancy. Intercourse can be commenced after these three days with a very low risk of pregnancy. This method is not effective if body temperature rises due to infection before ovulation.

Your temperature must be taken every morning before you get out of bed and before you have anything to smoke, eat or drink. You need to buy a thermometer from a pharmacy that is designed to detect very slight rises in body temperature. Place the thermometer under your tongue or into your vagina (always use the same place, don't interchange), and keep it there for three minutes to ensure an accurate reading. By keeping a record of your daily temperature on graph paper you will have a useful chart of your temperature patterns. These will indicate with accuracy, both fertile and infertile times.

SYMPTOTHERMAL METHODS

This is the term used to describe the combination of Temperature and Mucous methods to achieve contraception.

ASTROLOGICAL BIRTH CONTROL

This method involves avoidance of intercourse during your 'sun–moon' phase. This is the same 'sun–moon' phase that existed when you were born. It is calculated by an astrologer according to the time you were born, the date and your place of birth.

It is based on the belief by some astrologers that women release eggs twice a month. Once during mid-cycle and once during their 'sun–moon' phase. I have no information on success or failure rates of this method and as far as I am aware no scientific research is available on this method.

NO CONTRACEPTION

If you have sex without any form of contraception there is a strong likelihood that you will become pregnant. Simply telling yourself or convincing your partner that you probably won't fall pregnant does not work. There is an extremely high failure rate of around 80 to 90 per cent when no contraception is used.

Barrier Methods

THE CONDOM

This is probably the most ideal form of contraception available today. It is also one of the oldest methods still in use. Condoms were first designed to protect against STDs rather than for contraceptive purposes. They were worn in the sixteenth century to prevent the spread of syphilis and were made from silk and linen. In the eighteenth century they were made from animal intestines, then rubber and now they are much thinner and made from latex. They are worn over an erect penis and usually have a small teat in the end that acts as a reservoir to collect the ejaculated semen. They are around 15 to 20 centimetres long and will fit snugly around most penises.

Condoms are ideal for various reasons: they protect us from most sexually transmitted diseases; men are able to share the responsibility; they are readily available; and they are about 97 per cent effective as a contraceptive, provided they are used correctly.

Pregnancy is likely to occur from the incorrect use of condoms so the following information may be helpful.

Store condoms in a cool place and always check the expiry date before using them.

Don't keep them for too long as they can perish and develop small holes or tear during lovemaking, rendering them useless.

Use a fresh condom every time you have intercourse, they are not designed to be recycled!

Squeeze the pocket of air out of the reservoir tip of the condom before it is rolled all the way down the penis. If there is no reservoir, allow about one centimetre. This will ensure there is enough room at the top to catch and store the semen after ejaculation, otherwise it may leak down the sides and spill out.

Roll the condom onto the penis when it is erect just to make things easier, and put it on before there is any genital contact.
Condoms are often pre-lubricated, which makes them easier to put on and keeps them pliable to reduce the risk of breakage. If you do need a lubricant make sure it is a good water-based type that will not affect the rubber on the condom. Do not use Vaseline, as it is a petroleum-based product, or any oil-based substances as they can affect the latex and cause the condom to break.

When you finish, hold the rim of the condom at the base of the penis before withdrawal to ensure it stays on and do this before the penis becomes too soft.

There is really no need for a spermicide to be used with a condom as they provide enough protection by themselves. Some women find they are sensitive to the latex and can develop a tissue irritation. It may help to use a pure vitamin E cream or aloe vera gel to help this problem and to use a good water-based lubricant to avoid irritation from friction during intercourse.
Try to maintain a healthy attitude about condoms because they are effective contraceptives and offer good protection from STDs. Always carry one in your purse or pocket, just in case. Never allow yourself to be talked out of using one; regardless of how clean and honest a person might seem. Remember that the condom is the only effective protection against HIV/AIDS.
An added benefit of condoms is that they are an immediately reversible form of contraception should you desire pregnancy, with no adverse effects.

Note: If a condom breaks or comes off during intercourse, consult a doctor or family planning clinic within the next 48 hours to obtain the morning after pill if there is a risk of unwanted pregnancy.

THE FEMALE CONDOM

The female condom is made from transparent plastic and is designed to fit inside the vagina rather than over a penis. It is disposable, odourless and is an effective barrier method of contraception. The female condom has a small ring at the closed end that is inserted by squeezing the sides of the ring together between your thumb, index and middle finger until it is narrow, then sliding it inside the vagina. The larger ring on the open end remains outside your body and will comfortably rest up against your labia during intercourse. Put your finger into the open end which remains outside your body and feel up into the condom to locate the smaller ring. When you can feel it, push the inner ring up inside your vagina past your pubic bone which is located towards the front. The condom is now in place and should not feel uncomfortable. It can be inserted anytime before close genital contact.

The inside of the condom is pre-lubricated, however you can add extra lubrication if required.

When you are ready for intercourse, guide your partner's penis in through the open end and you should both enjoy lovemaking as normal without loss of sensitivity.

After intercourse, twist the outer ring to prevent spillage of sperm. Gently pull out the condom, wrap it up and throw it into the bin. Never dispose of condoms by flushing them down the toilet, we don't want them to end up in the ocean.

THE DIAPHRAGM

Diaphragms are dome-shaped rubber contraceptive devices that are very reliable as long as they are used correctly. If you are motivated to use one, they have a success rate of 85 to 95 per cent.

They are designed to cover your cervix and provide a barrier that will prevent sperm swimming in through the os, thereby avoiding fertilisation. The diaphragm tucks in behind your pubic bone, reaches back behind your cervix and is held in position by the muscles in the vaginal wall.

There are a number of benefits associated with cervical barriers:

Using a diaphragm for contraception will not interfere with spontaneity because it can be inserted several hours before sexual contact.

Except for the initial outlay, they are an inexpensive form of contraception and will last for several years.

They are handy for women who only need protection for a short time.

They can be used if you wish to have sex during your menstrual cycle to avoid staining. Take care to only leave your diaphragm in for short periods of time to enable your menses to flow freely.

Your diaphragm can be inserted in advance so it will not interfere with sexual arousal or reduce spontaneity. They have no unpleasant odour and if fitted correctly cannot be felt by your lover.

Unlike some methods of contraception the diaphragm does not interfere with your fertility and can be stopped at any time if you desire a pregnancy.

One problem that some women have with using a diaphragm is that it can put pressure on the bladder and aggravate cystitis. Urinating before and after intercourse can help to prevent this problem.

In the past it was recommended that you use a spermicide or jelly to improve the effectiveness of your diaphragm as a contraceptive. There is no research to indicate that there is an increased risk of pregnancy whether you use a spermicide or not. Spermicides can sometimes cause vaginal irritation in some women, they can be messy to use and they add to the cost of your contraception. Despite these factors, some women prefer to use a spermicide for added security and it really is a matter of personal choice.

Diaphragms are inexpensive, reusable and with care will last for several years. Be aware though, that the diaphragm does not provide protection against all STDs and should only be used in situations where women are absolutely certain they are in a monogamous relationship. Although it is a barrier method, it will only offer slight protection against wart virus, chlamydia and gonorrhoea because these organisms enter the upper reproductive area via the cervix. Diaphragms do not protect women against HIV/AIDS.

Fitting a diaphragm
If you decide to purchase a diaphragm you will need to see an experienced women's health worker for a fitting. This involves a pelvic examination to determine the depth and muscular strength of your vaginal walls and the size and shape of your cervix. They will then fit a few different diaphragms until they find one that fits snugly over your cervix and is held comfortably in place. There are various sizes of diaphragms available with several types

of springs in the rim to allow for differences in women's anatomy and muscle tone.

It is very important that you are given the opportunity to practise inserting and taking out your diaphragm before you leave the clinic. Make good use of your health practitioner and ask them to check that you have it in place correctly. It is better to make any mistakes at the clinic rather than experimenting at home. While you are there you should feel inside your vagina so you know what it feels like when it is inserted properly. Then you can be confident you are using an effective method of contraception.

You should never borrow someone else's diaphragm or simply buy one without finding out your size because proper fitting is essential. If you already have a diaphragm, be aware that changes in the vagina can interfere with its effectiveness as a contraceptive device. There are times when you may need to have an extra fitting to recheck the size because your diaphragm needs to fit well in order for it to seal properly. You will need an extra fitting:
* After pregnancy.
* If you have a significant weight change of say, more than 4 kilograms.
* If you have an abortion.
* If you have a miscarriage.
* Diaphragms eventually deteriorate and need to be replaced every two or three years.

How to insert a diaphragm
There is a certain amount of practise and skill required when inserting a diaphragm. After being shown at the time of your fitting, it is wise to practise in privacy a few times, until you feel you have it right. Then, it is a good idea to insert it yourself and go back to see your health practitioner so they can check if you have fitted it correctly.

Inserting a diaphragm can be like inserting a tampon for the first time. Try squatting or standing with one foot on a chair, the toilet or the bed.

Hold the diaphragm by its rim with the open side of the cup facing up. Squeeze the edges together between your thumb and first finger until it is a narrow, oval shape. Insert it and run the pointed edge up the back wall of your vagina until you feel it slide up behind the cervix. The front of it should then slip easily into place up behind the pubic bone. You may need to tuck it into place.

It is important to feel inside your vagina to ensure the diaphragm is in place over your cervix because that part of your vagina has no nerve endings. If you cannot feel your cervix, bear down or push with your stomach muscles until you can.

Once it is in position you or your partner should not be able to feel it during intercourse. If you can feel it, chances are it is not correctly in place or it may be the wrong size for you.

In order for your diaphragm to be an effective contraceptive device you must remember to insert it before any genital contact and leave it in for six hours after intercourse.

To remove it, hook your finger behind the front edge and pull it out. Always wash it in warm water with a mild soap, rinse it thoroughly and dry it well. Check to see there are no holes in it by holding it up to the light. You can dust it with a little cornflour to keep it dry and prevent it from perishing, and store it in its container in a cool, dry place. Do not use talc as it has a negative effect on the latex and it will cause the diaphragm to perish.

There is no evidence to show that a spermicide needs to be used with a diaphragm.

CERVICAL CAPS

Cervical caps are smaller than diaphragms and as the name suggests, they fit over the cervix and provide a barrier between sperm and the cervical canal. Caps are held in place by suction of the rim and they are fitted and used in the same way as a diaphragm. They can be a little harder to insert and the type of cap used is determined by the length of your cervix.

They are not as popular as diaphragms but may be a better option for women who are prone to urinary disorders due to pressure from their diaphragm.

Like diaphragms, cervical caps offer slight protection against some sexually transmitted diseases, but not HIV/AIDS.

Traditional herbal medicine and birth control

Herbal birth control has been used by women for thousands of years; there are records of remedies for the prevention of pregnancy dating from the first century AD.

Many indigenous women from a variety of cultures have used remedies that were highly effective in causing temporary sterility and preventing pregnancy. Many of the herbs used for this purpose contained hormonal substances that stimulated the uterus to contract and promoted menstruation. Some may have altered the endometrial lining of the uterus making it unsuitable for pregnancy. While we still have very limited research in this area of herbal medicine, we cannot guarantee the safety or the efficacy of these substances.

Medicinal herbs are powerful remedies that must be used with respect. While we do have herbs that can bring on a period, they are not given to women who have a desire to be pregnant or suspect they are pregnant because they may contribute to miscarriage.

For the purposes of contraception, herbal medicine can be used in conjunction with other methods of birth control to improve their effectiveness. For instance, natural family planning techniques, such as the Rhythm or Calendar method, are dependent on a regular menstrual pattern to improve their success rate. There are many 'safe' herbs that are highly effective in balancing and correcting an irregular menstrual cycle, and they can also help to maintain the health of our reproductive organs according to the specific action of the therapeutic and nutritional properties of the plant. It is rare to find a method of contraception that is actually healthy!

We have at our disposal many safe plants that contain hormonal substances and, in fact, wild yam provided the first materials used to make the oral contraceptive pill. This herb has been well-researched and well-utilised in traditional and orthodox medicine.

Women relying on lactation to prevent pregnancy can be helped by herbs that are known as galactagogues. These are safe for nursing mothers and they can improve a woman's milk supply. This may indirectly assist with contraception because it helps to prevent her milk 'drying up', which hastens the return of her menstrual cycle.

Although some herbal remedies have undesirable side effects, I strongly suspect that there were remedies that women could use with safety to prevent pregnancy. Unfortunately, information on herbal remedies for birth control methods cannot be shared. A traditional therapist cannot prescribe herbal medicines for the purpose of stimulating menstruation for contraceptive purposes.

It is ironic though, that it is acceptable for medical practitioners to legitimately prescribe chemical substances such as the morning after pill, to stimulate menstruation. These pills can cause dreadful side effects in some women, yet this form of 'menstrual regulation' using chemical intervention is approved. Women will simply have to rely on herbal medicines to complement the other natural family planning methods outlined above.

Chemical and conventional methods

THE ORAL CONTRACEPTIVE PILL

The oral contraceptive pill is a very popular method of contraception that was first produced in the 1960s. It was supposed to liberate women from the burden of unwanted pregnancies.

Undoubtedly the pill eliminated the fear of pregnancy so women could relax and enjoy lovemaking. For women who had complications with previous pregnancies and for whom any future pregnancy posed a health risk, the pill may have been a dream come true. However, there are women whose lives ended or became more difficult because of the pill.

The early pill contained very high levels of hormones that caused dreadful side effects. Some women suffered strokes and developed cancers because of the original formula used. Did they feel liberated? I doubt it.

While today's pill is based on the original formula, it has much lower levels of hormones, is much safer to use and is tolerated well by many women.

Effectiveness

The pill offers no protection against sexually transmitted diseases and women should keep this in mind when it is being used as a contraceptive.

It is most effective if it is taken at the same time every day. So if you are more than twelve hours late with the combined pill or three hours with the minipill, barrier methods should be considered because your pill may not be effective. Also, if you are taking broad-spectrum antibiotics or you have a bout of vomiting or diarrhoea, your pill may not be effective. In these circumstances you should continue to take the pill, but avoid intercourse or use barrier methods of contraception until your next period.

It is suspected that taking vitamin C in erratic and high doses can also interfere with the pill's effectiveness. There are a couple of possible explanations for this. Very high doses of vitamin C can cause diarrhoea which reduces its effectiveness. The level needed to cause this reaction will depend very much on the individual but often occurs above 2000 milligrams a day. If you have a virus or influenza and want to take short-term high levels of vitamin C to boost your immune response, and you continue to be sexually active, you should continue to take the pill and use a barrier method of contraception.

Unfortunately when you stop taking vitamin C, it is suspected that your blood level of hormones drops quite suddenly and may temporarily reduce the pill's effectiveness.

Daily doses of 250 to 500 milligrams of vitamin C actually increase the absorption of hormones in the pill making it more effective, which is good.

THE COMBINED PILL

This pill is based on the original 1960s formula; it contains the two hormones, oestrogen and progestogen (synthetic progesterone), in various levels according to the different brands available. Basically it prevents ovulation by stopping the ovaries from releasing an egg. If there is no egg then fertilisation cannot take place and no pregnancy will develop. The success rate is around 97 per cent.

Negative side effects of the oral contraceptive pill

There are a number of side effects associated with taking the oral contraceptive pill. The incidence of these is dependent on the type of pill taken and how these hormones will affect women. While every woman will react differently, some common side effects have been observed and most of these are completely reversible when the pill is discontinued. If you suspect your pill is causing undesirable side effects, talk to your doctor about alternative contraception.

Acne: if you develop acne from your pill it is usually because your ratio of oestrogen:progesterone is too low. Acne commonly occurs when progesterone levels are high and with some synthetic forms of hormones. If you wish to remain on the pill but find that it is causing acne, you will need to talk to your doctor about an alternative oral contraceptive pill. You may improve with one that has a different ratio of hormones.

Amenorrhoea (absence of menstruation): it is possible and sometimes desirable to deliberately stop a period by prescribing hormones in a specific way. An example is the treatment for endometriosis to prevent the further growth of endometrial tissue. In these circumstances it is done under close supervision and it is often beneficial. When women cease to have a period while taking an oral contraceptive pill without planning to, it is not necessarily a problem. It indicates that they are not producing enough oestrogen to build up a significant lining in the uterus. In this case, I feel it is a good idea to stop taking the pill every three to six months and allow your body to shed any lining that may have built up, even though it might only be minimal. Amenorrhoea can increase anxiety due to the suspicion of a pregnancy.

Breakthrough bleeding (unexpected bleeding): this is a common side effect of the pill. It usually occurs with low-dose pills such as the minipill or progesterone only pill, due to low levels of oestrogen. It can occur during the first few months of taking the pill or it can come on unexpectedly after being on the pill for many months. Sometimes it is an indication that your contraceptive pill is not being absorbed correctly and may not be offering you adequate protection from pregnancy.

Breast changes: It is normal to experience breast tenderness and a slight increase in their size when you first start the pill, as your body initially reacts to the change in hormones in your system. Breast tissue is sensitive to both oestrogen and progestogen so it is not surprising that women notice some change when they first start taking these hormones. This tends to settle down after the first three months and should disappear entirely. If your breasts remain tender and painful it is a strong indication that abnormal and undesirable changes are occurring in the breast tissue so it is advisable to stop taking the pill. You may find another brand of pill that will suit you better or change your contraception method altogether.

Chloasma or skin pigmentation: Some women develop brown patches on their face and neck when they take the pill. The pigmentation becomes much darker after exposure to the sun because ultraviolet light stimulates the release of the pigment melanin, which gives skin its colour. To control chloasma, wear a broad brimmed hat and sunscreen whenever you go out in the sun.

Depression: causes of depression are many and varied and so it can be difficult to know if your oral contraceptive pill is contributing. If you have noticed negative mood swings since you commenced the pill, or if you generally feel it is a contributing factor in your depression, stop taking it. Observe and record your moods through your next two cycles and use a barrier method of contraception if you take the pill for contraceptive purposes. This is the most accurate way of determining whether or not your pill is to blame. If you recommence taking the pill, keep in mind that you will need to continue using barrier methods for fourteen days because it takes that long for it to be effective again after a break.

Research shows that taking the oral contraceptive pill can reduce levels of certain B vitamins. Urinary output of tryptophan also increases in pill users and deficiency symptoms of this amino acid are insomnia, anxiety, depression and poor concentration. Vitamin B6 levels are greatly reduced when taking the oral contraceptive pill and a deficiency in this nutrient has also been linked with depression. Supplementation with vitamin B6 while taking the oral contraceptive pill has been shown to alleviate this problem.

Fluid retention: some women experience fluid retention when they take synthetic hormones. A deficiency of vitamin B6 can also contribute to fluid retention and we know that this nutrient is often deficient in women taking the oral contraceptive pill.

Gall bladder disease: an increased incidence of gall bladder disease has been observed in some young women taking the oral contraceptive pill. This is because it can cause us to have a greater concentration of cholesterol in the bile, and this can increase the formation of gall stones. These stones can easily become lodged in the bile duct, which leads to inflammation of the gall bladder and acute pain. It is not known whether the oral contraceptive pill causes gall bladder disease or accelerates it in women who are prone.

Headache: Some women experience headaches while taking an oral contraceptive pill with a high progestogen level. It is not uncommon for women to experience headaches when the ratio of oestrogen to progestogen falls too low. Try taking a pill with a higher oestrogen content to remedy this problem. If you still experience headaches it may be that you are sensitive to the synthetic hormones and the oral contraceptive pill is not suited to you.

High blood pressure: Some women develop high blood pressure when taking the oral contraceptive pill. It is wise to have your blood pressure regularly monitored when taking the pill and discontinue its use if your blood pressure becomes dangerously elevated.

Increased incidence of cancer: the pill most certainly increases the *risk* of cervical and breast cancers. The level of risk seems to be dependent on the amount of oestrogen the pill contains and whether a woman has other predisposing factors in her medical history that may increase her risk of developing certain cancers. We know that most cancers of the breast and cervix have been linked with high oestrogen because oestrogen encourages cell replication. The uncertainty lies in knowing whether the pill causes cancer or whether it stimulates the growth of cancer that may already be present. Women are more likely to detect cancerous changes by having a regular Pap smear and breast examination.

Recently it has been observed that a greater number of women under 35 have developed breast cancer. It has also been observed that the risk of cancer is greater in women taking the oral contraceptive pill before they have had a child. It is suspected that immature breast tissue may be more sensitive to synthetic hormones.

The oral contraceptive pill has been associated with the development of rare malignant liver tumours and benign tumours are more commonly found in users of the pill.

Migraine headaches: development or worsening of migraine headaches after commencing the pill is an indication that undesirable vascular changes are occurring. Stop taking the pill immediately and use another method of contraception.

Nausea: some women are very sensitive to synthetic hormones and can experience nausea and occasionally vomiting. This is normally associated with synthetic or ethinyl oestrogens.

Pruritus: a more common term for pruritus is itchy skin. Synthetic oestrogen can cause dermatitis in sensitive individuals. Some women successfully eliminate chronic dermatitis simply by discontinuing oestrogen therapy.

Reduced libido: some women find that taking the oral contraceptive pill suppresses their sexual desire and responsiveness. It has been suggested that this is due to high progestogen levels in some pills. If you are concerned that your pill is suppressing your libido then try one with a lower ratio of this hormone.

Thrombosis and embolism: some women have an increased risk of developing blood clots when they take the pill. This appears to be related to an increased level of blood clotting factors which are activated by the oral contraceptive pill. The risk was greater in the 1960s however, when hormone levels in the pill were much higher. If you develop symptoms of circulatory disorders such as swollen, painful legs, severe headaches, blurred vision or severe chest pain you must stop the pill immediately and see your doctor.

The risk of heart attack or stroke is considerably higher when a woman combines the oral contraceptive pill with smoking. All women taking the pill must be advised against smoking.

Vaginal discharge: I have observed that some women taking oral contraceptive pills that contain a high progestogen level are more prone to vaginal discharge.

Weight gain: It is very common for women to gain weight when they start taking any form of hormone therapy, including the oral contraceptive pill. We know that a side effect of taking oestrogen is fluid retention and that progestogen increases the appetite. Oestrogens contribute to our feminine curves and are stored in fatty tissue in various parts of our body, in particular our hips, buttocks and thighs. When women with a higher ratio of progesterone to oestrogen become overweight, they tend to develop upper body weight. They lose their waistline, develop a pot belly and increase the fatty tissue around their midriff. Changes in body shape are often observed within the first three months of commencing an oral contraceptive pill. Despite these observations there is no scientific evidence to prove any connection with increased weight and oral contraceptive pill usage.

Note: If you have any queries about the pill, you should consult your doctor or contact a family planning clinic.

Positive effects of the pill

* The pill has a high success rate as a contraceptive. Many women experience anxiety when they are at risk of pregnancy. Taking the pill often reduces this, and therefore can indirectly improve a woman's libido and make lovemaking more enjoyable.
* It can lighten and regulate the menstrual flow. This tends to eliminate cramping and reduces the risk of developing anaemia.
* Certain combinations of hormones in the pill can reduce benign breast disorders and the incidence of ovarian cysts.
* The pill helps to prevent pelvic inflammatory disease which is a major cause of infertility.
* It can assist in reducing inflammation in some cases of rheumatoid arthritis.
* Today's pill combinations have been shown to reduce the risk of ovarian and endometrial cancer, probably due to the addition of the progestogen component. It has not had any significant influence in the prevention of these cancers in obese women because oestrogen is stored in adipose or fatty tissue and obese women can be more prone to excessively high levels of circulating oestrogen.

THE MINIPILL OR PROGESTOGEN ONLY PILL

This pill contains no oestrogen and has less progestogen than the combined pill. Ovulation can still occur but the hormonal changes created by the minipill alter the cervical mucus causing it to thicken. This causes it to plug the cervical canal which renders it impenetrable to sperm. This pill also alters the endometrial lining of the uterus, making it less suitable for pregnancy.

Some women continue to ovulate while taking this pill and at 96 per cent it has a slightly lower success rate as a contraceptive than the combined pill.

Side effects

The minipill generally has less side effects than the combined pill, however it can create some serious health problems. It has been shown to increase the occurrence of ovarian cysts and if pregnancy occurs while taking this pill, it is more likely to be ectopic (*see* 'Women and healing'). The minipill can also cause irregular bleeding with a higher incidence of breakthrough bleeding or spotting.

Due to the absence of oestrogen in this pill, it can cause symptoms associated with low oestrogen in some women, particularly if it is prescribed to women who already have a low blood oestrogen level. This includes general dryness of the skin, vaginal dryness, headache and breast tenderness.

THE MORNING AFTER PILL

This is a very strong pill that can be prescribed for women who feel they are at risk of pregnancy. Accidents can happen and if a condom breaks or if you are worried that you have not had adequate protection to prevent an unwanted pregnancy, you can be prescribed a short course of hormones to prevent pregnancy occurring. You have three days to act because if you delay more than 72 hours the methods may be unsuccessful.

The morning after pill works by either delaying ovulation until the sperm has died or by altering the lining of the uterus so a fertilised egg cannot implant. The treatment is usually two doses of hormone given exactly twelve hours apart.

It is a very useful pill for women who are victims of rape and it should be offered under these circumstances.

Side effects of this treatment are at times unpleasant. It can make some women feel quite sick for a day or two and can cause vomiting. Antinausea drugs may be prescribed at the same time. Other side effects are sore breasts and a mild headache lasting for a few days.

Occasionally women will experience some breakthrough bleeding after the treatment which is not a normal period but a reaction to the hormone treatment. It is not unusual for your next period to be irregular.

If you are already pregnant from your previous cycle, morning after contraception will not harm the foetus. However, if you become pregnant during your current cycle, it is possible to cause ectopic pregnancy by using morning after methods. Consult your doctor immediately if your next period does not arrive or if you suspect you are pregnant.

This pill is highly effective as long as you act quickly.

RU486—THE ABORTION PILL

This is commonly called the 'abortion pill' and it is currently undergoing research in Australia. It has been used successfully in France for a number of years but is still causing some controversy with the anti-abortion lobby.

It is a single dose pill that is almost 100 per cent successful in preventing a pregnancy. A woman only needs to take it once a month, just before the period is due or if she notices her period is overdue. It has less side effects than the morning after pill and could be useful for women who do not have regular intercourse.

It works by preventing a pregnancy from holding in the uterus and is a better alternative to surgical termination. This pill only becomes an abortion pill when it is given in conjunction with another drug, a prostaglandin.

French trials have shown it to be relatively free of symptoms. However all drugs need to be studied over lengthy periods of time to determine any long-term health risks.

It is unlikely that this pill will be used for abortion in Australia but it may be used in the future as a menstrual regulator, like the morning after pill.

INJECTABLE CONTRACEPTION

Depo provera (Depot medroxyprogesterone acetate) is an injection of progesterone that is given every three months to women for contraception. It is not promoted in Australia but is obtainable.

It is a controversial drug because it has been given to some women, including women with disabilities, without informing them of possible side effects or gaining prior consent. This is a breach of human rights. One problem with the administration of hormones by injection is that we never really know beforehand how it is going to affect the individual. This drug is not instantly reversible. Once it is in the bloodstream we simply have to wait until the body can break it down. For those who experience negative side effects and alterations in mood and behaviour, the consequences can be devastating.

Some women experience irregular and unpredictable bleeding, headaches, weight gain and some may cease to menstruate. Return of fertility can be delayed for twelve months after taking this drug.

SPERMICIDES

A spermicide is a chemical contraception method which, when used alone, is highly ineffective. It comes in a range of products and ingredients and

87

they work by killing or immobilising sperm in the vagina. They may be in the form of a cream, foam, jelly or pessaries (bullet shaped tablets that are inserted into the vagina) and are available at pharmacists without a prescription.

Spermicides must be used correctly in order for them to be effective. They must be inserted no more than twenty minutes before intercourse. Use an applicator if one is provided because they need to be inserted high into the vagina, as close to the cervix as possible, to be effective. Each time you have intercourse, you must reapply the spermicide.

They only provide about 70 to 80 per cent effectiveness and have a high failure rate. For this reason they should be used as an additional contraceptive measure with a barrier method such as condoms or diaphragms. They are difficult to use in casual sex encounters and although they are odourless and lightweight, they can be messy. Some people complain that they have an unpleasant taste.

Spermicides can cause allergic reactions due to their chemical make-up. This can be in the form of local irritation or soreness.

They can offer some protection against bacterial STDs such as gonorrhoea and may prevent the transmission of thrush and herpes.

IUD—Intrauterine device

IUDs are small, flexible devices that are placed inside a woman's uterus in order to prevent pregnancy. They have been available for a long time and over the years have been made in different shapes and sizes. Some have caused problems in the past because the string attached to the device was made from woven fibres that made the wearer more susceptible to bacterial infection. The company that produced this device failed to provide the appropriate warnings to the user.

The ones available today are made of plastic that does not irritate the tissue in the uterus and the string is made from a different fibre. They have a small amount of copper added around their stem which does affect the lining of the uterus.

It is still relatively unknown how IUDs actually work. It is believed the IUD causes changes within the uterus that makes it unsuitable for a fertilised egg to imbed in the uterine wall. It is also possible that changes in the uterus prevent sperm swimming through. Copper is toxic to sperm.

If you have an IUD fitted that contains copper, you must be sure you do not have diathermy, shortwave or microwave treatment on your lower back or abdomen.

Fitting an IUD is generally a simple procedure that does not usually require anaesthesia. However your health worker must be certain you are not pregnant before an IUD is fitted. If you have recently given birth you must wait until your uterus returns to shape before an IUD can be fitted because it is held in place by the walls of your uterus. This is about six to eight weeks after childbirth.

The best time to have one fitted is during the last days of menstruation, after an abortion or during a postnatal visit. This is when the cervix is usually more dilated (open) and the device is easier to insert. It is not unusual to bleed lightly or cramp for a few hours after it has been introduced into the uterus.

The life span of your IUD is dependent on the type of device you have. Be guided by your health worker as to when it should be checked or replaced. As long as your IUD remains in place it will be an effective method of contraception. IUDs have a success rate of around 96 per cent.

Problems associated with IUDs
While it is possible for a woman who has never had a baby to have an IUD fitted, it is not always desirable to use one. These women can experience strong muscular cramps and heavy bleeding. As if their body is rejecting the device and trying to expel it.

It is possible that menstrual bleeding will become heavier when you have an IUD. Some women also encounter spotting between periods for a few months. To overcome this there is an IUD that contains progesterone so blood loss will be reduced.

Women who have experienced pregnancy before often have very few problems. However if you have heavy or irregular bleeding you may need to have the device removed and try another method of contraception.

The tail of most IUDs has a fine string attached that hangs through the cervix into the vagina. You should feel for it after each period to make sure it is still there. If it is going to be expelled it will happen during menstruation. The string makes it easier to remove the IUD when you no longer require it.

There is concern that the string sometimes allows bacteria easy access into the uterus and fallopian tubes which can accelerate some sexually transmitted diseases and pelvic inflammation. Research now shows that an IUD will only increase pelvic inflammatory disease in women who have already had sexually transmitted disease. Also women may not be aware that they have a sexually transmitted disease because they do not show any symptoms. Contact your health worker if you develop persistent lower abdominal pain, pain during intercourse or an offensive vaginal discharge. The risk of pelvic inflammatory disease is greatest during the twenty days after insertion of the device.

An IUD is not a good choice of contraception for a woman who has casual sexual encounters or whose partner has several sexual partners. Barrier methods are required for protection from STDs.

Occasionally the IUD can be forced through the uterine wall due to strong contractions. This occurs in about one insertion for every thousand made. When this occurs, the string is not able to be detected so you must see your doctor if you cannot locate the string of your IUD.

About two women in every hundred become pregnant while using an IUD. If you fall pregnant while you have an IUD, it is advisable to have the device removed. While it is possible for a woman to occasionally carry her pregnancy through without harm to her baby, IUDs tend to increase the risk of miscarriage and can cause serious complications.

IUDs increase the risk of ectopic pregnancy, this is a pregnancy that occurs outside the uterus. Women who have a history of ectopic pregnancy should not use an IUD.

Women with blood clotting disorders are also advised against having one.

Induced abortion

The decision to terminate a pregnancy is deeply personal and often very distressing. When a woman is considering a termination, it is important for her to contact people who will be understanding and helpful. She should have access to a well-equipped clinic or hospital where an induced abortion can be given without unnecessary delay or humiliation. It should be performed by a skilled medical attendant who can terminate the pregnancy with accuracy and safety. Information about these clinics can be obtained from the health section in the front of the phone book, women's health centres and some hospital clinics.

At abortion clinics women are usually given the opportunity to speak with a trained counsellor before a termination goes ahead. If the woman decides to proceed with the termination, counselling is usually provided afterwards to help her deal with any anxiety, depression, grief or guilt she may be experiencing. Information will also be provided about family planning to avoid unwanted pregnancy in the future.

Herbal abortion

Herbal remedies were traditionally used to bring about permanent sterility and abortion and some of these are still used today. They contain powerful active principles that can be highly toxic and dangerous to both the mother and her developing foetus.

Herbal abortion is not legal in Australia and women cannot expect herbalists to provide or prescribe herbs for this purpose. Although doctors are able to legally prescribe menstrual regulators a herbalist cannot provide herbal menstrual regulators for women who know or suspect they are pregnant.

Some women may be confused and unsure about the date of their last period and sometimes request herbs to induce menstrual bleeding. A desperate woman may tell me she is only a few days late for her period, when in fact she may be nine weeks pregnant. Women who are contemplating abortion often need a great deal of support as some can feel isolated and afraid. These women should be directed to the appropriate clinics where they will be shown the assistance and support they require.

Attempts at herbal abortion, successful or otherwise can have disastrous consequences.

Sterilisation

This is a permanent method of contraception that should only be considered when you are sure you never want to be pregnant.

A request for sterilisation is taken very seriously by most doctors. In order to make a well-informed choice, it is important to be aware of all aspects of the procedure and possible risks. These should be discussed with your doctor who can provide you with written information. You can also contact the Family Planning Association for current advice and literature. Do not allow yourself to be forced into a hasty decision because, although reversal has been successfully achieved in some cases, sterilisation must be considered permanent. While many people feel very clear about it at the time, circumstances can change.

It is important to consider future possibilities before reaching a decision. Take your time and think very carefully before proceeding.

TUBAL LIGATION

Female sterilisation is called tubal ligation. The procedure is relatively simple and involves blocking both fallopian tubes, which are the link between the uterus and the ovaries. The tubes are either cut and tied or clamped with clips or rings. By successfully blocking the tubes, the egg released from the ovary cannot be fertilised because sperm are unable to swim up and reach it.

This procedure does not generally interfere with the normal function of the ovaries. Our hormones are still able to be produced and we still experience normal ovulation and menstruation. The released egg will quickly disintegrate and be reabsorbed by the body.

Complications

There is always a slight risk of procedural complications associated with having a general anaesthetic and abdominal surgery. Discuss these possible risks with your doctor.

Some studies indicate that women who have been sterilised are more likely to experience menstrual irregularity and a heavier flow. There are rare instances of sterilised women experiencing an early menopause caused by restricted blood supply to the ovaries due to accidental destruction of blood vessels during surgical procedure.

Some women will suffer emotional distress due to a loss of fertility or regret over the decision.

HYSTERECTOMY

Hysterectomy is the removal of the entire uterus and sometimes the cervix and the lymph nodes. Occasionally a woman may be advised against tubal ligation and a hysterectomy may be suggested instead. There are some instances where a hysterectomy is inevitable and it would be pointless to undergo unnecessary surgery for tubal ligation. Situations where this may occur would be women with cancer, excessive tumour growth or a complete prolapse.

VASECTOMY

This is male sterilisation and it is a simple operation where the two tubes that carry sperm to the penis are blocked. Sperm are still produced but are unable to gain access into the seminal fluid. Ejaculation still occurs but because the fluid contains no sperm, fertilisation cannot take place.

Future methods of contraception

VAGINAL RINGS

Vaginal rings are made of plastic and contain synthetic hormones. They are designed to fit high inside the vagina where they release hormones into the bloodstream. There are two types of ring currently being researched in Australia.

A ring that contains progestogen only and is designed to be worn constantly for 90 days before it is changed. It can easily be removed for intercourse.

A ring that contains oestrogen and progestogen and follows a similar pattern to the oral contraceptive pill. It is designed to be worn for three weeks and then removed for a week.

Hormones from vaginal rings are rapidly taken up in the bloodstream, so lower doses of synthetic hormones are used in these devices.

PROGESTOGEN-RELEASING IMPLANTS

Norplant is a new method of contraception that is currently undergoing research for its release in Australia. It involves tiny capsules that contain the progestogen levonorgestrol, which is found in some oral contraceptive pills. The capsules are implanted under the skin of the forearm or upper arm where they slowly release the hormone into the bloodstream. They remain active for up to five years and are 99 per cent effective.

We should always exercise caution with hormonal implants. Once they are placed in the body they can release high levels of hormones that can cause side effects such as irregular bleeding. While it will be seen as an exciting breakthrough, an implant that provides us with five years worth of hormones needs to be evaluated carefully. At this stage we do not know if approval will be given by the Department of Human Services and Health for its use in Australia.

AND ALSO TO COME ...

There is currently a great deal of excitement amongst some scientists over the use of a super glue that can be injected into our fallopian tubes to prevent pregnancy. Experiments have been conducted on rabbits and apparently this glue shows promise as a future contraceptive method for women.

Are we really expected to embrace these breakthroughs in scientific research? I wonder if it will also be suggested as a method of contraception for men. Will they become excited over the thought of injecting glue into their ductus deferens or seminal duct, through which sperm travels! It would seem that there is no limit to the degree of intervention that women are expected to endure.

Recent surveys conducted for the Federal Department of Health and Deakin University have shown that many Australian women are rejecting more orthodox forms of contraception and prefer to use natural family planning methods which can be highly effective in preventing pregnancy. It has been observed that the birth rate has not increased and neither has the rate of abortion.

These surveys indicate that the decline in the use of chemical contraceptives is largely due to changes in our sexual behaviour. Women are more aware of the risk of sexually transmitted diseases and barrier methods such as condoms offer them protection while the pill and IUDs offer none.

It is not surprising that women are not choosing IUDs. Many women are concerned about their safety after the Dalkon shield was withdrawn from the market and doctors are also reluctant to fit them for fear of being sued if an IUD causes any problems.

Women are more aware of their choices in contraception but if sex does not have a high priority in their lives contraception methods will be of little consequence. Some women are opting for celibacy or lesbian relationships and are comfortable with their choices, and many women are prepared to have an abortion or take a morning after pill if they do conceive.

Many women who are only sexually active every few months or so see no point in taking synthetic hormones every day when they only need to use a condom when intercourse occurs.

Condoms are still popular as they are convenient, disposable, effective and they protect against disease. They have probably been our most ideal contraceptive for a long time.

Being Fertile

J UST as we need to prepare our garden in order for our plants to grow
and thrive, we need to prepare our bodies to nurture our children. The
best preparation for fertility is to establish a healthy eating pattern,
ensure regular moderate exercise and take action to reduce physical and
emotional stress.

When planning your pregnancy, work out an average time for conception to occur and be patient. Not every couple will be successful at first.
While some women conceive immediately, it is not uncommon for conception to take four to eight months to achieve, and sometimes it will take
even longer.

The fertile phase

All women can improve their chances for successful conception by observing body indicators that reveal fertile phases of the menstrual cycle. These
are natural family planning techniques and they are explained in detail in
the previous chapter. They can help you to understand the physical aspects
and indicators of fertility which will improve your chances of successful
conception.

In order for conception to occur a woman must produce an ovum (egg),
it must be picked up by the fine fimbria (fringelike projections) at the end
of the fallopian tube (oviduct) and sperm must be made available to it for
fertilisation. The fertilised egg then takes approximately three days to
travel back down the fallopian tube to the uterus where it will implant

itself into the prepared lining of the uterine cavity. If everything goes well, it will remain in the uterus where it will develop into a baby.

At the time of ovulation, when the egg is released from the ovary, it is capable of being fertilised for probably no longer than 24 hours. If fertilisation is to take place, it is important to time intercourse well, so that it will coincide with the release of the ovum.

It helps to keep sperm close to the cervix after intercourse so take care not to get up immediately after intercourse. The sperm is more likely to leak out of the vaginal entrance when you are standing upright and moving. Instead it should pool around the cervix to improve your chances of conception. You can try inserting a diaphragm after intercourse to hold the sperm in. Some people suggest lying with your legs high in the air or against a wall.

Keep in mind that sperm has an approximate survival rate of around 24 hours, although a few can remain alive for up to 72 hours. So if you have intercourse the day before ovulation you may still be able to conceive.

Try to relax and enjoy your lovemaking, the creation of a child should be a blissful experience rather than a stressful one.

Creating the perfect environment

A healthy vagina has a pH of 4 to 4.5 which is acidic, making it hostile to germs and bacteria. This tends to make fertilisation a little difficult though, because sperm prefers an alkaline environment for survival. Semen itself has a pH range of 7.35 to 7.50 which is slightly alkaline.

Nature generally doesn't get things wrong and so during intercourse our bodies produce alkaline secretions to protect the sperm. Both cervical mucus and seminal fluid that carries the sperm are alkaline and they neutralise vaginal acidity for about one to two hours after ejaculation. Our bodies also produce fluid from the bloodstream that seeps through the vaginal walls during arousal that has a pH of 7 which is pH neutral. The term pH neutral simply means it is neither acidic nor alkaline.

Unless you are following instructions from your health practitioner, it is best not to introduce anything into your vagina that can interfere with normal pH or mucous production. For this reason it is wise not to douche for long periods of time or use vaginal deodorants, sprays or body moisturisers as vaginal lubricants. These may interfere with your fertility.

Red clover and false unicorn root are herbs that can be taken orally as medicines to reduce excess acidity in the reproductive area. If necessary, your herbalist can prescribe these for you and they may improve your chances of becoming pregnant.

Successful ovulation

Some women, particularly those in their late thirties and early forties worry unnecessarily about ovulation. Despite changes in menstrual patterns or blood flow, most women still ovulate regularly at this age. Observing body indicators such as mucous and temperature changes will often confirm that ovulation occurs, however some women find it a bit of a chore to take their temperature every day.

If you are concerned that you are not ovulating you can purchase a do-it-yourself kit from your pharmacy that measures the amount of Luteinising Hormone (LH) in your urine. This hormone is produced for ovulation and if it is not present, ovulation will not occur. Alternatively, your doctor can arrange for you to have a blood test during the second half of your cycle which will confirm whether or not your blood contains progesterone. If it does contain this hormone then ovulation has usually occurred. Having this test can prevent a lot of unnecessary worry for those women who may be afraid they are no longer fertile.

Once you are aware that failure to ovulate is not an issue for you, it can be much simpler to observe changes in mucus that indicate fertile times (*see* 'Conception'). These physical signs are good indicators that let you know when your body is ready for conception and you may also find that your desire for intercourse is naturally stronger at this time, making it the perfect time for the creation of your baby.

Subfertility—discovering the cause

If you have been trying to become pregnant for nine to twelve months without success, you may decide to seek professional assistance. At first, the cause of subfertility must be determined. Couples may feel quite anxious because they are often afraid they might find that either one of them is infertile. Although it is not uncommon for couples to experience difficulty with conception it can come as a severe blow when it happens. It helps to discuss your fears and feelings with one another and try to determine how far you are prepared to go in order to have a child.

Help is available at hospital fertility clinics or family planning clinics. Some couples will prefer to see their doctor, gynaecologist or obstetrician

97

and some will consult with a natural therapist or a trained counsellor. These people can provide different forms and levels of assistance. If you decide you would like assistance, it is possible to successfully use a variety of methods in a complementary way to overcome subfertility.

There are a few standard medical procedures you can follow if you decide you would like to investigate the possible physical causes of your subfertility. Some couples have never achieved pregnancy before, while sometimes one or both partners have had previous pregnancies. The procedures will differ according to your history of pregnancy.

During your initial visit a thorough medical history will be taken and your health practitioner will generally carry out a physical examination. Couples must be prepared to disclose some fairly personal information and you may need to undergo some invasive diagnostic investigations. Listed below are some of the procedures.

SPERM COUNT

Providing there are no obvious physical problems preventing pregnancy, such as the absence of menstruation, the first person to be checked should be your partner to determine his sperm count, because if it is too low pregnancy will not occur. These tests are relatively simple compared to the complicated tests women undergo for subfertility, so if your partner is found to be sterile, it is often unnecessary to subject yourself to further testing.

In order to make a sperm count, your practitioner will require a fresh sample of semen. This can be provided at the clinic after masturbation or it can be collected at home in a jar and taken back for testing within two hours of collection.

If no sperm is found or there is a very low level of sperm, a blood test is then carried out to determine if the male is producing FSH (Follicle Stimulating Hormone). If this level of hormone is normal or low there is a possibility that the sperm count can be improved.

Factors that interfere with sperm count are:

* Excessive smoking and alcohol intake.
* Undescended testicles.
* A mass of varicose veins in the scrotum, referred to as a varicocele.
* Occupational factors, such as working in very hot environments or with certain chemicals.
* A past history of severe mumps, that affected the testes.

* Radiotherapy or chemotherapy.
* A previous history of gonorrhoea.
* Blocked spermatic ducts which are the tubes that transport sperm from the testes for ejaculation. Blockages can occur from scar tissue that was created from a previous infection, injury or operation.

Surgical procedures for clearing blockages or removing varicoceles in testicles can be successful in improving sperm levels in some men. By addressing some of these factors it is possible to improve sperm levels, however you will need to be patient because it takes at least ten to twelve weeks for sperm to reach maturity and become capable of fertilising an ovum.

If the sperm count is low, try not to have intercourse too regularly as this can deplete sperm numbers. Give them the opportunity to build up over a few days.

Herbs to improve sperm count
The following herbs are renowned for their beneficial effect on the male sexual system. While some are available in capsule or tablet form, best results will be achieved by consulting with a herbalist who can dispense them according to your needs.

DAMIANA, *Turnera aphrodisica*: can improve sexual function in both men and women.

FENUGREEK, *Foeniculum vulgare*: a nutritive herb that can assist the male reproductive functions.

KOREAN GINSENG, *Panax ginseng*: a very powerful herb that has a stronger action than the Siberian ginseng. It contains more steroidal substances that increase its androgenic action and therefore it is considered to be a yang herb, recommended for improving sperm count. Ginseng root is a tonic with a wide range of actions on the whole body. I recommend that it be taken at first light because it has a strong stimulant action. Taking a high dose, particularly late in the day, can cause insomnia in sensitive individuals.

While this herb is easy to obtain as an over-the-counter preparation it is often of inferior quality. Your herbalist can guarantee high quality Panax ginseng because it is laboratory tested for therapeutic properties by the manufacturers and suppliers of herbal medicines in Australia.

SARSAPARILLA, *Smilax ornata*: a good general tonic for men. The root of the sarsaparilla plant contains both progesterone and testosterone, which is why it has been traditionally used to treat sexual debility and impotence. It is available in a tablet form as an over-the-counter preparation.

SAW PALMETTO, *Serenoa repens*: very useful for men because it has an affinity with the prostate gland. It contains steroid substances and can assist with subfertility.

Homoeopathic remedies
Hamamelis: this is recommended for varicose conditions and may be helpful in treating a varicocele.
Serenoa: can be used for testicular inflammation.

Nutritional advice
Vitamins A, C, E, B complex, chromium, potassium, selenium and zinc may help to improve a low sperm count.

Subfertility in women

The causes of subfertility in women can be complex and your doctor might suggest some of the following procedures in order to determine the cause. The doctor may want to determine whether your subfertility is due to a failure to ovulate. They could check if your fallopian tubes are blocked or if there are any abnormalities within your reproductive area such as fibroids, endometriosis or cysts, that may be preventing pregnancy.

POST COITAL TEST
Occasionally women have changes with their cervical mucus making it hostile to sperm and preventing them from moving up through the cervix. Although this is rare, some women are allergic to their partner's sperm and they make antibodies in their mucus to destroy the sperm.

In order for your doctor to test for this problem, you would need to visit the surgery quite soon after having sexual intercourse. Provided that traces of sperm remain in your vagina, your doctor can take a sample of your cervical mucus and examine it under a microscope. This will determine whether the cervical mucus is destroying the sperm.

Improving oestrogen levels can help this problem by improving the quality of the mucus and I would also recommend taking betacarotene, zinc, evening primrose oil and vitamin E to improve tissue health. Couples can still achieve pregnancy despite having hostile mucus.

HYSTEROSALPINGOGRAM (HSG)
This is an X-ray that can determine if a woman's fallopian tubes are blocked and to see if the shape of her uterine cavity is normal. Either one

of the fallopian tubes need to be clear in order for the sperm to swim freely to the egg for fertilisation. Tubes can become blocked due to scar tissue from previous infections and surgery or from endometriosis.

During the hysterosalpingogram process a catheter is inserted into the vagina and directed up through the cervical opening. The catheter is connected to a syringe which contains a special dye that is slowly injected into the uterus. If the tubes are not blocked, the dye will move into the fallopian tubes and then spill out into the abdominal cavity. Because the dye is radio-opaque, its image can be picked up on a monitor in the X-ray room and the doctor can see if the tubes are normal and unobstructed. This test takes between ten and twenty minutes and does not require an anaesthetic. It can be painful, however, causing uterine cramping and pain at the tip of the shoulder.

LAPAROSCOPY

Laparoscopy is an alternative method to determine if the tubes are blocked and it requires a general anaesthetic.

While you are under anaesthetic your abdomen is filled with carbon dioxide gas and a narrow instrument, which resembles a telescope, is inserted into a small incision in the abdomen. The doctor then looks through the telescope at the pelvic organs and can detect blockages or abnormalities. It is possible to experience quite a lot of pain during the 48 hours after this test and you will naturally feel full of wind.

If blockages are found, surgery can be attempted to clear the tube. Due to the delicacy and narrowness of the tube, success rates are low, because scar tissue reforms after the operation.

BLOOD TESTS

One of the most common causes of infertility in women is failure to ovulate. This may be due to hormonal insufficiency when not enough stimuli are produced for ovulation to take place or from an abnormality occurring within the ovaries themselves, which inhibits their ability to function.

Some women fail to ovulate even though they may have a regular cycle and this is described as an anovulatory cycle. A blood test can be carried out to determine if you are ovulating. Blood is taken in the second half of your cycle, about one week before menstrual bleeding. If progesterone is present, there is a strong likelihood that ovulation has occurred.

Without ovulation your menstrual bleed may last longer and the flow may be heavier but it is usually painless. This commonly occurs during the year after menarche (beginning of menstruation) and also before menopause. Absence of menstruation can also indicate a failure to ovulate. If you have failed to ovulate then further investigation may be necessary to determine why.

Physical factors

Recent research has shown that women can fail to ovulate when they are 10 kilograms or more above their optimal body weight. When women lose this weight their hormonal balance improves and so does fertility. The development of cysts or endometriosis around the ovaries can also interfere with normal ovarian function. These can be treated quite successfully with herbal medicines, homoeopathy and acupuncture.

A major contributor to infertility is physical or emotional stress. It can interfere with the production of FSH and can prevent ovulation. Failure to ovulate leads to subfertility. Using Bach Flower remedies to treat the emotions, having a regular massage and practising some form of relaxation technique may be all that is required to deal with your stress and promote fertility.

There is a theory that women will improve their chances of ovulating by sleeping with the light on for three nights between Days 11 to 14 in the menstrual cycle. This is based on the assumption that many women ovulate in response to increased light when the moon is full. Leaving the light on may help to stimulate ovulation by imitating lunar rhythms. If you are a good sleeper, it might be worth a try.

THE SOLUTIONS

Many physical and emotional problems that cause subfertility are often able to be successfully treated. Listed below are a few ideas to assist men and women with fertility.

* Do not smoke and avoid being a passive smoker.
* Generally try to avoid alcohol.
* Avoid rapid weight loss and maintain a regular healthy intake of food. Keep a healthy amount of weight on your body as hormones are stored in your fatty tissue.
* Avoid strenuous or excessive exercise. Rises in body temperature can interfere with fertility.

In order to correct subfertility women can benefit from a range of natural therapies including herbal medicine, homoeopathy, osteopathy, dietary advice, stress management and acupuncture. The type of healing method required will be determined by the cause and nature of the problem and your natural therapist can suggest what is appropriate for you.

If subfertility is caused by a specific health problem, such as endometriosis or polycystic ovaries, refer to the chapter 'Your guide to good health' for a more comprehensive treatment program. If you decide to follow more orthodox methods to treat your subfertility, you can still complement these with natural therapies, and in doing so will increase your chances of success.

Herbs to improve fertility

The following information is provided to increase your awareness of traditional medicines and their ongoing role in improving women's reproductive health. Please do not try to self-medicate with these herbs. Instead consult with an accredited herbalist who has the expertise to dispense herbs according to your individual needs and can assist with your baby's conception in a safe and reliable way.

I have had a great deal of success using herbs to improve fertility even though the reasons for infertility were varied. We have many plants available that have been traditionally used by women all over the world with safety and reliability for centuries. Today we have the scientific understanding of how the properties within these plants work. It is interesting to see that the traditional use of many of these herbs was appropriate and can be supported with scientific research.

BLUE COHOSH, *Caulophyllum thalictroides*: an oestrogenic herb that is a uterine tonic and spasmolytic herb, which means that it reduces spasm and cramping. It is specifically used when the uterine muscles are weak and this is especially useful for preventing miscarriage. This herb should be dispensed by a herbalist who can prescribe it with safety and in the correct dosage.

DONG QUAI, *Angelica sinensis*: helps to balance the menstrual cycle. Your herbalist knows to use this herb in combination with other herbs and it will yield the best results if it is taken between ovulation and menstruation. To be effective this herb is generally prescribed well in advance of pregnancy and stopped before conception is attempted.

FALSE UNICORN ROOT, *Chamaelirium luteum*: a wonderful hormonal balancer and is specific for treating amenorrhoea (absence of menstruation). This makes it ideal for improving fertility and poses no risk to mother or

103

her developing child when pregnancy is achieved. It is a tonic to the uterus and like red clover, has an alkalising action.

RASPBERRY LEAF, *Rubus idaeus*: an astringent uterine tonic with a high calcium content. The wild herb is best. It is synergistic with red clover, which means the two herbs are best used together because they enhance each other's action. Low doses of this herb can improve fertility and strengthen the uterus.

RED CLOVER, *Trifolium pratense*: contains magnesium and calcium and is a nourishing tonic herb with a high vitamin content. It also balances the acid/alkali level of the vagina and uterus to favour conception. This herb can restore and balance hormonal functions and promote fertility. It has a strong connection with the uterus and ovaries and is specific for the treatment of ovarian cysts.

STINGING NETTLES, *Urtica dioica*: another uterine tonic that is a very nourishing herb with a high iron content. It strengthens the kidneys and adrenal glands and is considered to be a good general tonic for the hormonal system.

Preparing your body

Ideally we should strive for optimum health before we conceive so that we are more likely to have a problem-free pregnancy. Our babies deserve to have the best possible environment to encourage healthy growth and development. The most reliable way to do this is to maintain good nutrition as your ability to become pregnant is directly related to both your partner's and your own nutritional status and body weight.

Some essential nutrients to assist with fertility are zinc, vitamin E, folic acid, vitamin A or betacarotene, vitamin C, manganese, potassium, calcium, magnesium and essential fatty acids. Refer to the chapter 'Understanding nutrients and their sources' for information on foods containing these nutrients.

EXERCISE

Over the years we have been bombarded with exercise theories, so what is the ideal form of exercise for women? It is now recommended, unless you are training for a specific activity like sprint running or marathons, that the best exercise is walking. This should be maintained for about half an hour at a steady pace, to achieve maximum benefits. Walking exercises our large muscles without placing unnecessary stresses on our body and helps us to unwind.

When women exercise excessively they do not burn fat, they burn precious carbohydrates, which can deplete blood sugar levels leaving them tired, sometimes to the point of exhaustion. It is important to avoid excessive exercise such as high impact aerobics when we desire pregnancy, because a prolonged high body temperature can cause infertility. Some women experience a total lack of menstruation due to low oestrogen levels caused by excessive exercise. This will create a situation of subfertility.

Swimming can be an excellent way to tone muscles, improve circulation, stretch and relax from stress. Alternating swimming with walking is a great way to achieve ideal fitness without overkill. If you combine walking or swimming every day with a few floor exercises to passively stretch your body, you will feel the benefits immediately and improve your chances of fertility.

MEDICAL APPROACH

Fertility drugs may be recommended for a lack of ovulation. These drugs influence our hormone levels and encourage the ovaries to produce an egg. Sometimes they produce lots of eggs and multiple pregnancy becomes a possibility. Although these drugs stimulate ovulation in many women, only a small number will achieve a successful pregnancy.

Keep in mind that fertility drugs can have some undesirable side effects that can include enlargement of the ovaries, a bloated painful abdomen, dizziness, headache, insomnia, hot flushes and visual blurring. Ask your doctor to clearly outline any possible long-term risks, the cost, what the treatment entails and the chances of the treatment ending in the birth of a live healthy infant.

Before you commence any treatment, ask your doctor to refer you to a gynaecologist or endocrinologist who specialises in fertility, for their expert opinion. They are usually the best people to determine what tests need to be undertaken and your chances of success. If you are prescribed fertility drugs you will require regular gynaecological assessment and it is best to utilise the expertise of a specialist doctor in this field.

Assisted conception

If you have not been able to correct subfertility, you may be considering methods to assist conception. These include:

Artificial Insemination (AI): semen is introduced through a tube into the cervix or uterus.

Donor Insemination (DI): the semen of an unknown donor is artificially inseminated into the cervix or high in the vagina. Between 50 and 65 per cent of women will become pregnant with this method.

In-vitro (in glass) Fertilisation (IVF): eggs and semen are collected and fertilised in a glass dish. The fertilised eggs are then placed in the uterus.

Gamete Intrafallopian Transfer (GIFT): eggs are taken from the ovary and placed into the fallopian tube with sperm.

Note: It is very important for women who commence an assisted conception program to inform their doctor if they are taking any herbal medicines or nutritional supplements. As these programs require controlled environments to maximise success, your doctor needs all relevant information.

ZIFT, PROST, TEST AND MIF

These tests start with IVF and the fertilised egg is transferred into the tube rather than the uterus. The terms describe the various stages that the fertilised ovum is introduced into the fallopian tube.

ZIFT, zygote intrafallopian transfer: the transfer of a single cell embryo.

PROST, pronuclear stage transfer: the earliest stage, just after the sperm has penetrated the ovum.

TEST, tubal embryo stage transfer: the embryo is transferred after the cells have started to multiply.

MIFT, microinjection fallopian transfer. Sperm is injected into the ovum under a microscope and then transferred.

I have only provided a brief overview of these methods. Although they may sound simple, I can assure you they are not. If you are considering any of them it is very important that you are thoroughly counselled on all aspects of the treatment, success rates, short and long-term side effects and costs.

The entire process of assisted conception can be financially, emotionally and physically taxing. Couples who are successful with these programs are very fortunate because overall success rates are low.

The chances of assisted conception using IVF or GIFT ending in the birth of a healthy infant are about 15 per cent. GIFT is generally more successful than IVF, however the success of either method is highly dependent on a number of factors including the general health and age of the woman and whether or not it is a multiple pregnancy. Women under 25 generally have greater success than those over 35 and there are naturally more problems with multiple pregnancies.

Couples should realise that there is a risk of failure at every stage leading up to pregnancy. To start with, the ovaries must produce healthy ova or eggs. Then they need to be successfully collected and stored. After this they need to be fertilised and must reach a certain stage of development before they are put back into the woman's body. Then couples must wait to see if the fertilised egg will implant into the uterine wall. Even when implantation occurs, approximately 20 per cent of pregnancies will spontaneously abort, according to the 1991 figures from AIWH National Perinatal Statistics Unit at the University of Sydney.

For those who are successful, there is a high incidence of babies being born preterm (before 28 weeks of gestation). However the risk of this occurring depends on whether or not there is a multiple pregnancy which usually arrive earlier than planned.

Thoughts on infertility

Most people assume they will be able to choose when they want to have a child and who they will have it with. They usually don't consider the possibility of infertility until their attempts to achieve pregnancy are unsuccessful. When they discover they are unable to have a baby with the person they love, it can have a profound effect on their life.

It is not unusual to experience feelings of guilt, blame, frustration, grief and loss and it can place a great strain on some relationships. Couples need to decide why they want to have a child and how desperate they are to have one. They may require the assistance of a trained counsellor who can help deal with issues and tensions as they arise.

Some couples accept that they will not have a child together and decide to channel their energies into other things. Others will consider using donor insemination or adoption. There are many who see the IVF or GIFT programs as an opportunity for them to fulfil their dreams of having children together, even though the chances of success may only be slight. For some fortunate couples, the dream becomes a reality.

All couples who are making decisions about assisted conception will need to consult with a specialist in fertility management. Someone who can clearly outline the processes and implications if they decide to go ahead with assisted conception. They need to discuss with each other just how far they are prepared to go in order to have a child and set some boundaries. While their chances can improve with each attempt, it is not a natural process and there will be a certain level of physical discomfort and emotional distress. A friend recently compared the feeling of failure when IVF is unsuccessful with sitting for an important exam. You study hard and prepare as well as you possibly can. When you go in to do it you feel you have the best chance for success, but you still fail. For some women this happens every time they try and it can be psychologically devastating.

It is essential to have good support and hopefully your partner can provide this. If couples are able to communicate well with each other, and they are well informed, they are often able to work through these difficult times and carry on with their relationship intact. The way people deal with infertility is extremely personal and varies with every individual.

Gina's story

GINA came to see me after she had miscarried her first baby at eleven weeks. Naturally, she was still very distressed and coming to terms with the loss. It had taken her a year to conceive and she was concerned that she might never have another opportunity to have a child.

Gina was 38 and, like many women who desire to be pregnant toward the end of their fertile years, felt that time was running out. She had already decided not to consider fertility drugs or assisted conception methods because of the possibility of serious side effects.

I felt confident that I could help her as I have worked with many subfertile women in the past and have great faith in my medicines. I did not feel it would be too difficult. After all, she had already proven she was fertile.

There were several immediate indicators that I felt contributed to her subfertility. Gina had what we refer to as a thyroid body shape. She was reasonably tall and quite slender, with very little body fat. Like many women who have this shape, Gina had a rapid metabolic rate which meant whatever she ate would be burned off very quickly. As a consequence, she found it difficult to gain weight and had trouble maintaining a steady blood sugar level. She had a busy job, travelled long distances to work and was on her feet all day. This, coupled with her fear of not being able to have a child with the man she loved, contributed to a high degree of physical and emotional stress.

The first thing Gina needed before she could become pregnant again was reassurance. While it was important not to give her false hope, her mind had to be put at ease. Worrying about the possibility of infertility creates an enormous amount of stress and can be the very thing that can prevent pregnancy occurring.

I explained that there were to be three stages in her treatment program. The first would involve making some minor adjustments to her diet and we also needed to talk about appropriate methods that she could use to manage stress and help her to be more relaxed. Gina had also asked me if I could help her to control her emotional outbursts, because before her period she felt that she became fairly volatile.

After taking her medical history, I talked to her about her diet and made an assessment of her health by reading her body signs. Iridology (eye diagnosis) revealed that there was still some inflammation in her reproductive area and she had adrenal fatigue, probably due to the recent surgery and anaesthetic that was necessary after her miscarriage. There was slight fissuring (cracks) on her tongue which indicated that she was possibly low in vitamin B3. Her nails were flaking and she told me she had noticed an increased hair loss, revealing a folic acid deficiency. I suggested a multivitamin mixture that contained a good level of B vitamins and folic acid.

I prescribed some herbal medicine that contained nettles and raspberry leaf because these herbs are rich in nutrients, and some dong quai to improve her menstruation. A small amount of licorice was added for the adrenals, and some wild yam which is a good anti-inflammatory herb for the reproductive area. I topped the mixture up with hypericum: a nerve nutrient that has a mild sedative and antidepressant action. Gina was to take 3 millilitres of this mixture in a little water, three times a day. I always add Bach Flower remedies to my mixtures and Gina was given: Star of Bethlehem, to help her overcome the recent trauma of miscarriage; pine, for guilt, because she thought that maybe she was to blame for the miscarriage because she worked long hours; vervain, because she pushes herself too hard; mimulus, for known fear, because she worries it will happen again; impatiens, to help her relax and be patient.

Overall, the mixture was given to improve her physical and emotional health after her miscarriage. I explained to Gina that she would not fall pregnant for a few months because we needed to prepare her body first. I did not want her to despair each time her period came.

In order to improve her ability to conceive a child and reduce her risk of future miscarriage we had to increase her body weight slightly and develop a small amount of fatty tissue around her hips and thighs so she could improve her ability to produce and store hormones.

She always avoided fatty food but I explained that it would be good for her to eat more nuts and seeds, yoghurt, ricotta cheese, olive oil and oily fish such as cod. She did not need to eat things like chicken skin, cream or pastries because these are unhealthy forms of fat and are not desirable. I also asked her to eat five or six small meals every day that contained good quality carbohydrate or starchy foods and a small amount of protein to regulate her blood sugar. This was no problem for Gina who immediately decided she would eat lots of pasta, wholegrain breads and potatoes with seafood and occasionally some lean red meat.

We talked about ways of coping with stress in her life and she decided to cut back her working hours and start making a conscious effort to practise relaxation techniques. She also decided to go for a half-hour walk every day to clear her thoughts.

When I saw her again she had experienced another period and she was very pleased that she had only slight problems premenstrually. Her flow was steady with minimal cramping. It had previously been quite scanty, lasting for only two or three days. She said she had some fluid retention though, and her breasts were a little tender. She had made the necessary changes to her diet, looked forward to her daily walk and felt much better for it.

During the second stage of her treatment I concentrated more on balancing her cycle, so I changed her herbal mixture. I wanted to improve her cycle by rebalancing her hormones.

This time her mixture contained false unicorn root, which would help to balance her hormones and indirectly help her breast tenderness. Red clover was added for the health of her ovaries and blue cohosh because it is a tonic to the uterus. I decided to add St Mary's thistle for her liver function because this would improve her overall health and buchu was selected for her fluid retention. I continued using the hypericum to support her nervous system and replaced the Bach Flower pine for red chestnut because Gina was now starting to worry about her husband. Although I did not expect Gina to fall pregnant yet, I explained that these herbs would not harm her baby if she did. I expected that once again she would probably have another period. When she was leaving, I reminded her to pay attention to her vaginal mucus to see if she had fertile mucus in her next cycle.

Gina came to see me after her next period and she was feeling more positive. Her period had arrived on time and she had no premenstrual symptoms, pain or fluid retention. She was once again confident that she had a good opportunity to fall pregnant. Her flow had lengthened from three to five days, which indicated a healthier level of hormones, and she noticed fertile mucus in the middle of her cycle. There was no inflammation showing in her iris, her general wellbeing had improved, her nails were stronger and her tongue was clear. These were all very good indicators that her reproductive and general health were in good shape.

It was now time to move to the third stage of therapy and prepare her body for conception. A fertility mixture was prescribed using nutrient-rich herbs that would strengthen and nourish her reproductive organs. It contained red clover, nettles, raspberry leaf, blue cohosh, hypericum and a dash of ginger. I put in some of the Bach Flower remedies for fear as well as white chestnut because I did not want Gina to worry about the possibility of another miscarriage when she became pregnant. Although I was quietly confident, I included impatiens for patience, just in case.

I explained that it was safe to continue taking her mixture during early pregnancy and that it would actually help to prevent miscarriage. It was alright to continue with her daily multivitamin because it did not contain more than 2500 iu of vitamin A, which is a safe level for pregnancy.

Gina was pregnant within two months, had a problem-free pregnancy and gave birth to a healthy baby daughter without complications.

Pregnancy

THROUGHOUT pregnancy we nourish and provide emotional stability to our developing child. It can be a time of great joy and celebration, mixed with confusion, excitement and fear.

It is not unusual for parents to experience difficulty coming to terms with the feelings about this new life they have created. Pregnancy can come as a complete surprise and it can take some time before you are able to accept and flow with it. Becoming a parent brings an enormous amount of responsibility and many of us are unprepared. Even those who have planned their pregnancy, full of enthusiasm, can suddenly experience apprehension when they actually conceive. If you have a partner, it is important to understand that they may be struggling with their own conflicting emotions and possible insecurities. If they are comfortable with the idea of parenting and are encouraged to take part, they are more likely to be involved and provide the emotional support that is so necessary for the wellbeing of the mother and the developing child.

We usually draw on our own life experiences and intuitively feel our way. When we are ready to accept the relationship with our developing baby we open a channel of communication and love that some of us have never experienced before.

Confirming your pregnancy

Women who have a regular menstrual cycle will normally be alerted to a possible pregnancy when their period doesn't arrive. They may notice that their breasts are slightly larger and their nipples are tender. While these sensations can normally occur before menstruation, intuitive women will have strong suspicions about when they are pregnant.

It is now possible to buy a home testing kit from your pharmacy or have a blood test for speedy confirmation of pregnancy. Urine tests can confirm pregnancy from the eleventh day after ovulation and blood tests are sensitive enough to detect changes in hormonal levels nine days after ovulation. This is before your period is due to arrive. Gone are the days when women had to wait for several weeks after a missed period to have their suspicions confirmed.

Choices

Every woman expecting a baby is entitled to accurate information that will help her to have a healthy and trouble-free pregnancy. It is important for women to be aware of all the options available for health care during pregnancy and childbirth. There are many resources available that provide very useful information to assist with this decision-making process.

Women must always be shown respect for their choices during pregnancy and childbirth. These decisions may be strongly influenced by their spouse and other family members involved with the birth. Culturally there can be a certain level of commitment to their extended family and/or traditional beliefs. Ultimately though, it is the woman who must emotionally and physically give birth and every child and mother deserves to have a positive birth experience. I have witnessed many and I feel deeply privileged to have taken part in this process.

Pregnancy and birth support

During your pregnancy you will need to consider where you would like to give birth and with whom you would like to share this experience. Make sure that you are completely comfortable with those who will attend your baby's birth. It is important to have people around you who you can depend upon and who are reliable.

Exercise during pregnancy

A moderate level of exercise is highly beneficial during pregnancy. If you have been exercising prior to conception, providing the type of exercise you are doing is not too strenuous, you can safely continue. One of the problems with strenuous exercise is that it can increase your body temperature to a dangerous level. A sustained elevation of body temperature can be harmful to your developing baby and women who exercise excessively often have babies with a low birth weight. Vigorous aerobic exercise is not desirable.

Women who have not been exercising before their pregnancy can start by going for half-hour walks every day. There is no need to rush, just walk at a steady pace. This is a good level of exercise that will be beneficial. Drink a large glass of water before and after exercising to replace any fluid you lose.

If you attend a gym or exercise class, tell the instructor that you are pregnant. They can then modify your routine and let you know which exercises are unsuitable for pregnancy. It is best to avoid exercises that involve bending backwards and also those that put too much strain on your lower back and abdominal muscles.

Swimming is an excellent form of exercise for pregnancy. It helps to stretch your body, tone your muscles, regulate your breathing and is beneficial for your heart and lungs. Just remember to swim at your own pace and don't push yourself too hard.

Stretching is wonderful to prepare your body for the birth of your baby, as long as you do it the correct way. You can learn how to increase your flexibility at a yoga class. Many yoga centres also teach relaxation and breathing techniques.

Exercise classes for fitness during pregnancy are conducted at some maternity and local hospitals and also by some private organisations. Check your phone book or enquire at your hospital or community centre to find out what is available in your area. These classes can be commenced at any stage of your pregnancy and they will help to improve your flexibility, muscle tone and body control. This is excellent preparation for giving birth.

Dietary recommendations during pregnancy

The desired total weight gain in pregnancy is normally around 12 kilograms. It is calculated by taking into account the size of the baby and the extra weight that is caused by increased blood volume, fatty deposits and fluid. The weight gain is not evenly spread through the pregnancy. In the first twenty weeks women gain about 3 kilograms and in the last twenty weeks they gain about 9 kilograms.

Naturally there will be variations and women should not be alarmed if they don't follow this pattern providing they are eating regular, nutritious meals. On average though, women will generally gain about 0.5 kilo each week in the second half of their pregnancy.

We improve our chances of achieving a healthy pregnancy when at least 10 per cent of our body weight is body fat. The maximum amount of body fat desired is around 40 per cent. Therefore, underweight women should consider gaining some weight and overweight women should attempt to lose weight before they conceive. This can reduce the risk of complications during pregnancy. While it is possible, with supervision, to follow a weight-loss program during pregnancy, it is not desirable. If you haven't lost weight beforehand, it is best to postpone that weight-loss diet until after your baby is born.

SENSIBLE NUTRITION FOR PREGNANCY

All nourishment for a pregnant mother and her developing child will come directly from the mother's diet. In the past, pregnant women have been advised that babies obtained all the nutrients they needed from their mother's body regardless of what she ate and that pregnant women can virtually eat what they like without affecting their child.

This is a myth. Today we know that everything ingested has the capacity to cross the placenta and can directly affect the developing child. For this reason, sound nutrition is of the utmost importance for both the mother and her baby during pregnancy.

There is a constant need for the mother and her developing child to have a steady supply of nutrients. This will help them to achieve optimum health and reduce the risk of illness or abnormalities occurring. A mother has to be responsible in making sure her diet contains all the nutrients required by her baby. This does not mean you need to eat large amounts of food, there is no need to eat for two. It is more important to make good choices in foods. Fresh, unprocessed foods are the best sources of nutrients.

To maintain a healthy fluid balance and assist with elimination, pregnant women need to drink six to eight glasses of water every day. During pregnancy it is important not to overload the kidneys. They are working hard to remove waste from your body, so please start and end your day with a glass of fresh water. If you also drink two or three cups of herbal tea and two extra glasses of water throughout the day it becomes easy to meet your fluid needs.

Protein-rich foods must be eaten several times every day in order to meet the needs of your growing baby. They provide the building blocks for all growth and repair of body tissues. Good quality protein comes in the form of lean beef, lamb, pork and chicken, fresh and tinned fish, eggs, dairy products, grains, cereals, nuts, seeds and legumes.

Soy beans and soy products provide first-class protein, however other legumes need to be combined to meet protein requirements. This is not difficult, for instance, if you are having lentils serve them with barley. If you are having chick peas, serve them with rice. Eating vegetables with rice is not enough protein. You can improve this meal by having some yoghurt or tahini on the side. Alternatively you can make a cheese sauce to have on the vegetables or include some cashews in the dish.

Carbohydrate foods such as bread, pasta, grains, legumes, starchy fruits and vegetables will help to maintain healthy blood sugar levels. Eat these foods in abundance. They do not contribute to excess weight gain unless they are combined with fat. It is best to avoid pastries, cakes and biscuits. If you have a desire for something sweet, have a fruit scone or homemade muffin instead.

Vitamins and minerals are essential for the health of both mother and baby. Some of these nutrients for pregnancy and their food sources are outlined in 'Understanding nutrients and their sources'.

B complex vitamins: help to maintain a balanced emotional state during pregnancy. Vitamin B6 helps prevent morning sickness and regulates your fluid balance. B vitamins work together to prevent fatigue, insomnia and nervous tension.

Betacarotene, vitamin C and the bioflavanoids: keep your veins healthy and can improve your immunity. They help to form collagen which is essential for healthy skin and tissue in your developing child.

Calcium: this is important for the development of your baby's bones and teeth. By including calcium-rich foods in your diet every day you will also be taking care of your bone density and preventing osteoporosis. Calcium can also help to reduce muscular spasm and cramping.

Essential fatty acids: must be included in the diet every day because they keep the mother and baby healthy at a cellular level, and are necessary for healthy vision in your developing baby.

Folic acid: this is a very important nutrient for pregnancy. It is involved with the growth of cells in the infant; increased blood volume and tissue health in the mother. It helps to prevent birth abnormalities and can be taken as a supplement during pregnancy. Up to 400 mcg of folic acid every day will not harm your baby. When women experience hair loss during and after pregnancy it is often a direct result of a folic acid deficiency.

Iron: helps to meet the high demand for increased oxygen in the body during pregnancy. It is important for preventing anaemia and eating iron-rich foods every day is essential for the overall health of your developing baby. Adequate iron intake can also guard against miscarriage.

Low blood levels of iron can increase the likelihood of heavier bleeding after delivery and can make women more prone to infection.

Both iron and folic acid are needed to meet the demands of breast tissue for extra blood and oxygen during breastfeeding.

Magnesium: this is for the development of baby's bones and teeth. It prevents and eases muscular cramps, helps the liver deal with excess hormone levels and can be highly beneficial in the prevention of miscarriage.

You will greatly assist your body as it prepares for breastfeeding, by making sure you eat foods containing calcium, magnesium and protein every day during your pregnancy.

Vitamin E: helps to keep your veins healthy and can normalise blood pressure. It is not unusual for some women to experience low blood pressure due to relaxed veins caused by high progesterone levels during pregnancy. Vitamin E can help this and it also protects against miscarriage and toxaemia.

Zinc: prevents stretch marks in the mother and assists in the proper growth and maturity of your baby's sex organs.

To obtain these nutrients you need to include a variety of healthy foods in your diet every day. Eat from a broad range of foods and avoid those that are highly refined and highly processed, such as packaged white flour and white sugar products. If you do, you will increase the likelihood of a problem-free pregnancy, an easier delivery and a healthier child.

Dental care during pregnancy

It is best to visit a dentist before pregnancy in case you require an X-ray or drugs and especially if you have not had a dental check-up for some time.

Do not neglect your teeth during pregnancy. A good diet and proper oral hygiene will ensure that your teeth will not deteriorate during your pregnancy. Most dental work poses no risk to mother or baby and you can have your teeth thoroughly cleaned to prevent problems.

It is very important to care for your teeth during pregnancy because your gums can be more sensitive due to hormonal changes. Some women develop sore, swollen gums that bleed easily. This is often noticeable while you are brushing your teeth. Be sure to floss and brush your teeth regularly to remove plaque and bacteria.

Vitamin C can greatly assist the health of your gums and you can rinse your mouth with a good antiseptic mouth wash. Sage is specific for the mouth and you can make an effective mouth rinse by simmering a handful of sage in half a litre of water for about 20 minutes. Strain off the liquid and regularly swill it around your mouth. It is safe to swallow.

Reduce your intake of sugar and eat more fruits and vegetables instead. Also, include calcium and magnesium foods in your daily diet as they maintain tooth enamel and keep the teeth strong. Foods rich in phosphorous and calcium will benefit the formation of your baby's teeth, which begin to form in the first six weeks of pregnancy. Chamomile tea provides both of these minerals.

What to avoid during pregnancy

A mother has to carefully consider what she takes into her body during her pregnancy. Everything from food, drinks, drugs, exposure to pollutants, household and environmental chemicals, not only affect her but also her developing child.

Avoid exposure to the following substances before and during your pregnancy because they have been linked to birth defects, infertility or miscarriage.

* Radiation: avoid unnecessary X-rays.
* Caffeine: many people underestimate what a powerful substance caffeine is and are unaware that it has been linked with birth defects. Avoid medications containing caffeine and excessive amounts of cola drinks,

chocolate, tea and coffee. It is possible to purchase tea, coffee and cola drinks that are low in caffeine. Carob or an occasional cup of hot cocoa can be used as a substitute for chocolate.

* Laxatives: avoid harsh laxatives that can cause griping and spasm. This includes some herbal remedies such as cascara and high levels of vitamin C.

* Diuretics (fluid tablets): these drugs are not recommended during pregnancy because they can cross the placenta and be harmful to your baby.

* Hair dyes: some hair dyes contain heavy metals that can be absorbed through the scalp and can indirectly affect your baby. Check with your hairdresser for information on more natural products.

* Drugs: avoid taking drugs when preparing for conception and during pregnancy.

Tobacco: reduces your baby's birth weight and can cause breathing problems. Nicotine from cigarettes can affect your baby's growth and development. Do not smoke and avoid being around other smokers. Passive smoking is also dangerous to your baby; it can cause respiratory disease and has been linked to cot death.

Marijuana: this drug does cross the placenta and smoking large quantities can cause birth defects. Smoking marijuana can also prolong the length of your labour.

Cocaine: reduces birth weight and increases stillbirth rate. Babies of cocaine users usually suffer withdrawal symptoms.

Alcohol: absolutely no alcohol should be taken during pregnancy. Women are often told one or two standard drinks each day during pregnancy is safe. Research now shows that even small amounts of alcohol can be damaging to the unborn. A high alcohol intake can cause Foetal Alcohol Syndrome (FAS). Children with this syndrome have a low birth weight and facial abnormality. There can be varying degrees of intellectual disability and sometimes heart defects.

Opiates: these include morphine, heroin, codeine and opium. These drugs create a greater risk of stillbirth, growth deficiency, premature delivery, respiratory distress and there can be long-term effects on growth and behaviour.

* Roaccutane: there is a serious risk to your baby if you become pregnant while you are taking this drug.

* Vitamin A: it is recommended that pregnant women do not exceed taking more than 2500 iu per day because it has been linked with birth defects. Take betacarotene instead.

119

* Some herbal medicines: avoid taking herbal medicines that contain tansy, thuja, dong quai, licorice, golden seal, pennyroyal, mistletoe, pokeroot or high doses of cascara or senna.
* Hormones: it generally takes around three weeks for all oral contraceptives to be completely eliminated from your body. If you do fall pregnant while taking an oral contraceptive pill stop it immediately.
* Pesticides, herbicides and insecticides: many of these substances have been linked with birth defects and increased miscarriage.
* Heavy metals: many of these substances are highly toxic, for example, lead and mercury.
* Toxic substances, such as fumes from thinners, solvents, varnishes, have been linked with infertility.
* Cat faeces: contact with cats and their faeces can cause a parasitic infection called toxoplasmosis that can cause damage to your unborn child.

Special tests during pregnancy

Your medical centre or family planning clinic can provide information on the tests available for pregnant women that can detect chromosomal abnormalities, inherited disorders and neural tube defects such as spinabifida.

Women in high-risk categories are those in their mid-thirties and over; those who already have a child with a chromosomal disorder such as Down's Syndrome; or those with an inherited disorder in their family or their partner's family.

The tests usually involve CVS (chorionic villus sampling) or amniocentesis. During CVS a small amount of the placenta is removed for testing between the ninth to twelfth weeks of pregnancy, and the procedure has a miscarriage related rate of 2 per cent, or 1 in 50 pregnancies. Amniocentesis involves the removal of a small amount of amniotic fluid (which surrounds the baby) and it is performed between the fourteenth to eighteenth weeks of pregnancy. It carries a miscarriage related rate of around 1 per cent or 1 in 100 pregnancies. Cordocentesis is another test that involves taking a sample of the baby's blood for testing. It carries a miscarriage related rate of approximately 2 per cent.

The three phases of pregnancy

Once conception takes place, pregnancy is divided into three phases, which are referred to as the first, second and third trimesters. During these phases women experience physical and emotional changes that coincide with their babies' growth and development.

The first trimester is the first twelve weeks of pregnancy. This is the time when your body is undergoing a rapid process of change. In the first few weeks you will notice that your breasts are larger and firmer. Some women experience some sensitivity in the breasts because of tissue changes caused by increased hormone levels and an increase in blood volume. The veins in your breasts are usually more prominent and your nipples will start to darken.

MORNING SICKNESS

Once your pregnancy is underway and hormonal levels start to escalate it is not unusual to develop morning sickness. More than half of all pregnant women will experience nausea in the early months.

Morning sickness is a good indication that the natural processes of pregnancy are occurring; important changes in hormone levels are taking place and your body is trying to adapt.

Morning sickness will tend to come on at around six weeks and will generally end at around twelve weeks. For many women it will only occur in a mild form and is relatively easy to tolerate. Naturally, this will vary from woman to woman. It often develops as a slight feeling of nausea that is worse in the morning. If this is happening to you, try getting out of bed more slowly. Morning sickness doesn't always follow a regular pattern and can come on in waves at different intervals during the day or in the evening. Fresh air is usually helpful because some odours and perfumes can aggravate the nausea. There are some remedies that can be helpful for morning sickness. It is possible to safely use Bach Flower remedies, homoeopathic preparations, food as medicine and also some nourishing herbs. For instance, some women produce a lot of saliva, if this is happening you should probably see a herbalist who can include some sage in a morning sickness remedy. It will be easier to take 10 to 15 drops of herbal medicine in a little water than to try to drink sage as a herbal tea when you feel sick. If you can manage the tea however, it is highly effective in treating increased salivation.

Occasionally morning sickness can be quite debilitating and some

121

women are unable to hold any food down. When this occurs, it is important to eat the right type of food so digestion happens easily. The wrong foods can slow digestion and leave you feeling bloated and sluggish.

Vitamin B6 (100 mg for the first seven days then 50 mg daily) is specific for morning sickness. If it is taken as a supplement it is best to include a B complex vitamin with it to improve its absorption because all the B vitamins need to be present for any one of them to be absorbed properly.

Magnesium and vitamin B6 can help your liver to filter through the high level of hormones at this phase of pregnancy, which is considered to be a major cause of morning sickness. Magnesium has the added advantage of stopping cramping and muscular spasm. Therefore, this nutrient can also help to prevent miscarriage.

Your liver needs support at this stage because it is helping your body adjust to very high levels of hormones. Some good liver foods are beetroot, dandelion, chicory, garlic, onion, watercress and carrots. Drink a glass of carrot and beetroot juice daily and try dandelion beverage as a substitute for tea and coffee.

Hyperemesis
The most severe form of morning sickness is referred to as hyper-emesis gravidarum. In simple terms this means excessive vomiting in pregnancy. Women with hyperemesis often lose body weight and are constantly sick. This is very serious for the mother and her baby because they will both suffer from a lack of nourishment. When it is ongoing, it is sometimes necessary to admit the mother to hospital so she can be fed with an intravenous drip. In some rare instances drug therapy may be required. Women are often unaware that traditional herbal medicine and dietary changes can reduce and often eliminate these debilitating symptoms that can be associated with pregnancy.

Dietary advice for morning sickness
* Eat six smaller, nutritious meals rather than three large ones. This takes a load off your digestive processes and helps to maintain steady blood sugar levels.
* Avoid fried and fatty foods because they are slow to digest, place added stress on your liver and generally do not sit well.
* Make sure you eat cooked yellow vegetables and raw or steamed green vegetables every day. Beetroot is also highly beneficial and if you have a juicer, try a combination of beetroot and carrot juice.
* Rolled oats can be a good breakfast choice. They usually sit well and

are very nutritious. Alternatively, eat dry toast with fresh tomato, almond paste or avocado.

* Try soy milk if dairy products disagree with you. There are several brands on the market that are calcium enriched and they provide similar levels of calcium per cup as cow's milk.

* Pawpaw is very nutritious and great for helping to ease the discomfort of morning sickness. It is rich in nutrients and helps calm the stomach. If you don't enjoy it fresh then try the dried form.

* Acidophilus yoghurt or acidophilus powder is very good for the digestive tract. Eat yoghurt regularly or try taking an acidophilus supplement if you dislike the taste.

* Drink plenty of water so you don't dehydrate. Have small glasses of fresh water or soda water often.

Bach Flower remedies

Emotionally, morning sickness can be seen as not accepting and going with the flow of your pregnancy. Walnut is an excellent Bach Flower remedy that helps women adjust to situations of change.

Herbal medicine

A qualified herbalist has the expertise to safely and effectively prescribe herbal medicines, if required, for the treatment of morning sickness. The remedies are carefully selected and mixed together in a formula that will meet individual requirements. They often contain herbs to work on digestion and do not have any negative effects on the developing foetus or its immediate environment. I never encourage self-medication with herbal medicines, however there are some common herbs listed below that are readily available as pre-packaged herbal teas. They are easily prepared and can be useful for women who are looking for some simple self-help ideas.

* Dandelion is a good herb for the liver and has a similar flavour to coffee. Try drinking dandelion beverage instead of tea or coffee.

* Ginger has been shown to control morning sickness in clinical trials conducted on women whose nausea continued throughout their pregnancy. Results were very encouraging. Your herbalist can give a medicinal form of ginger that can be placed in a capsule if you have difficulty taking ginger in another form. Otherwise you can take ginger as a tea, eat glacé ginger or include fresh ginger root in your meals. Prepare the tea by simmering fresh ginger root in some water for about 20 or 30 minutes. Alternatively you can make weak tea and stir in one level teaspoon of ginger-root powder. Ginger is also great for abdominal cramps.

* Chew slippery elm tablets or prepare the powdered form as a drink and take it half an hour before meals and once before bed. This is highly beneficial for nausea and will help to prevent overacidity. Slippery elm is very protective and soothes the tissue in the digestive tract.
* Chamomile tea is very effective in relieving nausea and settling the stomach. Drink it regularly.
* Small amounts of peppermint tea will help if you have vomiting and it is also useful for relieving dyspepsia. It is very effective in combination with chamomile.
* Fennel is a nutritive herb that can be eaten as a vegetable or the seeds can be steeped to make a tea. It helps to calm the stomach and helps prevent wind and bloating.
* Raspberry leaf tea is a good nutritious tonic for morning sickness that provides gentle relief from nausea. It is a wonderful tonic to strengthen the uterus and it contains vitamins A, B, C, E and the minerals calcium, phosphorus, potassium and iron.

Homoeopathy
Homoeopathic remedies are highly effective during pregnancy and they are completely safe. They will not harm your developing baby, do not taste unpleasant and when they are selected well, they will work very quickly. See a homoeopath who can select the appropriate remedy for you.

Some remedies for morning sickness are:

Cocculus: a good motion sickness remedy. It is effective for women who have lost their appetite and who cannot stand the smell of food.

Ipecac: you may have heard of ipecac being used to bring on vomiting in children who have swallowed certain poisons. As a homoeopathic remedy it can be used to prevent vomiting and it is very useful when the vomiting cannot be relieved.

Nux vomica: this is particularly useful if there is nausea with lots of burping. It works best for those who feel worse in the morning.

Phosphorus: a good remedy for women who have a sour taste in their mouth and vomit as soon as any food or drink hits the stomach.

Tabacum: useful for women who are made worse by the smell of cigarette smoke. It is also effective during pregnancy when there is a constant need to spit.

PREVENTING MISCARRIAGE

Maintaining a healthy balanced diet will help prevent nutritional deficiencies in your baby and reduce your risk of miscarriage.

While it is very common for women to have some spotting or light bleeding during the first three months of pregnancy, any form of bleeding should be reported to your midwife or doctor. If you do experience any bleeding you should rest, stop exercising or stretching and abstain from intercourse until you have been advised that all is okay.

Self-help

Daily nutritional supplements of magnesium (400 mg) and vitamin E (500–1000 iu) can help to prevent miscarriage because they prevent cramping and improve circulation and oxygen distribution in the tissues.

You can drink chamomile and ginger tea to help relax and ease muscular cramping.

Stinging nettles are great for preventing spot bleeding. Try sipping nettle tea or include fresh nettles in a vegetable broth.

It is very important to have total bed rest until all cramping has stopped.

Herbal medicine

I usually provide women with a small bottle of herbs that can be used for first aid if they develop signs of miscarriage. Not only does it give them peace of mind but it is very important to have something on hand for emergencies. This is particularly important for isolated women. Consultation with a herbalist is required to obtain such a mixture. I cannot recommend self-medication with these herbs as strict dosage instructions must be followed to ensure effectiveness and safety. Some of the herbs used are valerian, blue cohosh, black haw, true unicorn root, cramp bark and nettles.

Homoeopathy

Some remedies for threatened miscarriage are sabina, pulsatilla and trillium. Consult with a homoeopath for the most effective remedy for your individual needs.

Bach Flower remedies for threatened miscarriage

The fear remedies are very important to prevent anxiety and panic situations. Tension and fear will contribute to muscular spasm. For this reason Rescue Remedy can help to calm both the mother and anyone else who is panicking around her.

TIREDNESS

It is not unusual to feel more tired during the early stages of pregnancy. Naturally, if you are not feeling well in the first few months, your tiredness can be directly related to morning sickness. Most people feel tired when they are feeling sick. Try to maintain good dietary habits and if you are having trouble keeping your food down, take a multivitamin tablet every day to maintain nutrient levels.

Abnormal fatigue can be a symptom of anaemia. The signs of anaemia can be dark circles under your eyes, red spots on your tongue, a pale face, flaking nails and sometimes there can be breathlessness and giddiness. Take some iron (ferrum) phosphate as a cell salt to help you absorb iron from your food. If this doesn't help have a blood test to check the level of iron in your blood.

There is usually no need to be concerned about feeling a bit tired, it may simply be nature's way of reminding you to take a rest when you need it.

FAINTING OR FEELING DIZZY

It is not unusual to faint or feel dizzy in the early stages of pregnancy. Your blood pressure can drop because of the effect of hormones on your blood vessels. Sudden drops in blood pressure, such as when you stand up quickly, can temporarily reduce the blood flow to your brain resulting in dizziness. Eat plenty of foods rich in vitamin E such as wheat germ, nuts and seeds, corn and fish oils. If you prefer to take a supplement, take 500–1000 iu of vitamin E every day to help normalise blood pressure.

FREQUENCY OF URINE

When women need to pass water more frequently during pregnancy they are often concerned they have a urinary tract infection. While this can occur, the frequency is usually due to an increased output of urine from the kidneys because of the pregnancy. As pregnancy progresses, the increased weight of the enlarged uterus will also put pressure on the bladder. This can make you feel the need to empty it more often.

Simply drink plenty of fresh water and do some pelvic floor exercises. Try taking nat mur as a cell salt to normalise your fluid balance. If it becomes troublesome, you may need to be checked for a possible infection. Talk to your herbalist or homoeopath about traditional therapies for urinary tract infections or see your doctor.

As your pregnancy progresses, your uterus will sit higher in the pelvic cavity and take the pressure off your bladder during the second trimester.

CONSTIPATION

Some women notice a general sluggishness with their digestion during pregnancy. This can be due to relaxed tissues caused by hormonal release or it may be the result of poor dietary habits. It is also possible to develop constipation from taking iron tablets. If this is the case, try taking a different brand of iron supplement and make sure it contains vitamin C and iron phosphate. This will help you to absorb it better.

Quite often constipation can be prevented by drinking six to eight glasses of water daily. Increase your fibre intake by eating fresh fruit and vegetables and choosing wholegrain breads and cereals. The fibre, husks and skin of these foods absorb water and add bulk to your faeces. This makes the stool softer and heavier so it will move through your intestinal tract much faster.

A good natural product for treating constipation is psyllium. This is available at health and bulk stores and it helps to regulate bowel habits.

SKIN CHANGES

It is not unusual for women to develop some pimples or acne in the first stage of pregnancy due to high progesterone levels. This will normally settle down once the body adjusts to the hormonal changes. You can indirectly help your skin by drinking dandelion beverage which is a good tonic for the liver and kidneys.

Chloasma

Some women develop what is referred to as the pregnancy mask or chloasma. It is caused by excessive release of a brown pigment, melanin, in your skin and it is stimulated by hormonal changes and it can be difficult to avoid. Exposure to heat and sun will darken this mask and make it worse so always wear plenty of sunscreen and a broad brimmed hat.

Cell salts for the first trimester

The cell or 'tissue' salts are excellent self-help remedies for pregnancy that are completely safe to use during all stages. Follow standard dosage instructions on the pack.

Calc fluor: for bone development in the baby and elasticity of connective tissue.

Ferrum phos: to increase the body's uptake of iron from food. This remedy can also help with morning sickness when there is vomiting of undigested food.

Kali mur: for morning sickness with vomiting of white phlegm.

Mag phos: for the prevention of miscarriage and to assist with healthy nerve development in the baby.

Nat mur: for morning sickness with vomiting of watery, frothy phlegm.

The second trimester

Once you are beyond twelve weeks you enter the second phase of your pregnancy, which is often a very positive time. Most women find that their energy has returned and they usually look and feel very well. They are moving along with the flow of their pregnancy and if there has been some morning sickness it will usually have stopped by now. There is only a slight risk of miscarriage now that will only affect a small number of women.

INCOMPETENT CERVIX

If you have reached inside your vagina and felt your cervix you would know that it normally feels very strong and firm. It has a narrow opening called the os that is meant to be sealed shut during pregnancy. Remember that the cervix is the entrance to your uterus and this is where your baby is encapsulated. As your baby grows larger, the cervix must remain tightly closed to prevent bacteria entering the uterus and also to prevent your baby falling out into your vagina.

Some women are at risk of miscarriage in the second stage of pregnancy because of a weakened or damaged cervix. Women who can be at risk are those who have torn their cervix during the second stage of a previous labour. This can occur when a woman starts to bear down in labour before her cervix is properly dilated or if the baby comes too quickly.

Occasionally the cervix can be damaged if a large part of it is removed during a cone biopsy or by a doctor using instruments to dilate it during surgical procedures. Although the cervix is capable of stretching apart to allow the baby to pass into the birth canal during pregnancy, it does so gradually and is softened by hormones released into the immediate area. Forcing it open during surgery can damage the muscular tone and this can prevent it from closing tight during pregnancy. This is an example of a routine surgical procedure leading to serious consequences for some women.

Ideally, an incompetent cervix should be treated prior to conception using astringent uterine tonics. Those women who are alerted to the problem during their pregnancy can still use the herbs but they may also require medical attention because the baby is growing rapidly in the middle stages of pregnancy. As the baby grows larger there will be a great deal of downward pressure. While I have great faith in my medicines to improve the muscle tone, complementary medicine at this stage will further reduce the risk of miscarriage. Medical treatment will involve having a couple of stitches inserted into the cervix to keep it closed until labour is due. The stitches will then be removed.

THE FIRST MOVEMENTS

When you are around eighteen to twenty weeks pregnant you will begin to feel some movement as the baby starts to stretch its limbs inside your uterus. At first it will only be slight but over the next few months these movements will become more powerful as your baby grows larger. This is a very exciting time for mothers who are now very aware of this new life inside them.

Cell salts for the second trimester

During this stage of pregnancy your baby's hair and organs are developing so the cell salt program for the second trimester will be:

Calc flour: to tone the uterus and prevent varicose conditions.

Ferrum phos: to improve iron absorption and oxygen transport in the blood.

Mag phos: if there is a risk of miscarriage or for leg cramps.

Nat mur: may be needed if there is fluid retention.

Silicea: to assist with the formation and strength of hair, teeth, bones and nails. Silicea also helps to prevent stretch marks.

The third trimester

At the beginning of the third trimester you will probably be feeling great. At last you are starting to look like you are pregnant; your uterus has increased in size and is now above your umbilicus or belly button.

As your pregnancy progresses there can be slight discomfort caused during the last few weeks. This, of course, differs from woman to woman and with each pregnancy.

As the pregnancy advances you may notice some mild contractions of the uterus called Braxton-Hicks contractions. These are painless and do not follow a regular pattern.

During the last month of pregnancy your baby will drop lower into your pelvic cavity and this will reduce pressure that may have been felt up under the ribs. When your baby moves closer towards the birth canal it is not unusual to once again experience some bladder frequency.

PREVENTING HEARTBURN

Heartburn is common in pregnancy and it can be due to a number of factors. It can be dietary, so avoid fatty or fried foods (including coconut or coconut milk and nuts). Try not to rush your food or eat on the run, instead, eat slowly, chew your food well and don't drink with meals. Drinking with meals tends to interfere with digestion because you flush through undigested food. Have a drink before eating and wait for half an hour after eating.

Try eating smaller meals more often and if the problem persists you could try taking one or two digestive enzymes immediately after you eat. These do not stop you producing enzymes, they simply add a few more to assist with digestion. There are several brands available from natural therapists, pharmacies or health stores. Eat enzyme-rich foods such as pineapple, pawpaw and kiwi fruit.

Try sipping chamomile or fennel tea.

Slippery elm powder or tablets (chewed) taken half an hour before meals and once before bed can help to stop the burning.

Sometimes the baby is situated high in the abdomen and may be pressing up onto the stomach causing digestive discomfort. Once baby moves again the discomfort will go.

Toward the end of your pregnancy heartburn may be due to tissue changes caused by the release of the hormone relaxin. This hormone causes the valve between the oesophagus (food pipe) and your stomach to soften, which can create heartburn or indigestion in the last few months of pregnancy. I was always told that it was because my babies had hair and yet when they were born, they were almost bald.

PREVENTING SORE NIPPLES

Some women develop sore nipples when they start breastfeeding. This can be due to feeding techniques, however preparing your nipples in the last stages of pregnancy will certainly reduce the risk of sore nipples developing.

* Expose your breasts to the fresh air as often as possible.
* Rub jojoba oil or vitamin E cream into your breasts in the last few weeks of pregnancy to keep the skin soft and supple.

* Do not wash your nipples with harsh soaps and keep talc away from them.

VARICOSE CONDITIONS

Varicose conditions occasionally occur in the later stages of pregnancy due to the added pressure of the baby and the release of hormones that can cause vascular walls to be more relaxed. Treatment and prevention of hae-morrhoids and varicose veins are discussed in detail on pages 247 and 249.

ITCHY SKIN

Toward the end of my first pregnancy I developed itchy feet. The itch nearly drove me mad and I was prescribed all sorts of lotions and potions, even though there was no sign of a rash. I now know that it was due to an increase in bile salts in the blood.

In order to bring the levels back to normal it is important to assist your liver function. Drink dandelion beverage and a glass of beetroot, celery and carrot juice every day. A great liver herb is St Mary's thistle, which is readily available in tablet form and is safe to take during pregnancy.

BACK ACHE

It is not unusual for women to experience some backache during the later stages of pregnancy. It is most commonly felt when they lie down on their back at night. This is because the weight of their baby has been pulling their spine forward all day, when they lie down, they push their spine flat and their stress receptors in the muscles respond. Muscular spasm and pain is a consequence.

Support your spine by placing a cushion in the small of your back when seated. As you lie down, do so gradually.

Try soaking in a warm bath that contains lavender or rosemary oil. Otherwise let the hot shower run onto your back.

A regular massage with a qualified therapist who knows how to massage during pregnancy can be highly beneficial, or see an osteopath or physiotherapist.

HIGH BLOOD PRESSURE AND PRE-ECLAMPSIA

Some women develop high blood pressure during the last few weeks of their pregnancy. While it should be checked regularly, it is expected that pressure will increase slightly because it is closely connected with emotions.

There is a great deal of excitement and anticipation building up before a birth.

If, however, your blood pressure rises sharply and/or you also have fluid retention, it is possible that you have developed pre-eclampsia and you should see your doctor immediately. This condition used to be referred to as toxaemia of pregnancy. Pre-eclampsia is very serious because if it is left untreated your baby can fail to thrive. In severe cases the baby can die.

As pre-eclampsia progresses protein will be detected in the urine. This is why blood pressure is monitored regularly during pregnancy and urine samples are taken. If high blood pressure and protein in the urine are detected early, pre-eclampsia can be treated and complications will be avoided.

Both mother and baby need to be closely monitored if any symptoms that indicate pre-eclampsia develop. These can include fluid retention, headaches, nausea, visual disturbances, vomiting, convulsions or epileptic fits. While naturopathic treatment of this condition will be helpful and complete rest is very important, medical supervision is necessary.

Self-help for the prevention of high blood pressure and pre-eclampsia includes:

Exercise: regular moderate exercise will help to prevent high blood pressure. Care must be taken however, to reduce exercise if you have pre-eclampsia because bed rest is required.

Stress management: tension and anxiety will contribute to high blood pressure. Find a relaxation technique that you look forward to doing daily. For example, tai chi, yoga, meditation or some type of deep-body relaxation technique. Cigarette smoking contributes to stress and can increase blood pressure. If you have not quit the habit yet, right now would be a good time.

Diet: avoid foods with a high fat content and do not fry anything.

Reduce your sodium (salt) intake. Do not add salt to your cooking or your food and read labels on packaging for processed foods to check their sodium content. You should aim for less than 600 mg of sodium each day. A level teaspoon of salt contains 2000 mg!

Eat lots of fresh fruit and vegetables, seeds, grains and legumes.

Avoid stimulants such as tea and coffee and drink herbal teas and fresh water instead.

Nettle, dandelion and rosemary are herbs that are safe during pregnancy and helpful for this condition. They are easy to obtain in a dried form or perhaps you have them growing in your garden. They can be made into tea or incorporated into your cooking.

Try to eat garlic every day because it can help to naturally reduce blood pressure.

BLEEDING IN THE SECOND HALF OF PREGNANCY

It is rare for women to bleed in the second half of their pregnancy, so if you notice you have bled enough to make a stain on your clothes or bedclothes you should contact your doctor immediately. It is very likely that either your placenta is positioned below your baby (*placenta praevia*) or it has separated from the wall of the uterus (*abruptio placentae*).

The placenta is the lifeline between mother and baby. It is through this organ that the baby receives nourishment and also clears waste, so the placenta must have a strong connection within the uterus in order for the developing baby to survive.

These are the two main causes of bleeding at this stage of pregnancy and a pelvic ultrasound is required for an accurate diagnosis. A picture is produced from ultrasound that will identify the position of the placenta. Sometimes an ultrasound done at 20 weeks will reveal a low placenta in some women. A low placenta at this stage, does not pose any serious risk because it can move higher as the pregnancy develops. Your doctor will repeat the ultrasound at around 30 weeks to check. If it is still low after this, you will be advised to rest in hospital.

When the placenta is positioned too low in the uterus, it can pose a health risk during the final weeks of pregnancy. It becomes serious if the placenta lies directly over the cervical outlet and is wholly contained in the lower portion of the uterus below the baby. As your pregnancy progresses, contractions begin and the lower part of the uterus enlarges. This can cause the placenta to separate and tear away from its attachment, resulting in a haemorrhage that may require a transfusion.

Many women with a low placenta are still able to have a normal vaginal delivery as long as both mother and baby are closely monitored.

Note: Although there are traditional medicines to prevent and treat haemorrhage, they will not alter the position of the placenta. If it is low you will require close medical supervision.

PREMATURE LABOUR

A small percentage of women will go into labour before the 37th week. It can be difficult to know why the onset of labour begins before the baby has completed its development. Premature labour can begin for no apparent reason or it can be a direct result of illness, nutritional deficiency or trauma. Labour sometimes starts early when there is a multiple pregnancy. In some circumstances, the infant may have a greater chance of survival outside the uterus.

While attempts can be made to delay delivery, they are not always successful or desirable. Your body will normally give you an indication that you are beginning to go into labour. You can expect to have the same symptoms as a full-term delivery although it can commence more slowly. Regular painful contractions that increase in frequency, or any signs of bleeding, can indicate the onset of labour. Sometimes the membranes surrounding your baby can rupture and you will either feel a gush of fluid or a slow leak of fluid from the vagina. If any of these occur, you will need to be taken to hospital where your baby can be monitored. The size of your baby will be checked and you will be examined to see if your cervix has started to open up. In order to slow the onset of labour, it is important for you to have complete bed rest.

Some remedies that can be useful for premature labour are:

* Magnesium phosphate to prevent muscular spasm.
* Rescue Remedy can be taken every fifteen minutes to reduce fear and anxiety.
* Drinking chamomile and ginger tea can reduce tension and muscular spasm.

BREECH PRESENTATION

Your baby will change its position quite regularly through the middle of pregnancy because the baby is small and there is plenty of fluid in which it can move around. In the final weeks before the birth the baby has less room to move and will settle into position for delivery: the ideal position is head down. A small percentage of babies will present the other way around, or bottom first. This is called a breech presentation.

While it is possible for some women to deliver their baby feet or bottom first, it is not desirable because it can result in a more difficult labour. The baby experiences more difficulty moving through the birth canal and dilation is slow. Some health practitioners will recommend an attempt to turn the baby. They refer to it as gentle manipulation and it is done by pushing and turning the baby from the outside; like a deep massaging movement.

Do not have this done without close monitoring of your baby's heartbeat. Your baby should be monitored before, during and after this procedure to check for signs of foetal distress. If your doctor is unsuccessful in turning the baby, an X-ray may be advised to check if its head will fit into the mother's pelvis.

I do not agree with either of the above procedures. Physical attempts to turn the baby and X-rays always carry an element of risk for your baby. The placenta can be damaged and nourishment to the baby can be cut off.

It is not unusual for breech babies to turn just before the birth, so I prefer to take a patient wait-and-see approach. There are other ways of encouraging your baby to turn without force.

Try taking a homoeopathic preparation of pulsatilla 30X. I have used this remedy on a number of occasions and it has been effective. It can be taken three to five times a day until the baby turns.

Swimming can be helpful, in particular breast stroke or just float around in the water. This often reduces muscular tension (unless the water is very cold) and can improve your baby's ability to move around and change its position. When you are standing upright, gravity is forcing the baby into the birth canal.

Visualisation is a powerful method of encouraging change. While you are swimming, visualise your baby lying in your uterus with its head down in the birth canal.

An alternative to swimming is to lie on your back with a couple of large thick cushions under your hips and buttocks. You can also put a cushion under your head. The idea is to have your hips higher than your head. Once again your baby drops away slightly from the birth canal. Gently massage your abdomen with the palms of your hands and communicate with your child. Try to adopt this pose quite regularly during the day and hold it for ten to fifteen minutes each time.

If your blood pressure drops when you are on your back try this position instead: get down on all fours, then drop lower onto your elbows. Allow your abdominal muscles to relax. In this position, your baby will naturally move away from the birth canal and be cradled in your mid to upper abdomen. This will also allow the baby greater freedom of movement, making it easier to naturally turn.

Another method is to lie on your back with your feet at the top, on a

135

slant board that has a fairly steep incline; about as steep as a slippery dip. Encourage your baby to disengage by gently stroking your abdomen.

If your baby does not turn, the most important thing is to be in the hands of a good midwife or obstetrician. Try not to worry, with gentle encouragement most babies will turn.

Cell salts for the third trimester

Calc fluor: for varicose conditions.

Ferrum phos: to help with iron absorption and oxygen transport to the tissues.

Kali phos: this is a nerve nutrient and it can also be helpful for an overdue baby.

Mag phos: for the prevention of heartburn or leg cramps.

Nat mur: to control the fluid balance. This is very useful for swollen ankles and fluid retention associated with pre-eclampsia.

Silicea: to prevent stretch marks and maintain the health of the skin, hair, bones and nails.

Herbal medicines

Your herbalist will prepare a birth tonic to prepare your body for childbirth. There are also some safe self-help remedies that can be taken as herbal teas.

Raspberry leaf is a very useful herb at the end of pregnancy; it can be used alone or in combination with squaw vine and blue cohosh to encourage a good steady labour. Drink raspberry leaf tea regularly in the last few weeks of pregnancy as it is a highly nutritive tea that can prepare your body well for birthing.

Stinging nettles are nutritive herbs that contain vitamin K. Vitamin K is important for reducing the risk of haemorrhage after delivery. The effectiveness of stinging nettles at this stage of pregnancy is hard to prove, nevertheless they are safe to use. Nettles can also help to reduce haemorrhoids because they are mildly astringent and will strengthen blood vessels.

Bach Flower remedies

These are very helpful during pregnancy and childbirth because they help to balance emotions. See the list of remedies in 'Moods and the mind' and select the remedies that you feel are appropriate for your needs. Some useful pregnancy remedies are walnut, mimulus, cerato, sweet chestnut, vervain and Rescue Remedy.

OVERDUE BABIES

At the end of your pregnancy, hormonal secretions will soften your cervix so that it can gradually open and allow your baby to come through. If the cervix is tight and unyielding, labour will be delayed. There are a few self-help methods to ripen the cervix and encourage labour.

* Stimulating your nipples can help to trigger the release of hormones that help to soften the cervix and initiate the birth.
* Visualise your baby being born. Imagine your uterus is contracting and with each contraction, your cervix is beginning to open.
* Sexual stimulation can be beneficial. Orgasm is a good way of encouraging rhythmical muscular contractions and stimulation of the cervix.
* Go for long walks. When you are vertical, gravity pushes baby down and places more pressure on the cervix which encourages it to open.
* Crouch in a squatting position regularly. If you have haemorrhoids, put a cushion or a couple of thick books under your bottom for support.
* Take homoeopathic caulophyllum 200X morning and night until labour commences.
* Some Bach Flowers can help. Try rockwater to help loosen up, impatiens for patience and red chestnut if you can't stop worrying about the baby.
* Your herbalist can give you some black cohosh tincture if your baby is overdue and you can take ten drops in a little water every two or three hours until labour commences.

If you prepare your body for childbirth you can help to prevent premature or late deliveries and you can help to facilitate labour in a more natural way.

INDUCED LABOUR

Your doctor may want to facilitate labour artificially by induction. This will be done by either placing a prostaglandin gel on your cervix; artificially rupturing the membranes surrounding the baby; and/or administering an intravenous drip that contains oxytocin.

Unless there is a serious risk to the baby if it is not born soon, try to avoid inductions. In the final stages before a natural birth, your body releases hormones that soften ligaments and tendons in preparation for labour. When you have inductions, your body is not prepared and your labour will be different. When birth does not follow a natural process, everything is forced and your contractions will be stronger and more painful.

137

It is possible to have your baby monitored each day so you know there is no foetal distress and you can safely wait a bit longer for a natural labour to begin. Talk to your doctor about this possibility.

The birth

Birth is the gradual transition of an infant from the womb to its mother's arms. It is the arrival of a new soul and it is both sacred and instinctual. Trust in your own ability to give birth naturally, without the need for intervention.

Women have every reason to feel confident in their ability to give birth, yet doubts and fears begin to emerge as the pregnancy progresses. It is perfectly natural for a woman to be concerned for the safety of her baby, and it is understandable that she might be worried or fearful about the experience of childbirth.

These fears are often reinforced by a medical model that does not believe that women are capable of going through this natural and enriching experience without intervention. It is important however, to be around experienced midwives or birth attendants who know how to provide support and encouragement to women in childbirth.

They are often there from the very first stages of labour, right through to when the baby is born, attending to the mother's needs, answering her questions and providing encouragement. They keep her feeling positive because they have complete confidence in natural childbirth methods.

Women will find encouragement and support if they decide to opt for an active and natural birth process for their child.

Women who assist others in childbirth understand the entire emotional, spiritual and physical processes of labour from start to finish. They remain in tune with the rhythm of the birth and try to ensure a positive experience for the mother and the infant.

When we only consult with doctors during our pregnancy, we are dealing with people who may have limited birth experiences. As a birth support person, I have never seen a doctor remain with a woman throughout her entire labour. They are often called in for the final stages of delivery and very few of them resist the temptation to intervene.

Partners are welcomed and encouraged to participate in the birth of their child. They provide a woman with a great deal of love and compassion, and love that flows freely during childbirth will also be passed on to the infant. Witnessing the birth of a child establishes a strong connection and will provide a solid foundation for their relationship in the future.

It is not unusual for a woman to relive her own birth experience and some women find comfort in having their mother or a sister present to provide emotional support.

By surrounding yourself with the right people you can overcome your fears and help to create a positive birth experience.

WHAT TO EXPECT

Your baby has moved right down into your pelvis and will slowly move away from the comfort and safety it has experienced in the womb. It is ready to leave your body and with the aid of muscular contractions, ever so slowly, your baby will travel down into the birth canal.

The first indication that you are starting labour can be the painless contractions that you have been experiencing in the last few weeks have intensified and become more frequent.

The hormones that soften the ligaments and muscles before birth can affect the bowel and you may have some diarrhoea just prior to labour.

Some women will notice a small amount of blood-stained mucus on their pants. This is called a 'show' and it can come away from inside the cervix when it starts to stretch open.

Occasionally women develop a strong urge to clean or organise their house and some women just sense that the time is near and feel a need to rest.

All of these signs can be indicators that labour is not far away. Whether you notice them or not is irrelevant because you will know when your labour has begun.

FIRST STAGE

Sometimes labour will start with the waters breaking. The water is the amniotic fluid that has been surrounding the baby during pregnancy. Pressure from the baby's head on the membranes that contain the fluid cause them to rupture and the warm fluid will either trickle out gradually or gush out all at once. This is referred to as the waters breaking and if labour has not commenced already, it will usually start within a few hours of this occurring.

Women are often encouraged to go to hospital once their waters break because they are at risk of infection. There is generally no need for you to rush to the hospital, however you should not take a bath or put anything into your vagina once the membranes that surround your baby have broken. This means no vaginal examination unless the hands are scrubbed beforehand and definitely no sexual intercourse.

Occasionally the membranes are ruptured artificially by the doctor to induce or accelerate labour. This should not be done as a routine procedure, however it is sometimes necessary if there are indications that your baby is in distress, in order to speed up the birthing process.

By observing the colour of the amniotic fluid, your birth attendant will know if it contains meconium, which is your baby's first bowel evacuation. It stains the fluid brown or green and if it is present, it confirms that your baby may be in foetal distress.

If you are at home and you notice that the fluid is stained brown or green, you should go to the hospital immediately so that your baby can be closely monitored for signs of distress.

Contractions

Your baby is assisted through the birth canal with the aid of muscular contractions. With each contraction, the cervix is opening and the baby is pushed ever so slowly down towards the vagina.

During a natural labour, the contractions are usually fairly mild and easy to cope with at first. Women may feel a dull ache in their abdomen or lower back, a bit like the cramping associated with period pain. It is not constant, lasting only as long as the contraction or tightening of the uterine muscle.

The contractions often continue like this for a number of hours. They are easily tolerated at the start of labour and may only last for 15 to 30 seconds. They will be felt about every 20 to 30 minutes or they may be spaced further apart with no distinct pattern. During this stage women are often very excited that their baby will soon be arriving, however if it is the middle of the night, try to get more sleep if you can. Labour is often a slow process and you will appreciate the rest. If it is the middle of the day just continue with your routine for as long as you can.

If you are hungry eat lightly. Soup can be good because it sits well and is very nutritious.

During labour it is important to walk around as much as you can to facilitate the birth process. Don't exhaust yourself though, and have short periods of rest. Have a shower and ask your partner or support person to give you a massage to help you relax.

Be prepared that you might regularly feel the need to open your bowel or urinate. This is not unusual as your baby moves deeper into the birth canal.

Pain relief

It has been my experience that women who are educated in natural child birth techniques during labour rarely need to use pain relieving drugs. For this reason I encourage women to approach childbirth from a positive perspective.

There are times however, when women will require assistance to overcome pain and they need not feel guilty for having it. The gas provided in labour wards and birth centres can be very useful during the transitional stage when contractions can become quite intense. It is important to remember though, that if you need to use gas, do not take too much. Breathing the gas for too long can make women feel giddy and disorientated. You should remain clear and focused during this stage of your labour. Wait until you feel the contraction coming on and then start to slowly breathe the gas. When the contraction reaches its peak, put the gas down because its effects will last through the remainder of the contraction. If you use it in this way, you take the edge off the pain and you will still feel clear between contractions.

Keep in mind that drugs such as Pethidine can slow down the birth, make the mother sleepy and will directly affect the baby. Some women are given an epidural anaesthesia, which is an anaesthetic injected into the spine. This will result in a loss of feeling from the waist down and is sometimes given to women who have a long and difficult labour. If these drugs are given towards the end of labour they can prevent the mother from effectively delivering her baby, which often results in a forceps delivery with episiotomy.

Episiotomy

This is a surgical cut that is made to enlarge the vaginal opening during childbirth. Although it was only meant to be used in emergency situations, it has become a routine obstetric procedure.

Women are told that a cut heals better than a tear. There is no real evidence to support this and in fact there is a lot of evidence that a tear heals better than a cut. This type of surgical incision requires stitching, can be slow to heal and often creates excessive scar tissue that can lead to future problems with intercourse. Having an episiotomy can be a very traumatic experience for women.

Avoiding perineal tears

One of the most effective ways of avoiding a tear is to have confidence in your body's capacity to stretch during your baby's delivery. If you are nervous and fearful you will be more likely to tighten up and prevent the stretching and expansion that our skin and tissue is able to achieve. Your vagina is made of the same type of tissue as your mouth and lips and it is extremely flexible.

There are a few self-help techniques that you can use to prevent tearing during the birth.

* Massage jojoba oil or vitamin E cream into your vaginal area and perineum every evening after your bath or shower. Do this for the last four to six weeks before the birth.
* Stretch your body regularly during your pregnancy and do pelvic floor exercises.
* Do not use talc or vaginal sprays that can be drying.
* Avoid washing your vaginal area with harsh soaps, use sorbolene instead.
* Adopt active birth postures such as squatting, kneeling down or being on all fours.

Do not rush the delivery and force the birth. Be guided by your midwife or birth support person.

Self-help in the early stages

This can involve meditation and stretching to keep you supple and relaxed. Take homoeopathic caulophyllum 200X as soon as labour begins. If you are anxious, drink some chamomile tea and take some Rescue Remedy to help overcome fear.

After a while, your cervix will start to dilate and draw back, allowing your baby to come through a little more. This is when contractions will be closer together, last far longer and become more intense. At this stage, they may be ten minutes apart and can be felt for 30 to 40 seconds. They will start to build in intensity and you will need to centre yourself and breathe steadily through each one.

If you start to feel shivery try to relax until it passes. It is an indication that you need to deal with your tension. Drink some chamomile tea and get your shoulders or feet rubbed. Your birth attendant may have some specific Bach Flower remedies or homoeopathic remedies that can help. If not just take some Rescue Remedy and play some quiet, soothing music. A short meditation practise will keep you connected and tuned in with your baby. Try to relax and flow freely with the rhythm of your contractions.

Some women will vomit during the earlier stages of labour. While this can be a nervous response it often happens and may simply come from a need to empty the stomach contents. If you are sick take one dose of homoeopathic nux vomica 30X. I have used this remedy many times and it is great for stopping nausea. Do not use it as a preventative measure, not every woman will be sick and you should only take medicines if you have to, this includes the natural ones.

When to leave for hospital

If you are having your baby in a hospital or birth centre, you will need to decide when the best time is to leave. If you have a birth attendant with you, they can help with this decision. It will depend how far away the hospital is, the condition of the road (bumpy roads can be difficult during contractions), and how quickly labour is progressing. It is usually a good idea to stay home as long as possible because it is not much fun spending ten hours in a birthing room. However, you do not want to leave your run too late.

As a guide, it is time to leave for the hospital when the contractions are about two to three minutes apart, as long as you do not have to travel far. If you are anxious and not comfortable at home then you might leave sooner.

Women who are having a home birth obviously do not have to make this decision.

143

An active birth

At this stage of your labour you must try to keep moving around as much as possible, with short rests in between. It is good to regularly change your position so you can discover the most comfortable one for you. Remaining in a vertical position, leaning forward against a chair, kneeling on all fours or squatting will allow gravity to assist the birthing process and take pressure off your spine.

Drink water regularly and empty your bladder or bowel when required.

Soon your contractions will be three to five minutes apart and lasting from 40 to 50 seconds. Your midwife will regularly monitor your baby's heart rate and check your blood pressure. If your midwife does a vaginal examination at this stage it will usually reveal that your cervix is almost fully dilated and your baby is starting to move down into the vagina.

By now, your contractions are very powerful and may be difficult to cope with. This is a transitional stage when you will need the comfort and support of those around you more than any other time. This is probably the most difficult stage of the entire birth process and you may become irritable and distressed. It is not unusual to withdraw to your inner self in order to focus all your energy on working through the powerful contractions. Your partner or birth assistant will probably need to massage slowly and deeply into your lower back and sacrum. Keep breathing regularly as you work through this stage.

It is too soon to start pushing, even though you will have an incredible urge to do so. You will need to be encouraged and reminded that your baby is very close.

Many women experience back pain during this stage and they benefit greatly from having someone massage their lower back. A warm shower or being draped with hot towels can also help. Women will often begin to intuitively sway or rock their pelvis from side to side in an attempt to loosen their muscles and let go of tension.

Continue to breathe deeply and take your awareness to your baby in the birth canal. You can assist your baby's passage by visualising your body opening up to allow the infant more room to move through. Try not to fight against the birth process, it is time to let go and help your baby complete its journey. If you need to call out or make any sort of noise you should do so.

This is not a good time to be lying on your back. In this position, the pain will be stronger and the space in the birth canal will be reduced by one fifth. Try kneeling on some cushions or over a bed. You may prefer to let your body hang loosely while being supported under your arms or you may want to adopt a squatting position. Between each contraction you should still be moving around as much as possible. Your support people will need to let you lean on them if you feel weak.

SECOND STAGE

Your cervix is fully dilated now and at last you are ready to help push your baby out of your body.

It is impossible to know what birth position you will favour during the final stages of the birth or how well you will cope with the situation. There are many factors to consider, including the baby's position in the birth canal, the mother's energy and state of health, the length of the labour and whether there are any complications.

Work with your contractions at this stage. As you feel them coming on, take a breath and push down into your bottom as you slowly exhale. The contractions will last much longer now so take another quick breath and push again. It is important to have controlled breathing at this stage and try to breathe the baby out. Rest between contractions.

Try not to be frightened or anxious about the birth. If you are anxious, your muscles will become tense and this will slow down the birth process and intensify the pain. Let go of fear; you have already come through the most difficult phase and soon you will hold your baby close.

Before long your baby's head is visible at the vaginal entrance and if you reach down, you will be able to feel it with your hand. Now, with each contraction, you will feel some pressure and a burning sensation as the skin around your perineum stretches. Your birth attendant can gently massage some oil into the area to make the tissues more resilient. Surrender to the birth process at this stage and remember that your body is extremely flexible and resilient. Your vagina is capable of stretching, without tearing or splitting, to accommodate the size of your baby.

By draping a hot towel across the perineum the midwife can encourage blood into the tissues which can improve flexibility. Pour some boiling water over a clean handtowel and when it has cooled slightly, wring out the water, fold it and hold it against the perineum. This can be very soothing and relaxing to the tissues.

It is important for the birth of your baby to be well controlled at this stage. If you push too hard as the head emerges, you may cause your skin to tear. Your birth attendant can talk you through this stage of delivery so that you can exercise greater control over the muscles around the entrance to your vagina. She may ask you to breathe lightly or grunt as the head emerges. 145

Then she might get you to push very gently as each of the shoulders are released.

During this phase it can help if you reach down and feel your baby coming through. You can gently stretch and massage your own perineum and when a mother helps deliver her baby she is less likely to tear.

Once your baby's head is through, the body follows with the next contraction and it doesn't hurt any more.

After the baby slips from its mother's body, it will be held face down for a moment to allow any fluid to drain from its mouth and nose and then handed immediately to its mother, or gently placed between her legs where she can reach down to pick it up. The cord that attaches the child to its mother is pulsating. It is still providing your baby with oxygen at this stage and should not be cut immediately.

A mother will instinctively hold the baby close to her skin. Drape mother and child with a cotton blanket for warmth, especially if you are in an airconditioned room.

These first moments after delivery are very important for the bonding between a mother and her baby. If the father of the baby is present he will also welcome this new infant. This is a lovely time to share a few peaceful moments together.

After five or ten minutes the baby is usually breathing well and the cord can be cut and tied. I usually encourage a mother to offer her breast at this stage, and babies will often instinctively start sucking. Do not be worried if they reject the breast. Some babies need encouragement to suckle and some mothers are a bit apprehensive initially. Breastfeeding doesn't come easily to all of us and it can take time to develop.

THE THIRD AND FINAL STAGE

The final stage of labour is the delivery of the placenta and it needs to come away in one piece. Once the placenta is delivered the blood vessels in the uterus will seal off and prevent haemorrhage.

Stimulation of the nipples can trigger the release of the hormone oxytocin which causes the uterus to contract allowing the placenta to come away more easily. This is why it is good to offer the breast to the baby after birth.

The placenta is easy to deliver and usually comes away within an hour after the birth.

At this stage I give the mother one dose of homoeopathic Arnica 200X for bruising in the birth canal. This remedy will prevent her from feeling sore over the next few days.

THE SAFETY NET

There is always an element of risk with childbirth and if complications arise during or after the birth, there can be a genuine need for medical intervention. There are times when the life of the mother or the baby is at risk and an emergency caesarean delivery will be necessary.

Midwives attending home births are trained to act quickly when things go wrong and will immediately transfer the mother to the nearest hospital without delay. If your midwife says it is time to go to hospital, do so immediately. While it is perfectly natural for women to feel disappointment, try not to feel inadequate. Remember, whether you give birth at home, under a bush, in a vehicle, or in a hospital, naturally, actively, induced or by caesarean, it will still be possible for you to have a high level of involvement in your child's birth experience.

THE NEXT DAY

* Arnica 200: to be taken morning and night until bruising in the birth canal subsides.
* Herbal baths: your herbalist can mix together comfrey, calendula and hypericum tincture. This can be added to a bath and is excellent for healing bruises, tears or grazes.
* Salt baths can be helpful if you have stitches.
* The addition of lavender to a bath will help with haemorrhoids and helps to heal tears.

Stillbirth

The tragedy of the stillbirth will remain with a mother forever. Words cannot describe the physical and emotional emptiness and the incredible sense of loss.

It is important to try to express your feelings even though the emotional release can be overwhelming and painful at times. You will experience a wide range of feelings that include shock, anger, frustration, despair, guilt, depression and incredible sadness.

It will still be possible to have an active birth and it is important for you to do so. You will have the opportunity to hold your baby and, although you might be afraid to do this, it will help you to come to terms with the reality of the situation. If you do not see your child, it will be more difficult to accept what has happened. When you see your baby you will know immediately that the child is at peace. A stillborn child does not suffer in death, and in time you may come to understand that although your time together was cut short, your relationship was perfect in every way.

. . . wrapped in a patience and warmth of expectation and love,
dreams of the love and care you would bestow on the child of your loins,
the only thing this child knew was the warmth and comfort of the mother's womb,
the wealth and comfort of the mother's sounds while a mother's love surrounds.

Norman Charles Grierson

Breastfeeding

Breastfeeding provides the best nourishment you can give your baby and while you are breastfeeding, you are developing an intimate relationship with your child.

Some mothers experience difficulty with breastfeeding, and while it is true that some babies will suckle instantly, it can take up to two weeks for others to settle into a good pattern of feeding. Remember that you have lots of time. Be patient and try not to feel inadequate.

Start by making sure you are relaxed and in a comfortable position. Prop yourself up with some pillows. Grasp your nipple firmly between your fingers and gently encourage it into your baby's mouth. Talk softly to your child and hold it close to your skin. Your baby might start by licking the end of the breast and after a while it will begin to suck. Try not to be distressed if it doesn't, some babies do not have a good sucking reflex. When your baby does latch on, make sure it has the nipple well into its mouth. If you feed incorrectly your nipples can become red and sore. If they do, apply vitamin E cream, comfrey cream or aloe vera gel after feeding. Wash these off with warm water before commencing the next feed. Within a few days they will improve and breastfeeding will no longer be painful.

For the first few days your breasts produce a thick yellow fluid called colostrum, that is rich in protein and contains antibodies to protect your baby from infection. This provides all the nourishment your baby needs for the first few days.

Let your baby nurse regularly, but don't leave them to suck for a long time as this can make the nipples tender. Start with just a couple of minutes on either breast and slowly increase it over the next few days as your breasts become used to baby sucking.

After two or three days your milk will 'come in' and your breasts will become harder and much fuller. Make sure you get plenty of rest and feed your baby 'on demand'. When you feed regularly, your breasts are less likely to become lumpy and engorged with milk.

Breastfeeding has many advantages. Mothers must be assisted and encouraged to try to establish a feeding pattern with their babies, even if it is only for a few months.

* Breastfeeding establishes a good relationship between mother and baby.
* It protects against illness and allergies.
* It is economical and convenient.
* It is sterile and easy to prepare.
* Breastfeeding protects against obesity later in life.
* The essential fatty acids in breast milk help to prevent mental illness.
* Mothers will regain their figure more quickly.
* Breastfed babies are more likely to thrive.

Herbs to improve your milk supply

There are many traditional herbs that can improve a dwindling milk supply. We refer to these as galactagogues and they are highly nutritive for both the mother and her baby. Some can be made as teas and others included in soups or salads. Alternatively, your herbalist can make up a medicinal preparation that can be taken in water three times a day.

ALFALFA, *Medicago sativa*: this is a highly nutritive herb that helps increase milk quantity. The sprouted seeds are a rich source of vitamins and minerals.

ANISEED, *Pimpinella anisum*: stimulates the mammary glands for milk production and is also a digestive aid.

DILL, *Anethum graveolens*: an ingredient in gripe water used for babies with colic. The addition of dill in a mixture for a nursing mother can indirectly assist the baby.

FENNEL, *Foeniculum officinale*: a nutritive herb that can also reduce abdominal bloating. Use the seeds to make tea or eat the whole plant as a vegetable.

FENUGREEK, *Trigonella foenum-graecum*: use this in your cooking or make a tea from the dried seeds.

HOPS, *Humulus*: this is an old remedy for mothers of twins who needed an abundant milk supply.

PARSLEY, *Petrosillium crispum*: A great iron tonic that can be used in cooking.

While I encourage every woman to breastfeed, a mother has not failed her child if she cannot. As long as you still cuddle your baby during bottle feeding and maintain close, intimate contact, it is possible to develop a healthy bond with your child and they will not feel deprived of your love. If you want to 149 wean your child, sage will help to dry up your milk supply. See your herbalist who can dispense it in a medicinal form that is easy to take.

The first six weeks

BACK CARE

Be sure to see your chiropractor or osteopath within the first six weeks after delivery. The ligaments in your pelvis are still fairly soft due to the secretion of the hormone relaxin which is produced before delivery. Your therapist can easily make any necessary adjustments to your lower back before these ligaments harden once again. If your lower back is out of alignment it becomes harder to adjust after the six-week period.

During childbirth the pelvic bones open up a little and the coccyx, or tail bone, moves back to make room for baby in the birth canal. After delivery it is not uncommon for your coccyx to turn inwards too far when it flicks back into place. This can be worsened by sliding backwards onto your bed or onto a chair, because you have stitches or are a little bit tender. You must be sure always to sit down squarely on your bottom to avoid this problem.

LIBIDO

It is understandable to have a lower libido after childbirth. Apart from the sudden decline of hormones, a new mother is usually occupied with caring for her baby, feeding on demand and having broken sleep. If a woman has required an episiotomy she may find intercourse leads to discomfort and it may be painful until she has thoroughly healed. This can also be true for women who have had other abdominal or reproductive surgery.

PREVENTING POSTNATAL DEPRESSION

While it is not uncommon to feel a bit flat when all the excitement of a new baby has worn off, some women lapse into a lasting depression that can be very distressing. It can be triggered by low hormone levels, fatigue, isolation, nutritional deficiencies, relationship problems and alcohol or drug dependency. A demanding baby can also cause a mother distress. If a baby is not sleeping well because it has colic, a mother can find it difficult to cope. Some women will have experienced trauma during childbirth and this can also contribute to depression in the weeks following the birth.

In severe and chronic depression women will need to see a doctor who may suggest counselling and/or prescribe hormones or antidepressants.

If you can find the motivation to help yourself the following ideas can be useful.

* Take care of yourself and eat nutritious food every day.
* Contact a women's help line or community health centre to find out if there is a local support group.
* Contact a friend who you can talk to about how you are feeling.
* Go outdoors regularly with your baby.
* Try to organise some time for yourself and do something you enjoy.
* Exercise for 30 minutes every day.
* Do not smoke or drink alcohol (they are depressants).
* Take a B complex vitamin every day, a good multivitamin tablet that includes zinc and magnesium and essential fatty acids.
* A herbalist can mix a good tonic to improve your wellbeing and help balance hormones.
* Drink lemon balm tea.

In conclusion

Pregnancy and birth are natural processes. There is no need to be afraid of the experience of childbirth, your body will be prepared for it.

Turn to the many intuitive and experienced women who are our midwives, birth educators and support people. They will help you prepare for childbirth so that you are more likely to give birth in a confident, active and intuitive way.

Remember that you can give birth naturally in complete control, without complications. Things seldom go wrong and with the right preparation, the birth of your child will be a positive and wondrous occasion.

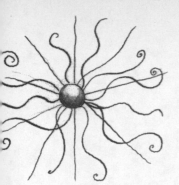

PARt 3

A
POSItIVE
TRANSITION

Menopause:
A Natural Event
in a Woman's Life

THERE comes a time when a woman's body will cease to be fertile. Her ovaries will no longer produce ova and menstrual bleeding will stop. This is known as the menopause and it is a natural event in a woman's life. Many women come through menopause without difficulty and begin another phase of their lives without experiencing any distressing symptoms. In fact, for many it is a time of liberation. Menstruation has ceased and contraception is no longer an issue. Children are usually at an age where they are independent and mothers can let go and focus on themselves once again.

In many cultures, women welcome menopause because when menstrual bleeding stops they are free from taboos and restrictions and they often gain a higher status and greater respect.

What are the physical signs?

Changes in menstruation are usually the first indicators that the transition into menopause has begun. These changes differ considerably between women, but for most the bleeding will become lighter or irregular before the period actually stops.

This will not tend to follow any particular pattern. For example, you can skip a period and then you may have a period six weeks later that lasts for ten days. Then another one will come in three weeks, followed by no period for three months. This irregular pattern occurs because the ovaries are functioning erratically, just as they do at menarche, when menstruation begins.

During menopause, the ovaries produce lower levels of hormones and they stop producing eggs. The hormones that are normally produced by the ovaries have a powerful influence on a woman's body and when they are no longer produced, the body responds and physical changes occur.

When the ovaries stop functioning, your body will try to stimulate them into working again by releasing higher levels of Follicle Stimulating Hormone (FSH) and Luteinising Hormone (LH) from the pituitary gland. If the ovaries still fail to respond, these levels can become abnormally high and this is when some women can experience side effects such as hot flushes, headaches, increased urination, skin dryness, insomnia, poor memory, joint pain and mood changes. Not every woman will have all these symptoms, of course, and for most women they will be temporary.

Your body has very good self-regulating mechanisms, and it will eventually get the message that the ovaries are not going to function like they used to. When this happens, the FSH and LH levels reduce and the adrenal glands, which are just above the kidneys, will start producing a weaker form of oestrogen that continues to be produced after menopause.

This is the natural process of menopause and it is an important biological process.

EMOTIONS AND MENOPAUSE

While we know that hormones influence mood, we must be careful not to overlook other factors that influence emotions at menopause. This is a time when a woman reflects on many aspects of her life. The absence of menstrual bleeding is a powerful reminder to women that they are entering the last phase of their life. Although they may still have another 30 or so years left, women at this stage tend to make some important decisions about their future.

Women I talk to think a lot about their life and their happiness when they reach menopause. They make decisions about their relationships and whether they are living according to their values. Sometimes they discover that their life has been filled with compromise, that they have strayed from their path and their destiny is no longer clear. They often make some serious changes and many women, for the very first time, decide to take control of their own lives.

For some women, menopause is the catalyst that leads them into a journey of self-discovery. Their inner strength surfaces and often brings with it aspects of themselves that have been repressed during the years of being a wife and a mother. Menopause is a time of change on many levels and the emotional aspects associated with the end of menstruation can override the physical. At times they can be overwhelming and women need to keep open the channels of communication with those who are close to them.

It is wrong to assume that confused thoughts and emotional outbursts, which many people associate with menopause, are all a result of hormones. Menopause is a time when women can flow with the tide of change and trust in their own ability to make decisions about their own destiny.

A SMOOTH TRANSITION

Women who have a difficult time during menopause are often those who are experiencing ongoing anxiety in their lives. During stressful situations the body releases high levels of the hormone adrenaline. This is produced in the adrenal glands, and when stress is extreme and ongoing, the body can find it difficult to cope and adrenal fatigue can result. Remember these adrenal glands need to be functioning well during menopause because they take over the function of oestrogen production when the ovaries stop producing eggs.

The time when the ovaries stop producing oestrogen and the adrenal glands start, is the time when women usually experience the physical symptoms of menopause associated with low oestrogen levels. In order to have a smooth transition into menopause, it is important to support the adrenals so that they can function effectively and provide the body with the oestrogen it requires quickly and effectively.

When women consult their doctor during this phase of their lives, they are more likely to be offered hormone therapy or tranquillisers, rather than practical ways to manage their stress. As a traditional therapist who understands menopause I prefer to take a different approach. Like lots of natural therapists, I have been trained in many systems of medicine; I know that women under stress can be helped with herbal medicine, dietary and nutritional therapy and massage therapy. They should be encouraged to learn a deep-body relaxation technique that they are comfortable with and reminded to practise it regularly. When they consult with a natural therapist, they will generally find they are not rushed and they are given the opportunity to express themselves in a confidential environment.

What most of these women are experiencing is a transitional phase, and with education, guidance and support they will be able to make a smooth transition through their menopause.

I encourage women to use the natural systems of medicine and consult with an accredited health practitioner who can offer assistance on many levels.

Bridging the gap with herbal medicine

Traditional herbal medicine is a highly effective form of medicine when it is employed in the management of menopause. It can be used before menopause to balance fluctuations in ovarian function and hormonal output and it can bridge the oestrogen gap during the transition.

There are a number of herbal medicines that contain oestrogenic and other hormonal substances that influence our glandular system. These seem to reduce any negative side effects of low oestrogen at the time of menopause. Some of these herbs are sage, Korean ginseng, false unicorn root, alfalfa, red clover, black cohosh and wild yam.

There is a great deal of research material available that supports the effectiveness of these traditional medicines in helping women achieve a natural menopause without the need for drug therapy that can include Hormone Therapy (HT), tranquillisers and antidepressants. The role of herbal medicine in the management of menopause is not limited to the use of plant oestrogens. As a traditional herbalist, I have many medicines at my disposal that can support the adrenals and alleviate stress. Good examples are licorice, Korean ginseng, hypericum and passionflower. These herbs help you to relax and they are tonics for the nervous system.

It is also advantageous to improve the function of the liver so that excessive levels of hormones can be effectively cleared from the bloodstream. Dandelion and St Mary's thistle are excellent for this purpose. There are herbs to reduce pain and spasm associated with headaches, for example, rosemary, cramp bark, valerian and black cohosh.

Natural anti-inflammatory herbs such as feverfew, willow bark and guaiacum can be used to treat arthritic and rheumatic conditions. They are good alternatives to steroid medication that increases the risk of osteoporosis.

Herbs with an antidepressant action are hypericum, lemon balm and damiana, and they will help to elevate mood.

Valerian, skullcap, hops, chamomile and passionflower are all herbs with a sedative action, and they can help with sleep patterns.

None of these herbs have a risk of addiction or serious side effects. What is more, they do not have to be taken for long periods of time to achieve a lasting effect.

Let's look at some common symptoms of menopause and how to manage them in a natural way.

HOT FLUSHES

The scientific world is undecided as to why some women get hot flushes at menopause. We do know that hot flushes are more frequent and distressing when you are anxious or rushed because there is more blood pooling under the surface of the skin. When you become stressed or rush about, your peripheral circulation increases and this creates more heat under the skin. Your body then tries to cool down by stimulating the pores of the skin to open and perspire. This is an effective natural cooling mechanism, which occurs too frequently for some women at menopause.

The herb to treat hot flushes is sage. Try drinking cold sage tea mixed with apple juice as a self-help remedy. Include it in your cooking or, alternatively, see your herbalist who can incorporate it into a herbal tonic.

Homoeopathic Lachesis 30 is also very effective for controlling hot flushes. It is usually taken three to six times a day until symptoms improve.

The tissue salt nat mur will also help to control your fluid balance.

VAGINAL DRYNESS

When oestrogen levels fall at menopause, some women experience dryness of the skin. This dryness affects most of the tissues in the body, including vaginal tissue. Some women abstain from intercourse because of vaginal dryness and the discomfort that can occur when the oestrogen levels decline. While women have a right to abstain from intercourse if they desire, abstinence from sexual contact can make the problem worse. Sexual stimulation encourages production of hormones necessary for improving the libido. Try not to feel inadequate, communicate with your partner, use a lubricant and take more time.

If you find you do not lubricate well or have vaginal dryness due to low oestrogen levels, don't despair, this problem is easily overcome. There are some good water-based lubricants available at your chemist that are designed for this purpose. They are a neutral pH and are not perfumed so they will not irritate the vagina. The only problem with them is that they can get a bit sticky during a long session of lovemaking and they may be expensive.

If you have chronic dryness from low oestrogen levels your vagina can become quite raw and sore. This can make lovemaking either difficult, painful or impossible. In order to overcome this you will need to use a substance that will heal the vagina as well as provide lubrication.

You can purchase some very good soothing gels from the chemist or health store which contain approximately 98 per cent pure aloe vera. Simply ask for aloe vera gel. It is very effective in lubricating and healing the vagina as well as providing a coolness that can relieve the burning that is often felt with this condition. It is wise to test the gel on a patch of soft tissue near the entrance to your vagina in case of sensitivity. Do not use these gels with condoms if you are practising safe sex because, like vaseline and baby oil, they may cause the condom to break.

It is possible to obtain a *pure* vitamin E cream that is free of petroleum products, which is available from a registered naturopath or herbalist. I have prescribed this cream for many women who have found it soothing and helpful in healing damaged skin and tissue.

Your doctor may suggest a hormonal vaginal cream containing oestrogen that is available on prescription, however it is not meant for everyday use. At times, women tell me their partners complain of burning and redness on their penis after intercourse. This may be due to an acid/alkali imbalance of the vagina and its secretions. You can test this with litmus paper or with a urinalysis stick to determine vaginal pH. The normal pH of the vagina should be around 4, which is acidic. If the vagina is acidic it will turn litmus yellow/orange and if it is alkaline it will be blue/green.

URINARY PROBLEMS

The urinary tract can also be prone to tissue changes when oestrogen levels fall. This can contribute to increased infections, frequency and loss of control (*see* 'Your guide to good health').

It can help to increase the intake of cooked yellow vegetables to improve vitamin A levels or take a supplement of betacarotene. These nutrients keep our internal body tissues in good health and prevent dryness and inflammation.

Homoeopathic phosphoric acid 6 can help to prevent increased urination and there are a number of herbs that can be prescribed that can also assist.

Doing pelvic floor exercises regularly will assist with urinary problems generally.

Sleeplessness

Some women have trouble sleeping during menopause. This is often due to night sweats and urinary frequency that naturally disturb normal sleep patterns. Night sweats can be related to liver function and it can help to drink dandelion beverage instead of tea or coffee.

Have a cup of chamomile or valerian tea before bed and avoid sugary snacks.

Regular exercise can help to improve sleep patterns enormously.

Early menopause

Most women experience menopause sometime between the ages of 45 and 55. Occasionally a woman can experience menopause before age 40. Sometimes this can be a direct result of radiation therapy that is given to treat cancer, however it is not clear why it occurs naturally. In some cases it is considered to be hereditary if mothers or sisters have also experienced it.

In my clinical experience, I have had a great deal of success using herbal medicine to stimulate menstruation in women who have gone through a natural early menopause. In all cases menstruation that had stopped for six months to two years recommenced within two to three months. I have great faith in the effectiveness of traditional medicine in restoring menstrual bleeding and reproductive functions.

Surgical menopause

Women who have had their ovaries removed, have an immediate menopause, regardless of their age, and the medical term for this is oophorectomy. These women often require hormone therapy, particularly if their surgery occurs before age 45. If only one of the ovaries is removed, the other can function normally and menopause does not occur.

During a hysterectomy, the uterus is removed but the ovaries remain, and while menstrual bleeding no longer occurs, hormonal output continues. Women who have had a hysterectomy still experience an emotional pattern on a monthly basis and it is not unusual for them to consult with their health practitioner when they reach their mid forties to find out if they are menopausal. It can be difficult for women who do not menstruate to know when they have reached their natural menopause.

It has been observed that women who have had a hysterectomy are more likely to have an earlier menopause and they often have more severe symptoms. These women sometimes need to be given herbs for longer stretches of time. If symptoms are severe or overwhelming they can use a low-dose oestrogen pill and a natural therapist will work in a complementary way with nutritional therapy, herbal medicines and massage therapy.

BONE HEALTH

Bones are made of living cells and they are constantly being broken down or being built up. This process is performed by two main types of cells—osteoblasts and osteoclasts.

Osteoclasts wear away the bone and osteoblasts fill it back up again. It is believed that oestrogen either reduces the rate at which bone is broken down or it increases the activity of osteoblasts which form new bone. It also helps our bodies to absorb calcium, so there is no doubt that oestrogen provides a protective mechanism to the bones.

It is not the only important factor however, and a reduction in oestrogen levels at menopause is not the only cause of bone loss in women. There are also a number of nutrients required to maintain the health of our bones and they are calcium, magnesium, phosphorus, silicea and vitamin D. It is important to keep these nutrients in the correct balance. Some other specific essential nutrients are boron (found in rose hip tea), copper, zinc, manganese and vitamin C.

Vitamin D is essential for bone health because it helps the body absorb and utilise calcium and phosphorus. Calcium is the main component of bone and phosphorus is required for bone formation. Magnesium keeps the bones strong and it is essential for the proper absorption of calcium. Silicea is like the formwork in cement, without it, other nutrients have nothing to latch onto.

I have found that a large percentage of women over the age of 35 who consult with me do not maintain adequate dietary levels of calcium. While opinions differ on how much calcium is needed, it is generally considered that women require around 800 to 1200 mg of calcium every day. To keep this calcium in balance, it is best to obtain it in a form that is easily utilised, such as calcium orotate.

Chamomile, oatstraw and alfalfa tea all contain calcium, silicea and magnesium. Other good sources of calcium are:

Milk (250 ml or 1 cup)	–	300–450 mg of calcium
Yoghurt (200 g)	–	240 mg of calcium
Ricotta cheese (30 g)	–	100 mg of calcium
Sardines (100 g)	–	350 mg of calcium

Tuna with bones (100 g)   –   290 mg of calcium
Almonds (approx. 25)   –   70 mg of calcium
Tofu (half cup)   –   130 mg of calcium

Calcium should also be buffered with magnesium and good sources of magnesium include almonds, cashews, soy beans, molasses and whole-grains. Silicea is found in all the stringy fruits and vegetables such as rhubarb, celery, mango and squash. Vitamin D is provided by the sun and it is also abundant in fish oils.

Bones are very much like teeth; they have a dense, hard outer shell and the inside is like a woven structure. The strength of bone is dependent on the density of this structure.

Moderate exercise can greatly improve bone density because when bones are stressed, they become stronger. Walking or dancing are both good forms of exercise to help keep the bones healthy.

OSTEOPOROSIS

Osteoporosis is a disease where there is a loss of bone density and the bones become porous. Instead of the bone having a dense and thick texture, it develops a honeycomb appearance. As we get older, our bones can start to reduce their density. This can result in the bones becoming more fragile or brittle, which means they can break more easily.

One of the causes of osteoporosis is an inadequate intake of calcium over a number of years. Other causes and risk factors of osteoporosis can be:

* A lack of exercise.
* Low oestrogen levels.
* Drinking too much high-phosphate or fizzy drinks.
* High tea or coffee intake.
* Drinking alcohol.
* Steroid medication (including the oral contraceptive pill).
* Thyroid or diuretic medication.
* Anticonvulsant medication.
* Antacid medications that contain aluminium.
* Laxative abuse.
* Smoking (lowers natural oestrogen levels).
* Having an Asian background or fair skin with a small delicate frame.
* Hereditary factors, such as having a mother with osteoporosis.

If women are concerned that they may be at risk of osteoporosis they can have a bone density scan to check the strength of their bones. Because bones reach their peak at age 35, there is not much point in having this test until you are in your forties unless you are in a high-risk category, such as those women who had early removal of their ovaries.

If you have the test and your bone density is good, you can simply maintain the correct level of nutrients in your diet and exercise on a daily basis. If density is low and you have already developed osteoporosis, you have several treatment options available.

You may decide to take hormone therapy or your doctor can prescribe a drug that contains vitamin D, such as Rocaltrol. If you decide to take Rocaltrol, you will require a rigid dietary program and you will need to be monitored regularly for side effects. It would also be advisable to start an exercise program.

If the osteoporosis is a direct result of prescription medication (and it often is), such as drugs used to control asthma, it is possible to use traditional therapies in a complementary way. For instance, your natural therapist may help to reduce the incidence of bronchial infections by improving your immune system, this will lessen the need for steroid medication that contributes to osteoporosis. The other option is to rely on nutritional therapy and maintain an exercise program.

Until recently there was no research material to show that taking calcium could improve bone density; we maintained adequate levels of calcium to prevent further loss. Now we are seeing the results of nutritional research which indicates that by taking magnesium, with calcium as a supplement, we can actually restore density in bones that have previously lost density. So we need to make sure that any supplement we take provides us with calcium and magnesium in a ratio of 2:1.

Keep in mind however, that not every woman will develop osteoporosis. There are women who have very healthy bones because they have had regular exercise and maintained good dietary calcium levels *before* they reached their menopause. Prevention is always better than cure.

HORMONE THERAPY (HT)

Hormone therapy has been with us now for a number of years and many women have tried it. Over the past few years, I have worked closely with women who were taking various brands and combinations of hormone therapy and I have observed that very few women stay on it. There are a number of reasons for this.

Although doctors can attempt to prevent bleeding, many women continue to menstruate while taking hormone therapy and they usually would prefer not to. This is not a true period but a breakthrough bleed caused by the hormone therapy.

Some women develop breakthrough bleeding that is unpredictable.

Some women dislike taking medication when they do not feel sick or have any health problems.

Hormone therapy can influence eating behaviour and weight gain is common. It can also interfere with weight loss in women on reduction programs. We know that progesterone increases the appetite, with a tendency to create cravings for salty foods and when oestrogen is high, we are more likely to crave sweet, creamy foods.

Changes in the breast tissue are common and women often have very painful breasts while taking HT. Women also become very concerned about possible cancer risks.

Some women taking HT develop aching legs and have a higher risk of developing blood clots.

Sensitivity to the synthetic hormones can cause headaches and migraine.

Skin rashes and dermatitis are a side effect of taking HT for some women.

HT can cause fluid retention.

Endometriosis can flare up under the influence of the synthetic hormones.

While there are a few women who do feel better for taking HT, many who try this type of therapy do not continue it.

I have heard it said that HT should be given to all women over the age of 45. While women will make their own decisions about this, I think they need to be very cautious about taking long-term hormone therapy. Although the oral contraceptive pill has been thoroughly researched, there is not enough known about the effects of HT on older women.

While there are a few women who will certainly benefit from hormone therapy, there are others who cannot take it, such as those with a history of breast cancer. These women are often afraid that they will develop osteoporosis because they cannot take hormone therapy. This is due to the way HT has been promoted. The campaign for hormone therapy has focused fairly exclusively on slowing down the ageing process, and the prevention of osteoporosis and heart disease.

Those women who cannot or choose not to take HT should not be made to feel helpless, guilty or irresponsible. Not every woman will get osteoporosis and not every woman will develop heart problems. In the majority of cases, both of these health problems can be treated with nutritional therapy and lifestyle modification. Scientists are still unsure about the role of oestrogen in preventing cardiovascular disease. While it can make our arteries more efficient, hormone therapy also increases levels of fat in the blood and increases the risk of angina. There are many ways to reduce the risk of heart disease without taking hormone therapy.

Many doctors promote the use of HT and they tell women that the increased risk of cancer from taking synthetic hormones is low or minimal. During lectures by advocates of hormone therapy we are often told, with great enthusiasm, that the benefits of this type of therapy far outweigh the risks. Somehow this is supposed to make us feel better about using a carcinogenic substance. I suspect that those women who have developed cancer after taking synthetic hormones find little comfort in this information.

In conclusion

I have worked closely with women at every stage of menopause and my clinical experience extends beyond traditional therapies. I encourage women to consider using traditional therapies if they need assistance with managing their menopause. HT should only be considered for women who have had a surgical menopause or where there is significant bone density loss due to osteoporosis. In my opinion, hormone therapy should only be used when other systems of medicine have failed.

When women arrive at menopause they often still have 30 or 40 good years to look forward to. For many women it is a liberating time and some begin a new path. There need not be an expectation of rapid ageing or illness simply because your menstrual bleeding has ended. Women can achieve a smooth passage through their menopause and they will do it easily with the assistance of traditional medicine and the guidance and support of their natural therapist.

Dianne's story

DIANNE was 48 when she first came to see me. One year before this, her period had been irregular for about three months and then had ceased altogether. When her period stopped, she had hot flushes that kept her awake at night. She recalled dreadful mood swings, tiredness and a constant dull headache. Her doctor had explained that she was menopausal and prescribed hormone therapy. This caused her to have a regular period again and stopped her hot flushes, which meant she could get a good night's sleep. Although she still had an occasional headache, she was not as tired and her moods were steadier.

Dianne was happy with the result at first, but as the months progressed, she was not altogether comfortable with taking hormones. Like many women I consult with, Dianne questioned the need for taking prescription drugs for the rest of her life and worried about possible side effects.

She had noticed subtle changes in her body, such as a general feeling of puffiness and despite regular exercise and a low-fat diet, she couldn't lose the extra six kilos she had managed to gain since starting HT. Her breasts were a little tender and lumpy and it worried her that there might be some changes occurring in the breast tissue.

Dianne had been reading about menopause and had decided that she would prefer a natural approach. She was hoping I could help her get off the HT but was worried that she would have the same symptoms that she experienced before.

I explained that when she stopped HT, she had to expect a reaction because her body would immediately experience a sudden lack of oestrogen. It would respond by increasing blood levels of pituitary hormones in an attempt to stimulate her ovaries. Because it was unlikely that her ovaries would respond, her bloodstream would contain high levels of pituitary hormones such as FSH and LH while her oestrogen would remain low. This situation of extreme hormonal imbalance usually causes symptoms such as flushing, night sweats and headaches at this stage of menopause. I explained to Dianne that she would still have to physically and emotionally adjust to her menopause, and it would be an easier transition if she took some herbal medicine. There was a possibility that her period would return.

The mixture I prescribed contained herbal extracts of black cohosh, false unicorn root, licorice, dandelion, sage and hypericum. Several of these herbs contain plant oestrogens and the others would help her body adapt more quickly to menopause, preventing side effects such as hot flushes and headaches. I also included some Bach Flower remedies: honeysuckle, walnut, wild oat and Rescue Remedy. Honeysuckle would move her out of the past, walnut would help her adjust to change and wild oat would help her to move on. Rescue Remedy was added to help her feel balanced and in control. Dianne was to start taking her herbs in a low but consistent dose twice a day, two weeks before finishing her HT. This was planned to coincide with the time that she would normally have a breakthrough bleed to enable her body to shed any lining that had built up in her uterus from the HT. The weaker plant oestrogens would initially lower the blood oestrogen levels because they compete with the synthetic oestrogens for the receptor sites. Then, once the herbal medicine was in her system, Dianne could stop the HT and continue taking the herbs in a slightly higher dose three times a day. While the oestrogen levels would drop once again when the HT was stopped, the weaker oestrogens would continue to fill the receptor sites and usually prevent wild swings in pituitary hormone levels.

Dianne was willing to take the herbs and I asked her to come back to see me in three to four weeks' time. I also asked her to write down everything she ate for the next two weeks so that I could assess her diet next time I saw her. I needed to be sure that she was meeting her daily nutritional requirements.

When we next met Dianne was feeling fine. She had a headache for a couple of days when she first stopped her HT, but that settled down. She had felt unusually hot a few times when she was under stress at work, but she didn't perspire excessively.

I made up a repeat of her mixture but this time I added a bit more sage in order to eliminate the flushing. When I checked her diet, I found that Dianne's eating habits were good, however some days she did not get quite as much calcium as she needed. I recommended a good nutritional supplement of calcium that she could take on the days when her diet did not meet her calcium needs.

Dianne was in the habit of exercising every day, and she was not really in a high-risk category for osteoporosis, however I still recommended that she consider having a bone density scan to determine the strength of her bones. I saw her again six weeks later and she was feeling terrific. She was symptom-free and had lost all her puffiness as well as the extra weight she had gained from taking HT. Her bone density results were very good, so as long as she continued to exercise and maintain her calcium intake, she would not be at risk of osteoporosis. I recommended a repeat scan in about eight to twelve months to make sure.

Dianne continued to see me on and off for the next twelve months. Her repeat scan showed no changes in her bone density and her period did not return. Although she could have stopped taking her herbs, Dianne continued taking a low dose once a day together with a good daily multivitamin, simply because she felt so good while she was taking them.

PART 4

WOMEN
and
HEALING

Your Guide to
Good Health

ILLNESS and disease are signals from our body that make us aware
that something is wrong. By developing an understanding of what
these signals mean you can take an active role in the treatment and
prevention of disease.

This chapter is an A to Z of women's health imbalances. It provides self-
help information that clearly explains how to use safe and effective natural
remedies and treatments that are inexpensive and easy to obtain, such as
cell salts, Bach Flower remedies, homoeopathic remedies, essential oils,
nutritional supplements, herbal teas, as well as dietary information. Your
body has a healing potential of its own and in this section you will learn
how to become involved in these healing processes. I have included information on some naturopathic and conventional medical approaches to the
treatment of various women's health disorders in order to offer you a
range of options in health care.

The suggested treatments are simply intended to be a guide and you
should keep in mind that a face-to-face consultation with your health practitioner is essential for an accurate diagnosis and an effective treatment
program.

Acne

Acne is a common skin disorder that mainly affects adolescents but can
continue right through to the thirties. It ranges from the occasional pimple to
severe cystic acne that can leave permanent scars. Most people with acne feel
that it is unsightly and it can have devastating effects on self-esteem and
confidence.

The main cause of acne is the overreaction of the glands in the skin to the production of androgenic hormones. We all produce androgens in our bodies but only those women who are sensitive to them will develop acne. During adolescence there is often a high production of androgens and these hormones influence the sebaceous glands in our skin. These glands secrete sebum, which is an oily substance that keeps our hair and skin soft and resilient. When androgen levels are too high they cause the glands to discharge higher levels of sebum which makes the skin oilier. Androgens also cause the skin that lines the tiny ducts through which sebum escapes to thicken. This causes the ducts to become narrow and at times they can completely close over. The sebum can't escape and it continues to build up under the skin, which leads to the formation of a whitehead. The sebum often darkens when it is exposed to the air and the whitehead then turns into a blackhead. If sebum production continues without being released from the skin, bacteria can cause inflammation in the surrounding tissue. This is how we develop a pimple. If the duct is very tightly closed, it can force inflammation to spread into deeper layers of the skin which will lead to painful blind pimples.

The most severe form of acne is cystic acne, where large lumps called cysts form in the skin leading to chronic inflammation that can take months to heal. This type of acne usually causes scarring and pitting of the skin. This severe form sometimes requires medical treatment which is particularly effective when combined with external applications of herbal skin lotions and creams as well as dietary changes.

Other causes of acne can be allergy, emotional stress, some oral contraceptive pills, a bad diet, poor hygiene and a weakened immune system.

Treatment Like our kidneys, lungs and bowel, our skin can be an organ of elimination. If any of these other areas of elimination are not functioning well, the body may seek another outlet, the skin. Have you ever noticed the way the smell of your skin can change according to what you eat or drink?

Sweat glands are distributed throughout most areas of our skin and they are surrounded by tiny blood vessels. We perspire in order to regulate body temperature and eliminate waste. Our perspiration is a mixture of water, salts, urea (a by-product of protein metabolism), uric acid, amino acids, ammonia, sugar, lactic acid and vitamin C. We know that some of these substances can affect the health of our skin. While our body has very good regulating mechanisms, certain people are more sensitive to some of these substances than others.

If you have acne it is important to maintain a good diet, drink lots of fresh water and exercise every day. It can be easy to overlook what may be happening on the inside of your body when the problems are showing on the outside. Your skin must not be seen as being separate to your body.

Acute outbreaks of acne can be triggered by stress, environmental toxins, oily make-up preparations, coming off the oral contraceptive pill, binges on junk food, fever or illness. Acne is primarily a hormonal problem, so the hormones must be balanced in order to resolve the problem. Keep in mind that our hormones can be altered by stress and dietary habits.

After determining the causes of your acne, your herbalist can dispense the appropriate herbs to help clear your skin. The approach may involve using herbs to correct hormonal irregularities, drainage and detoxification, improving digestion and elimination, counteracting stress and boosting immune function. Treatment will be determined according to individual needs.

Dietary advice While dermatologists may correctly inform you that a poor diet does not necessarily cause acne, I feel it is important to consider that a good diet can certainly speed the healing process and may well prevent its return. In the treatment of any health disorder we rarely find a cure in any one form of therapy. Dietary changes are often necessary in the treatment of acne for a number of reasons. Acne is primarily caused by too many androgenic hormones and a diet that is high in animal products can increase these levels further as many beasts that are grown for human consumption often contain hormonal substances, androgens, to encourage rapid growth.

Women with acne should select protein foods from vegetarian sources such as legumes, soy products, wholegrain cereals, nuts and seeds.

Nutrients required are vitamins A, C, E, B complex, calcium, zinc and essential fatty acids.

Have a large variety of cooked yellow vegetables to obtain a good source of vitamin A which is vital to the health of your skin and immune system.

Eat raw or steamed green vegetables every day for B vitamins to help with stress.

Have fresh fruit and raw salad vegetables every day for vitamin C and fibre. A sluggish digestive system can be a big contributor to acne.

Zinc helps to heal acne, reduce inflammation and repairs the skin; good sources are wholegrains, pumpkin seeds and oysters.

Vitamin E will help with hormonal imbalance, is specific for healing acne and prevents scarring; good sources are almonds, corn and wheat germ.

Essential fatty acids can reduce inflammation and improve hormonal imbalances. Include fish oils in your diet, linseeds and tofu for natural sources.

Try to eat yoghurt every day to keep your intestines healthy and maintain calcium levels. Calcium maintains the acid/alkali balance of your blood and this is necessary for a clear complexion.

Eat garlic every day (if tolerated) or take garlic capsules.

Avoid refined carbohydrates such as white flour or white sugar products. Try wholegrain cereal products instead, such as corn breads, pumpkin breads, sunflower and barley bread and eat more rice.

Eat no fried foods. A little oil in a salad dressing or marinade is fine.

Keep coffee, tea, alcohol and cordials to a minimum. Instead drink fresh water every day. If you enjoy hot drinks try herbal teas such as chamomile, rosehip, hibiscus and dandelion beverage.

A good multivitamin or antioxidant daily with evening primrose oil or fish oil capsule may help.

Self-help Wash your skin twice a day with a mild cleansing lotion or simple soap and pat dry.

With a painful pimple that has a head, prick it with a sterilised needle and gently wipe the pus away with a soft swab dipped in tea-tree oil.

Masks can be helpful to draw out impurities; use once or twice a week. You can make a cold face pack using oatmeal made into a thick porridge and allowed to cool, honey and 'flowers of sulphur' (from the pharmacist). Spread it onto your face, leave it on for ten minutes and wash off with tepid water.

Do not use steam or heat treatments on oily skin, heat only encourages the skin to bring more oil to the surface.

Do not stand with your face directly in front of the hot water from the shower.

Do not lie out in the sun. While fresh air and ultraviolet light can help, too much sun is damaging and increases oil production.

Do not use harsh facial scrubs. They can increase inflammation and can stimulate extra skin cells that may block ducts.

Do not try to squeeze out pimples, whiteheads or blackheads. You can introduce infection from your fingers or nails and can increase inflammation.

Do some form of stress management technique every day. It may be meditation, yoga, deep breathing, walking or swimming; whatever works best for you.

Herbal medicine There are many herbs used in the treatment of acne, some of these are:

BLUE FLAG, *Iris versicolor*: specific for oily skin and is considered to be a good herb for the liver.

BURDOCK, *Arctium lappa*: a good anti-bacterial herb specific for the skin.

QUEENS DELIGHT, *Stillingia sylvatica*: for skin problems associated with lymphatic congestion.

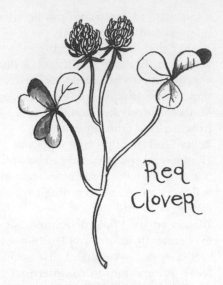

Red Clover

RED CLOVER, *Trifolium pratense*: contains plant oestrogens and is specific for chronic skin disease.

YELLOW DOCK, *Rumex crispus*: particularly good for acne on the shoulders and back. It has a mild laxative action.

Bach Flower remedies Emotional problems are often linked with acne. Some Bach flower remedies worth considering are crab apple, walnut, larch, agrimony and white chestnut.

Essential oils Chamomile oil is good for delicate skin and helps reduce redness in the skin.

Geranium oil regulates the oil balance on the surface of the skin.

Lemon grass oil is cooling to the skin; works as an astringent and is a perfect toner for the skin.

Tea-tree oil: research in Australia has shown that this is as effective as Benzoyl Peroxide in the treatment of acne. Benzoyl Peroxide is sold by pharmacies and while it can be a good treatment for acne, it does tend to dry the skin and can cause irritation. Tea-tree oil doesn't dry the skin, prevents scarring and is a very good antiseptic agent.

A few drops of these essential oils can be mixed into some vitamin E cream, aqueous cream (water-based cream sold in pharmacies) or sorbolene cream and applied as a moisturiser.

Homoeopathy Sulphur can be a good clearing remedy, especially if the skin is red, hot and itchy. Be prepared though, that the skin may initially get worse when you commence treatment, as sulphur heals from within to out. I have used hepar sulph for suppurative acne and achieved good results, especially when the pustules are large with yellow centres.

Graphites can be particularly good for treating cystic acne that has a tendency to scar.

Cell salts Calc sulph: for pimples with pustular heads. Calc cleanses the blood.

Kali mur: for facial acne with glandular involvement.

Kali sulph: for dry and peeling skin on the outside but the pimple itself is pustular with a watery discharge that crusts over.

Silicea: for acne that leaves scars on cheeks, back and chest.

Other We can speed the healing process by using a skin lotion or cream. If the skin is particularly oily it will help to use astringent herbs with antibacterial herbs as a lotion or toner. A good combination of herbs can be equal parts of golden seal, calendula and yellow dock. If the skin is itchy you can add some chickweed. If the skin is dry, this mixture can be blended with pure vitamin E cream or sorbolene: one part herbs to three parts vitamin E cream.

It can often help to see a beautician who will treat your skin externally and may give good advice regarding its proper cleansing. In some cases your beautician may need to open some of the pores to help release blocked sebum.

Medical approach Your doctor may suggest drugs that lower androgenic hormones in the body or prescribe an oral contraceptive pill such as Diane. While this pill can be quite effective in reducing acne while you are taking it, you will be unlikely to achieve a cure. It is more important to get to the source of the acne in the first place.

Antibiotic therapy has shown to help in a few cases but long-term therapy takes its toll on your immune system and can cause yeast infections. If you do take antibiotics make sure you eat yoghurt every day and/or take an acidophilus and bifida supplement.

In severe cases of acne your dermatologist may prescribe a synthetic form of vitamin A which can heal cystic acne very effectively. You cannot take this drug if you are pregnant and you must not take supplements of vitamin A while you are on it.

Alopecia—Baldness

Women lose, on average, about 100 hairs from their scalp every day of their life. There are times however when we may lose hair faster and in larger amounts. This can occur after fevers, nutritional deficiencies, hormonal imbalances, or during pregnancy. Some drug therapy can also cause serious hair loss. By far the most common cause of hair loss in women is stress and it can be either a primary or secondary cause. There is a genetic baldness that can occur in women but it is extremely rare.

If you have lost hair due to any of the problems listed above, rest assured it will always grow back once the problem is corrected. The more you worry, the more hair you will lose and

177

so you can perpetuate a negative cycle. Take action and learn to deal with your stress, talk to a natural therapist about possible deficiencies, stress management and how to rebalance your hormones. By utilising their advice, you will usually find your hair will grow back very well.

Treatment In order to overcome stress and improve nutrition it is important to eliminate or reduce the impact of contributing factors.

If you are a smoker, take action to give up your habit. You may need some help because smoking is a powerful addiction and there are various groups and organisations that can assist you. Keep in mind that smoking does not help with stress, it contributes to it.

In order to deal with stress you usually need to release it in some way. Talk it out; shrug it off; laugh it off; write it out; play some sport; go for a walk or a swim; attend a relaxation or stress management class; learn to meditate; bellydance or sing. It doesn't matter what it is just find something that works for you.

Dietary advice A well-balanced diet is essential for the maintenance of healthy hair and a healthy scalp.

Nutrients required are vitamins A, B and C, zinc, copper, iron, folic acid.

In order to cope with stress in our lives our diet needs to be rich in vitamins B and C. These are found in fresh fruits, green peppers, tomatoes, wholegrains, egg yolk and fresh or steamed green leafy vegetables.

Vitamin A is beneficial to the scalp which indirectly influences hair. It is found in all yellow and dark green vegetables and yellow/orange fruits. Eat plenty of cooked pumpkin, sweet potato, corn and carrots and fruits such as apricots, pawpaw, nectarines and mangoes.

If your hair is coming out in patches, particularly after pregnancy, you may be lacking folic acid. This is found in lentils, organ meats, eggs and green leafy vegetables.

Low levels of zinc can be a problem so eat wholegrains, pumpkin seeds and oysters.

Iron deficiency anaemia can cause hair loss. Iron is found in lean meats, dried apricots, pine nuts, parsley and sunflower seeds.

A lack of copper can cause baldness. Natural sources are almonds, oysters, mushrooms and prunes.

Try not to skip meals and avoid drinking large amounts of coffee and other stimulants.

Make sure your source of energy comes from starchy foods rather than sugary foods. For instance bread, rice, pasta and potato rather than cakes, biscuits and lollies.

Self-help The health of your scalp will greatly influence the health of your hair. Many hair products contain harsh chemicals. Try to buy more natural products that will not be harmful to your scalp.

If you are losing hair do not be tempted to use hair spray as it can make the hair more brittle so that it is more likely to be pulled out when combing or brushing.

Bleaches and some hair dyes can be damaging so talk to your hairdresser about hair products.

Allow your scalp to breathe, massage it regularly to improve circulation and encourage the release of natural oils.

Herbal medicine The following herbs illustrate the variety of ways that your herbalist can use plant remedies to help reduce hair loss in women.

FALSE UNICORN ROOT, *Chamaelirium luteum*: a female corrective herb for hormonal imbalance.

HORSETAIL, *Equisetum arvense*: rich in the mineral silicea, helps to strengthen hair.

HYPERICUM, *Hypericum perforatum*: a specific treatment for anxiety and depression.

KELP, *Fucus vesiculosis*: a nutritive herb that can help to correct thyroid insufficiency.

ROSEMARY, *Rosmarinus officinalis*: specifically for hair loss and is also a good treatment for poor memory and headaches.

Note: Add a handful of fresh or dried rosemary to a litre of water and simmer for 20 to 30 minutes. Strain and cool. Use this water as a final rinse after shampooing, it should leave the hair shiny and it will benefit your scalp.

VALERIAN, *Valeriana officinalis*: good for excessive stress and sleeplessness.

Bach Flower remedies Bach Flower remedies can be very helpful for emotional problems associated with hair loss. Consider using mimulus, sweet chestnut, larch, star of Bethlehem or white chestnut. Keep in mind that Rescue Remedy is always helpful during stressful times.

Essential oils Rosemary oil is specific in the treatment of baldness. Apply directly to the scalp or add to a carrier oil and massage the scalp.

Jojoba oil is an excellent oil for overcoming scalp problems and baldness that can be associated with these conditions. Use 100 per cent pure jojoba oil and massage into the scalp (a little bit goes a long way) twice a week. Leave it on the scalp as long as possible and then shampoo your hair as normal to remove it. It is a highly unsaturated oil that penetrates into the deeper layers of the skin. Try adding a few drops of rosemary to this oil treatment.

Homoeopathy I have had a great deal of success treating baldness with Phosphorus 6X. It needs to be taken 4 to 6 times a day, away from food. Phosphorus is a nerve nutrient and on many occasions the new hair growth has occurred quite rapidly. Talk to your homoeopath about other constitutional remedies that may be required.

Cell salts Kali sulph: for bald spots and hair loss.

Nat mur: for dandruff and hair loss.

Amenorrhoea

Amenorrhoea is a temporary or permanent absence of menstrual bleeding. If a young women in her late teens has not started menstruation, it is referred to as primary amenorrhoea. Secondary amenorrhoea is when a women has already commenced menstrual bleeding and her cycle has stopped for one or more periods. It is

Rosemary

not unnatural for a woman to occasionally skip a period or have a period delayed due to stress or excitement. It is important though, to test for pregnancy in heterosexual women with amenorrhoea who are sexually active and it is wise to have this test before commencing any treatment. If a woman is not pregnant, there is no real problem unless the period has not returned within six to nine months. Further investigation may then be required.

It becomes serious if a woman ceases to menstruate due to eating disorders or from excessive exercise. This can be made worse by following a vegetarian diet that does not provide enough iron-rich foods. Sometimes obesity can cause a lack of menstruation due to ovarian dysfunction. In fact, any sudden change in bodyweight, either gains or losses, can cause amenorrhoea.

It is often caused by hormonal changes created from deficiencies of pituitary or ovarian hormones when there is a failure to ovulate because oestrogen levels fall too low. Our ovaries must produce a particular level of oestrogen in order to perpetuate our menstrual cycle. If the ovaries secrete low levels of oestrogen, it can be months before menstrual bleeding can occur. When bleeding does recommence it is not unusual for the flow to be quite dark in colour. Sometimes the ovaries do not function correctly due to the formation of cysts.

In rare cases there can be a tumour growth on the pituitary gland. This can cause an increase in the hormone prolactin, which can switch off the ovaries. An indication of this can be milk secretions from the breasts without breastfeeding. See your health practitioner if this occurs.

Certain drugs such as Tertroxin used for thyroid disorders, some oral contraceptive pills and chemotherapy or radiotherapy can also cause amenorrhoea. Occasionally women will experience irregular periods when coming off the oral contraceptive pill. This is not unusual, particularly if your cycle was irregular before you commenced the pill.

For women in their late forties, amenorrhoea can be the first indicator of menopause. It is possible to skip periods for up to six months as we approach menopause due to fluctuations in oestrogen levels caused by ovarian dysfunction.

After childbirth bleeding does not usually recommence, or can be irregular, for six weeks to a few months and lactating women do not usually experience menstrual bleeding until their child is weaned.

Iron deficiency anaemia can also cause amenorrhoea.

Many women are not aware that herbal medicine, homoeopathy and acupuncture can be highly effective in correcting many of these hormonal imbalances.

Dietary advice It is difficult to provide specific dietary advice for amenorrhoea because it is highly dependent on the cause.

Nutrients required are vitamin E, B complex, folic acid, calcium, iron, magnesium and essential fatty acids.

If the amenorrhoea is created by eating disorders, psychological and emotional factors must also be addressed. In order to stimulate the appetite in anorexic women, the diet must be rich in the B Complex nutrients and in particular vitamin B1 and vitamin B3. When there is a deficiency in these nutrients there can also be a loss of appetite. Foods rich in these nutrients are legumes, wholegrains, nuts, eggs, wheat germ, salmon and sardines.

There must be some fatty tissue around the hips and thighs in order to store oestrogen. If your body weight is particularly low and oestrogen levels are also low, try to include some dairy products such as cheeses and yoghurt, coconut milk, olive oil, nuts and seeds and wholegrain cereal products. The addition of these foods with good quality protein in the form of lean meats, eggs, legumes, nuts and seeds will greatly enhance your ability to store oestrogen in your body.

On the other hand, if your ovaries are not functioning well because you are overweight, it is important to eliminate saturated fat from your diet. Do not eat chocolate, fried foods, full-cream dairy products, pastries, cakes and biscuits, chicken skin and the fat on meat. Instead, eat lean cuts of meat, fish, legumes, wholegrain cereal products, fresh vegetables, salad and fruit every day.

Vitamin B6 can help with emotional distress and hormonal dysfunction. You may benefit from this nutrient if you are coming off the oral contraceptive pill. The pill has been shown to deplete vitamin B6 levels. Foods rich in this nutrient are tuna, salmon, walnuts, legumes, oats and egg yolk.

It is important to correct any iron or folic acid deficiencies that may be causing anaemia so try to include foods rich in these nutrients in your diet every day. They are apricots, parsley, liver, lean beef, dark green leafy vegetables, lentils, oysters and eggs.

Calcium and magnesium levels must be maintained to avoid losses in bone density due to low oestrogen levels. To do this eat low-fat dairy products, sardines, hommos, almonds, cashews and wholegrain cereals.

The addition of vitamin E rich foods and essential fatty acids will help with the manufacture of your hormones. Try linseeds, egg yolk, nuts and seeds, cold pressed olive oil, tofu or fish oils.

Herbal medicine Your herbalist may incorporate some of these remedies in a tonic to restore menstruation.

BLUE COHOSH, *Caulophyllum thalictroides*: helps to promote menstruation. It has a strong affinity with the uterus and has a long history in the treatment of menstrual irregularity.

FALSE UNICORN ROOT, *Chamaelirium luteum*: a good corrective herb for menstrual irregularities.

LOVAGE, *Levisticum officinale*: specifically for delayed menstruation.

MUGWORT, *Artemisia vulgaris*: can help with delayed or irregular periods, particularly when they are associated with anorexia.

PENNYROYAL, *Mentha pulegium*: a powerful emmenagogue, which means it brings on menstruation. It is important to only use the leaf of this plant, not the oil which is extremely toxic.

SOUTHERNWOOD; LADS LOVE, *Artemisia abrotanum*: can be used in combination with false unicorn root to treat amenorrhoea that is caused by stress. Best results are achieved if it is combined with herbs to treat the nervous system such as hypericum.

Bach Flower remedies Some remedies that can help amenorrhoea are vervain, elm, walnut, white chestnut and mimulus.

Homoeopathy Aconite is a helpful remedy if the period is delayed from emotional trauma or shock.

Dulcamara is used when the amenorrhoea is due to excessive exercise.

Lycopodium may be of use when there are oestrogen deficiency symptoms and pulsatilla is often good for young women at puberty who have erratic ovarian function.

Cell salts Calc phos: for absence of menstruation caused by anaemia.

Ferrum phos: for amenorrhoea associated with iron deficiency anaemia.

Kali mur: for ovarian dysfunction and sluggish liver.

Kali phos: for delayed menstruation with depression.

Kali sulph: for late menses with abdominal fullness.

Nat mur: when menstruation is scanty or does not appear for long periods of time.

Other Acupuncture can be a highly effective form of therapy for absence of menstruation.

Medical approach Your doctor will possibly investigate the cause of your amenorrhoea. The treatment program will depend on the results and whether or not you desire to be pregnant. The oral contraceptive pill is often prescribed to regulate the cycle. It does not promote ovulation though, and the bleeding created by the pill is not a true period but a withdrawal bleed.

Anaemia

Anaemia is a sign that there is a reduced amount of oxygen available to the cells in your body. The red blood cells contain a protein, haemoglobin, that makes oxygen available to your body. Haemoglobin contains iron particles that bind to oxygen in your lungs, transport it via your bloodstream and release it into body tissues. If you have insufficient numbers of red blood cells and/or if these cells are an irregular size or shape and are fragile, your ability to carry oxygen in your blood will be reduced. If iron is not made available to the body, there will be a reduced production of red blood cells.

Anaemia is usually the end result of an iron deficiency or caused by an infection, kidney disease, blood loss or digestive disorders. Symptoms can include tiredness, breathlessness, pale skin, intolerance to cold, irritability, brittle nails and dizziness. You may also find that you have a lower resistance to infections.

There are several different types of anaemia, however, and a variety of causes. If you suspect you have symptoms of anaemia it may be worthwhile to consult with your health practitioner who may organise for you to have a blood test. This will accurately measure the amount of haemoglobin or iron-containing red blood cells present in your blood and it will also show if they are fragile or oddly shaped. Iron levels in the blood vary from day to day and it is possible to have a normal pathology reading of haemoglobin and still be anaemic. Good indicators of iron deficiency are blood tests that reveal iron storage and iron uptake in the body.

Treatment Once you have been diagnosed with anaemia, you should be guided by your health practitioner as to the best form of therapy. This will be highly dependent on the type of anaemia you have. Some women may simply need to improve dietary levels of iron while others may need a series of iron or B12 injections. The most common type of anaemia in women is iron-deficiency anaemia and this is usually corrected by improving dietary levels of iron or by taking a supplement. Do not take more than the dosage recommended by the manufacturer. When red blood cells die, the iron they contain is recycled in the body. So unless we are losing blood through excessive menstrual loss or an internal bleed, we do not require large amounts of iron.

Dietary advice Iron-deficiency anaemia can often be corrected by eating iron-rich foods such as liver, dark green leafy vegetables, pine nuts, parsley, apricots, oysters, soy beans and lean red meats.

Sometimes the iron is not being absorbed from the small intestine. You can improve your absorption by eating foods containing vitamin C at the same time as eating iron-rich foods. For example, tabouli salad is great because it contains iron-rich parsley and tomatoes which contain vitamin C. By including a wedge of pawpaw or pineapple with a green salad or by making a fresh tomato sauce to serve with lean steak you will absorb more iron from the meal. Vitamin C is also contained in citrus fruits, capsicums, strawberries, guavas and rosehips.

Another simple measure for improving iron levels is to cook some meals in cast-iron cookware. The iron in the cookware will be absorbed into your food.

Excessive tea and coffee drinking can severely deplete your iron levels due to their tannin content. Try to limit your intake to two cups daily. Alternatively, drink herbal teas or buy tea that has a low tannin content.

Other things that interfere with iron absorption are antacids or an excessive calcium or zinc intake.

In addition to the foods listed above you should try to include the following nutrients in your diet to improve your ability to manufacture healthy red blood cells, improve iron absorption and avoid anaemia.

Biotin: soybeans, wholegrain cereals, egg yolk and bean sprouts.

Copper: almonds, prunes, oysters, seafood, wholegrains, legumes and mushrooms.

Folic acid: green leafy vegetables, eggs, liver, lentils, yeast and dried beans.

Molybdenum: legumes, cereal grains, sunflower seeds, wheat germ, lentils and butter.

Vitamin B6: egg yolk, tuna, salmon, walnuts, legumes.

Vitamin B12: animal protein such as kidney and liver, dairy products (especially non-fat dry milk powder), eggs, fish, molasses, mushrooms, shellfish, tempeh, wheat germ.

Vitamin E: nuts and seeds, corn, egg yolk and wheat germ.

Zinc: oysters, pumpkin seeds, wholegrains and liver.

Herbal medicine Many herbs used to treat anaemia are selected because they are rich in nutrients. Some of these are: alfalfa, burdock, dandelion, gotu kola, meadowsweet, mullein, parsley, raspberry leaf, red clover, stinging nettles, and yellow dock.

I often incorporate the herb berberis in mixtures for women who are prone to anaemia because it is a tonic to the spleen, the organ that recycles your red blood cells.

Other Some women become constipated when they take certain iron tablets and they notice that their bowel motion is black in colour. This is a good indication that the iron is not being absorbed well. The addition of vitamin C and homoeopathic ferrum (iron) phosphate, taken as a cell salt,

183

can greatly improve your body's ability to absorb iron.

Breast pain

Having painful or tender breasts can be quite common for many women. It is not unusual for the breasts to become larger and more sensitive in the second half of the menstrual cycle due to increased progesterone levels. Progesterone creates tissue changes that can stimulate the release of inflammatory prostaglandins which leads to swollen, irritable breasts. The degree of tenderness varies considerably from woman to woman. Some will simply notice a tingling sensation in the nipples, while others experience extreme soreness and discomfort.

Breast abscess

Occasionally an abscess may form in the breast tissue following an infection in the glands of the breast or a duct beneath the nipple. On examination the lump will feel warm and extremely tender.

It is possible to develop an abscess in the breast due to a blocked milk duct when breastfeeding. If this occurs it is important to continue breastfeeding as this will unblock the duct and speed your recovery. It is completely safe to feed your baby as they will not pick up the infection. If you stop feeding, you may reduce or endanger your milk supply. Your baby may be affected by any antibiotics you need to take however, because they can cross into your milk supply.
Note: Care should be taken to observe your baby closely because some antibiotics can cause colitis in sensitive children. Symptoms of colitis will be abdominal distress and occasionally blood will be present in baby's stool.

Self-help Observe strict hygiene and place a warm compress over the abscess. A poultice is a good way to heal an abscess and reduce inflammation in the breast. Slippery elm powder has excellent drawing qualities. To make a simple and effective poultice place one or two heaped teaspoons of slippery elm in a bowl or cup. Add a small amount of freshly boiled water to it, mixing as you go until it forms a soft ball. To improve its effectiveness, you can add a small amount of calendula or golden seal tincture to it because they are good antiseptic herbs. Place this mixture onto a piece of clean gauze or cloth and apply it to the abscess while it is still fairly hot. Tape it to the breast and leave it on overnight. When it is removed in the morning you will see that it has absorbed the contents of the abscess and relieved a great deal of soreness and pressure.

Other useful drawing substances are oats (porridge), bread and grated raw potato.
Medical approach Antibiotic therapy may be recommended.

In some stubborn cases of abscess, your doctor may need to lance it to release its contents.

Breast cysts

Breast examination or mammography will sometimes reveal one or more lumps within one or both breasts. Although they are very common, women will naturally feel alarmed at their discovery. While it is important to have them checked immediately to rule out the possibility of malignancy, often these lumps are benign and may be cysts.

Cysts in the breast are round, fluid-filled pockets that can be moved easily. They may be very small or as large as a walnut. They generally make the tissue surrounding them more fibrous and so women who are prone to breast cysts often have increased fibrous tissue in their breasts as well. Cysts tend to increase in size and become more tender in the week before the period, revealing the link between hormonal secretions and breast changes.

Just like cysts in any part of the body they can come and go with minimal treatment. Our bodies are capable of reabsorbing them. If you have cysts in the breast, it is not unusual for them to disappear completely after menopause. This indicates that breast cysts, like ovarian cysts can be stimulated by oestrogen. This is why a combined oral contraceptive pill or oestrogen therapy can increase the incidence and size of cysts in the breasts.

It is important to examine your breasts after every menstrual period and report any changes to your health practitioner without delay.

Medical approach Sometimes your doctor will want to remove the fluid from the cyst with a needle.

Hormone therapy to reduce oestrogen or prolactin levels may be advised.

Diuretics are sometimes prescribed for fluid retention.

Breast infections

It is possible to develop a bacterial infection in the breast ducts. The signs and symptoms of a serious infection may be a discharge from the nipple that is yellow, green or greyish in colour. The breasts will be tender, especially around the nipple, you may have a fever and your lymph glands under your arms may be swollen.

Self-help A poultice can be applied over the infected site (*see* 'Breast abscess').

Medical approach The breast infection may be caused by some fairly nasty bacteria. It may be streptococcus, staphylococcus or pseudomonas. The latter is very rare, usually causes a green discharge, and can be life threatening.

Drug therapy must be given to achieve a cure. Seek medical attention.

Breast inflammation: Mastitis

Mastitis is an inflammatory disease of the breast that primarily affects nursing mothers. One or both breasts will become painful, lumpy, hot and swollen. There will also be a fever and you can become extremely ill.

Self-help Place a warm cabbage leaf inside your bra.

Apply hot compresses to your breasts several times a day.

Phytolacca ointment can be gently rubbed directly into the breast.

Continue to breastfeed your baby, however make sure you are feeding correctly. Your nipple must be well inside the baby's mouth and you must take care to empty the contents of your breast at each feed. If you don't, your breasts can become engorged and mastitis may be the result. If your baby does not take all your milk, stand under a warm shower and lean forward. Gently stroke your breast with the palmar surface of your hand to encourage the release of milk. Try not to express excessively with a breast pump because this stimulates a greater production of milk.

Make sure you get plenty of rest in order to speed your recovery.

Homoeopathy Phytolacca: this is specific for mastitis and can achieve rapid results.

Belladonna: for hot, red, swollen breasts that are throbbing, with an accompanying fever.

Bryonia: specifically for milk fever with hot, hard, painful breasts.

Medical approach A mild antibiotic is often prescribed and also medicine to reduce pain and fever.

General remedies for the breasts

Dietary advice Specific dietary advice for problems with the breasts will be dependent on the nature of the problem and the levels of oestrogen and progesterone in a woman's body. If you have a high level of oestrogen, you will benefit by including foods that are rich in phytoestrogens such as soy products and sprouted seeds (*see* 'Soy solution' on page 190). These foods can effectively reduce excessively high oestrogen levels that can predispose women to breast cancers.

If you have too much progesterone and are experiencing tender, lumpy breasts before a period, you may benefit from eating a low-fat, low-sodium vegetarian diet that includes some low-fat dairy products.

In general, if you are having problems with your breasts, there may be a possible lack of iodine in your body. This is especially so for women with low thyroid function. These women can be prone to high levels of circulating oestrogen. If you do not use salt in your diet, you could try including a small amount of iodised salt on your food. Supplementation with kelp can be helpful, especially for women who need to keep their sodium intake to a minimum. Other sources of

iodine are cod, oysters, mushrooms and sunflower seeds.

Definitely avoid caffeine if you have sore, tender breasts because it can be a major contributing factor. Caffeine is found in tea, cola drinks, coffee and chocolate. Drink dandelion beverage instead. If you really enjoy tea or coffee, try removing them only in the week before your period and see if it makes a difference.

Avoid full-cream dairy products which tend to contribute to lymphatic congestion in the breast area and under the arms.

Do not drink alcohol and avoid foods that may contain hormonal substances, such as some meats, poultry and eggs.

Selenium is a good antioxidant mineral that can assist with breast tenderness. It occurs naturally in garlic and tuna.

Vitamin E and the essential fatty acids are very helpful in overcoming breast problems. These are found in fish oils, sunflower seeds, evening primrose oil, linseeds and wheat germ.

Evening Primrose

Keep calcium in balance by eating magnesium-rich foods such as almonds, cashews, soy beans and wholegrains.

Do not smoke cigarettes and reduce exposure to passive smoking.

Drink vegetable juices, such as carrot and celery, to reduce fluid retention and increase vitamin A levels.

Increased body fat can be a problem so avoid fats in your diet and start a sensible weight reducing program that includes exercise today.

Herbal medicine BUCHU, *Agothosma betulina*: a good diuretic herb that is useful in combination with hormonal regulators. Helps with swollen painful breasts.

CLEAVERS, *Galium aparine*: an astringent herb for enlarged lymph nodes.

ECHINACEA, *Echinacea angustifolia*: one of nature's antiviral herbs.

GERMAN CHAMOMILE, *Matricaria recutita*: an anti-inflammatory herb that is very calming.

WILD THYME, *Thymus serpyllum*: can be effective as an addition to a poultice or hot compress.

YARROW AND PEPPERMINT: in combination as a tea. These herbs can be very helpful in reducing fever.

Bach Flower remedies Rescue Remedy can be helpful to reduce anxiety associated with breast changes. Other useful remedies can be hornbeam, oak, red chestnut and vervain.

Essential oils Try gently massaging the breasts with a few drops of essential oils in a good carrier oil such as 100 per cent jojoba oil to reduce lymphatic congestion. Some good essences are lavender, chamomile, hypericum or sandalwood.

Homoeopathy Bryonia: for painful breasts at the menstrual period, worse

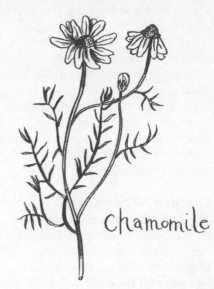

chamomile

on the right side.

Calc carb: for tender, swollen breasts before menses.

Conium: for when the breasts become large and painful before menstrual bleeding.

Helonias: for swollen breasts with painful, tender nipples.

Hepar sulph: for tender nipples during menses and breast abcess.

Iodum: for fibrocystic breasts.

Phosphorus: for when there is a burning, watery discharge from the nipple.

Phytolacca: for irritable breasts before and during menses, glandular swellings, cysts and tumours.

Silicea: for hard lumpy breasts.

Cell salts Calc fluor: for hard fibrous tissue and cysts in the breasts.

Calc phos: for burning and soreness in the breasts.

Calc sulph: for mastitis and a discharge from the nipple.

Ferrum phos: For the first stages of inflammation or infection where there

187

is a fever. A good remedy for cracked nipples.

Kali phos: For brownish offensive smelling discharge from the nipple.

Nat mur: For chronic swollen lymph glands.

Silicea: For hard, lumpy painful breasts.

Other Lymphatic drainage massage or herbs to reduce lymphatic congestion can be highly beneficial.

Cancer screening

The high incidence of cervical and breast cancer in Australian women reinforces the need for regular screening to ensure early detection and treatment of these life threatening disorders. Although many women die each year from these cancers, the good news is that early detection has a high rate of cure, so make sure you have the following routine health checks.

PAP SMEARS

The regular test for cervical cancer is called the Pap (Papanicolaou) smear. During a vaginal examination your health practitioner will use a speculum to gently hold the vaginal walls slightly apart. This will provide a clear view of the cervix and will enable them to gently scrape off a sample of the cells just inside the cervix. This is not unlike scraping the inside of your cheek with your fingernail. It should not hurt and it does not take long. The cells are wiped onto a slide and sent to a laboratory for testing. When the results come through after a few days, they will either give a negative or positive result.

Sometimes the smear result will recommend the test be repeated because endocervical cells were not seen. This simply means that there were not enough cells present on the slide for an accurate assessment.

If your practitioner does not let you know your result, it is a good idea to phone and ask for it. There have been instances where results of tests have been overlooked and filed away. Never assume it is alright just because you haven't heard anything.

A negative result means that no abnormal cells were seen. If your test has shown abnormal cells, there is no immediate cause for alarm. It does not automatically mean you have cancer. Sometimes there is an infection or inflammation. Your health practitioner will explain what your positive result means and will discuss the advisable form of treatment. Your Pap result may indicate that genital wart virus or Human Papilloma Virus (HPV) is present. Women with this virus have a higher risk of developing cervical dysplasia. Therefore this virus should be promptly treated (*see* 'Wart virus' page 227).

If your smear indicates you have dysplasia, it is wise to see a specialist doctor who can monitor the progress of cellular transformation. They can advise you on the degree of dysplasia and recommend treatment options. If cervical dysplasia is treated promptly there is a very high success rate with the cervical cells returning to normal.

If a woman prefers to use natural methods of treatment in the early stages of dysplasia, providing she has a Pap smear every three to six months, there is really no danger. The most important thing is for her to have a regular check by a qualified health practitioner. If the dysplasia has not improved after three months, it may then be advisable to seek medical intervention.

There are differing opinions about

how often women should have a Pap test and recommendations vary from every one to three years. It has been suggested that older women need a smear every year because their risk of cancer is higher than younger women. I feel that there are many young women who are sexually active with several different partners and they are also in a high-risk category. Women who have a sexual partner who has several sexual partners are also at higher risk. The risk is not only about developing cervical cancer. It also includes the risk of contracting genital wart virus which can increase the incidence of developing abnormal cells.

The incidence of cervical cancer in women who have never had sex is rare while it increases in women who have a number of sexual partners. For this reason I would recommend that women have a Pap smear every twelve months as long as they are sexually active. If they are not currently sexually active but have been in the past, they require a smear every two years. Women who have never been sexually active do not require a Pap smear.

If you have a positive Pap result, your health practitioner may want to see you every three or six months.

It is not unusual for some women to feel uneasy about having a Pap smear. The majority of doctors are men and not all women are comfortable with the idea of seeing a male doctor for screening. All women must have access to screening services provided by other women. It is important to reach all women including those in minority groups, such as women with disabilities, non-English speaking women, lesbians, Aboriginal women, isolated women and those whose cultural or religious beliefs require them to be attended by another woman.

These women need to be informed that there are women available who can do their Pap smear and where to find them. Pap smears can be done by women's health nurses in community health centres, staff in women's health centres and family planning clinics, Aboriginal health clinics and some natural therapy centres.

BREAST SELF-EXAMINATION
It is important to examine your breasts regularly to improve your chances of detecting changes that can indicate breast cancer. It is best done after each menstrual period when the breasts are soft. Hormonal changes before the period can create lumps and swellings in the breasts of some women that are not serious, but can create false alarms. If you do not have a period, make a point of checking your breasts on the first day of every month. A women's health practitioner can check your breasts professionally and with accuracy. They can then show you how to do it for yourself and explain what to look for.

Start examining your breasts at about age 21. Although it is extremely rare for breast cancer to occur in women under 25 it is important to make breast examination part of your routine. Many doctors advise mammography screening in all women over 40 years of age.

Cancerous cells can affect the body in different ways. Sometimes women notice other changes in the breast such as a discharge from the nipple, changes in the size or shape of the breast, puckering, dimpling, roughness, redness or turning in of the nipple. Any of these changes should be investigated.

189

If you detect a lump in your breast, do not ignore it or worry about it. Have it checked at your health clinic. In most instances breast lumps are benign, however it is best to leave the diagnosis to the experts. It is wise to attend a breast clinic or see a specialist doctor for an accurate assessment. These people are more skilled at making an accurate diagnosis and are also more likely to understand your anxiety and concerns.

Breast cancer does not carry a death sentence if it is detected early. Methods of diagnosis may include a diagnostic mammogram, an ultrasound or a biopsy.

What causes breast cancer? There are some factors that increase the risk of breast cancer in women.

Age is a factor because the incidence of cancer is higher in older women.

A family history, such as having a mother or sister with breast cancer can increase the risk. It is suggested that this is carried by a specific gene and some women are encouraged to embark upon a treatment program if the gene is detected in their body, even though they have no symptoms. While this of course is an individual's choice, it always concerns me that women often choose these types of therapy out of fear. Even if women carry this gene it does not necessarily mean they will develop cancer. I would suggest that other factors are more likely to create cancers, such as dietary habits, high oestrogen levels, cigarette smoking and high stress etc. Prevention can take other forms, such as using natural methods to balance hormones, maintaining good dietary practices, stress management, regular exercise and avoidance of drugs and environmental pollutants. A large amount of women with breast cancer do not have a family member with the disease.

Women who have previously had cancer in one breast are at increased risk of developing it in the other breast.

There is an increased risk of malignancy when the body naturally produces high levels of oestrogen. High oestrogen levels may be unnaturally created from, for example, obesity, taking some oral contraceptive pills, and having oestrogen therapy in the form of implants or injections.

Hormone therapy has definitely been linked to a higher incidence of breast cancer in women.

Is soy the solution? Currently research is being carried out in various parts of the world on the effects of plant oestrogens in the treatment of cancer. Strong evidence reveals that the addition of soy bean products in your diet can reduce the risk of breast, ovarian and endometrial cancer.

Soy beans are rich in vegetable hormones known as phytoestrogens. These plant oestrogens are significantly weaker than the oestrogen produced in the ovaries, however because they are a similar shape to the natural hormone, they can bind to the receptor sites on cells in the human body. It is believed that these oestrogens then assist in balancing oestrogen in the body. The weaker plant oestrogens will have a diluting effect on the more powerful oestrogens because they will prevent the stronger oestrogens from binding to the receptor sites. A major contributing factor to breast and endometrial cancer is a high oestrogen level in the body. High oestrogen increases the risk of malignancy.

Long menstrual cycles of around 32 days lower the risk of cancer. Research at the University of Cincinnati revealed that women in a test study who were supplemented with soy protein increased their menstrual cycles by an average of two and half days. When they resumed their regular diet, their cycle shortened again.

While these women were on the soy diet, they increased the length of the follicular phase of their cycle, before ovulation. In doing so, they reduced excessive stimulation to the breast cells that normally occurs in the second half of the cycle, after ovulation. It was concluded that this would significantly reduce cancer risk. It seems the more soy product eaten, the greater the benefit.

We may find from this research that plant oestrogens might be an effective and much safer alternative to Tamoxifen in preventing breast cancer. This research supports my own clinical experience of working with specific herbal remedies that contain plant hormones. It amazes me that most research into hormone therapy focuses so heavily on the production of synthetic substances. We have many traditional plants that have withstood the test of time, and continue to yield excellent results, with safety, in the treatment and management of hormonal imbalance. Although research into herbal medicines is limited, the results so far are very encouraging.

Boosting the immune system
Chemotherapy and irradiation techniques for destroying cancers lower the amount of oxygen in the tissues. While this is necessary to destroy the cancer cells there are various things that can be done after therapy to assist recovery in a complementary way. This information is only intended to be a guide. An effective naturopathic program requires face-to-face consultation. I would recommend that you discuss any complementary therapy programs with your specialist doctor for their perusal and opinion. Cancer therapy is very specific in its action and your oncologist may not support the use of complementary medicine at certain stages of cancer treatment.

Herbal treatment KOREAN GINSENG: 3–5 ml to be taken on waking (ginseng is always given in the morning as it is a stimulant and can cause insomnia if taken late in the day). It improves oxygenation of tissue, and intensifies cellular defence.

SWEET VIOLET, *Viola odorata*: this herb has anticancer (antineoplastic) properties.

For other immune system herbs see entry for HIV and AIDS.

Anti-inflammatory nutritional supplements Garlic: fresh is best so include it in your cooking.

Magnesium: 400–800 mg per day.

Selenium: your doctor can prescribe

Selemite B—50 micrograms (mcg) per day.

Vitamin A: can be taken in the form of betacarotene (5000–10,000 iu).

Vitamins B complex and B6 (100 mg).

Vitamin C with bioflavanoids: intravenous administration will be tolerated better than oral doses. High levels can cause headache and diarrhoea. (Supplement with 1000–2000 mg.)

Vitamin E: 500–1000 iu per day.

Nutrients that reduce the stickiness of platelets Cancer needs the platelets to be sticky to help it latch on. To reduce the stickiness the following substances can be taken before chemotherapy, irradiation or surgery.

Gingko biloba tincture: ten drops per day in a little water.

Essential fatty acids: evening primrose oil, linseed, borage or marine lipid oil. These can be purchased in one formula.

Antioxidant vitamins A, B, C, E. Follow dosage recommendations according to the manufacturer.

Eat ginger, garlic and onion regularly.

To reduce the side effects of chemotherapy you can take co-enzyme Q 10.

Assisting digestion Depending on where the cancer is, chemotherapy can damage the lining of the gut which will affect digestion.

Freshly squeezed fruit and vegetable juices are rich in enzymes that help to breakdown food. Drink juices 5-6 times a day. Wheat grass juice and beetroot juice are particularly good. Beetroot contains betain which is a great tonic for the liver. Your liver will need support because it is responsible for removing toxic substances.

Alternatively, you can take digestive enzymes in a tablet form. These supplements do not prevent your body from producing enzymes, they just add more.

Acidophilus and bifida may be required to recolonise the bowel with healthy bacteria.

Research has shown that two highly nutritious meals are preferable to the usual three to five in combating cancers. You may find that you do not have a good appetite anyway.

Do not eat foods that contain nitrites. These are found in pickled, cured, smoked or processed meats, like devon, sausages, saveloys etc.

Avoid foods that are known carcinogens, or cancer-causing substances, such as cyclamate, saccharin, artificial colours, nitrates and nitrites.

Do not eat margarine. You can have small amounts of butter, olive oil, linseed or canola oil. These should be added to salads or mashed into vegetables etc. Do not use them for frying food and avoid fried fatty foods at all costs. Cancer loves to migrate to fatty tissue.

Choose foods that are fresh and organic where possible and avoid highly processed irradiated food.

Eat an abundance of cruciferous vegetables such as cabbage, cauliflower, brussels sprouts and broccoli. These green vegetables should be steamed not boiled as their nutrients are heat sensitive. Other greens should be eaten raw or steamed.

Cancer protective foods are cabbage, broccoli, green pepper, eggplant, shallots, pineapple, apples, ginger, mint, wheat sprouts, lettuce, spinach and mustard greens.

Cooked yellow vegetables will provide

vitamin A. This nutrient is very important for your immune system and it keeps the mucous membranes in good health. This includes the skin, lungs, intestines etc. You will get more vitamin A from cooked yellow vegetables than raw because it is a fat-soluble vitamin and it is locked within the cellulose fibres of the plant. When they are cooked they soften and the nutrient is easier to absorb and utilise. Vegetables with a high level of vitamin A are carrots, pumpkin, sweet potato and broccoli. Most yellow fruit and vegetables contain vitamin A. Pawpaw is excellent because it is high in vitamin A and it assists digestion. If you like it you should eat lots of this fruit.

Eat fibre-rich foods such as wholegrains instead of highly refined foods like white flour and white sugar products. Wholegrains are a good source of zinc and B vitamins.

Eat yoghurt regularly for a good source of acidophilus and bifida.

Avoid vegemite, promite, bonox, marmite and yeast powder.

Eat small amounts of protein in the form of fish, some lean chicken and legumes (dried beans and peas like soy beans, chick peas etc). Don't eat red meat in large quantities too often. It is a good source of iron but difficult to digest. Avoid beef and chicken that is hormonally treated.

Eat parsley on salads and in your food to boost folate levels.

Have a low salt intake.

Eat garlic every day.

Don't smoke cigarettes and keep alcohol to an absolute minimum.

Drink herbal teas such as dandelion beverage, rosehip or chamomile instead of tea and coffee.

Most of the nutrients listed above can be found in these foods, however you will probably need supplementation to boost these levels and achieve a therapeutic dose. I do not personally megadose with vitamins—more is not always better. Many of these nutrients are available in combination so it is not necessary to take heaps of pills in order to benefit from them.

It is not my intention to suggest that taking all these nutrients will lead to a cure. Start nutritional therapy by ensuring that your diet is meeting your needs and be aware that not all of the supplements will be required.

Self-help If you have cancer seek out some individual or group counselling. It often helps to talk about things or share experiences. Reduce anxiety by learning and practising deep-body relaxation. Daily meditation, affirmations and visualisation techniques will also be helpful. Dietary therapy and relaxation are not expensive forms of therapy and can be highly effective in improving the general wellbeing of women who have been diagnosed with cancer.

Try not to be afraid of cancer, it will thrive on fear. Find peace within yourself and remember that cancer doesn't need to be life threatening. Treat it like any other illness and develop ways to improve your overall health and quality of life.

Note: Women participating in research programs into gene therapy must inform their doctor of any herbal medicines or nutritional supplements they may be taking. In order for these studies to be conducted accurately, they normally require strict controls.

Cervical cancer

Dysplasia should not be ignored because it can develop into *carcinoma in situ*, which is cancer of the cervix.

This is a common form of cancer in women. Cancers are not always detected from Pap smears, so seek medical advice if you have any sores or ulcers on your vulva that do not heal, abnormal bleeding, pain and/or bleeding during intercourse, pelvic pain and abnormal bleeding after menopause.

If cervical cancer is left undetected, it can spread to other areas of your body via the lymphatic vessels. This is referred to as invasive cancer and although it rarely occurs, it is life threatening.

While promiscuous sexual behaviour can increase the risk of cervical cancer, it is not the only factor. Cigarette smoking in women is a strong contributor because it weakens the immune system. Stress, drug therapy, nutritional and environmental factors can also cause abnormal changes in cells and must be taken into consideration.

Recovery from all forms of cervical dysplasia and cervical cancers require a strong and healthy immune system. Even if you decide to have medical treatment, a natural therapist can work in a complementary way to improve immunity and general wellbeing.

Cervical cysts

Some women develop small clear cysts on the cervix that are about the size of a pea. These develop as a result of a blockage of the ducts in the glands that open into the cervical canal. This leads to the formation of mucous filled swellings called Nabothian cysts. They can easily be felt on vaginal examination and feel slightly firmer than the tissue of cervix. Usually no treatment is required. If there is chronic inflammation in the area, your

doctor may recommend drainage.
Homoeopathy Silica 200 is available from a homoeopath and in this potency, can help to break down cervical cysts.
(*See* 'Ovarian cysts', page 214, for dietary and herbal advice for cervical cysts and polyps.)

Cervical dysplasia

The tissue within the cervical canal is built from cells that have many layers. The cells on the surface, like the cells of our skin, are constantly being sloughed off and new cells come up from underneath. When there are cell abnormalities, this normal process of cell development and sloughing off changes. Disordered cell development occurs and this is referred to as dysplasia.

There are various stages of dysplasia. When it is a mild level it will be referred to as CIN 1. A moderate level of abnormal cells is described as CIN 11 and severe dysplasia is CIN 111. The progression from CIN 1 to CIN 111 usually occurs over many months. This, of course, is dependent on various emotional and physical health factors that differ from woman to woman.

There is evidence to show that in some instances of mild dysplasia, the cells can be shed without intervention, and providing there is regular monitoring, it is possible to wait and see if the cells are shed naturally. This will be dependent on the woman's current state of health and medical history. Once women are informed of the degree of dysplasia and the treatment options, they can decide for themselves how they wish to approach treatment.

There is a link between the health of

the cervix and sexual intercourse. Using barrier methods of contraception will reduce the incidence of cervical cancer and other sexually transmitted diseases. Women with abnormal cell changes also have a greater chance of the cells returning to normal if their partner uses a barrier method.

Women who are not in a monogamous relationship should not feel guilty about having an active sex life, however they must realise the importance of using a condom. Carry your own condoms and insist that your sexual partner wears one.

Cervical erosion or eversion

Cervical erosion is a benign (non-cancerous) growth of the cells around the os or opening in the cervix. On examination the cervix sometimes has a red and angry appearance and may look a little bumpy. Doctors in the past thought this was abnormal because it resembled an ulcer, however, we know today that it is simply the cells from inside the cervix growing just outside.

The cells that line the cervical canal are clear, occasionally they grow outside the cervical canal and the blood vessels underneath show through them. This gives the red angry appearance of erosion. Erosion is actually a bad term because the tissue is not being worn down, instead the cells are pushing out or everting.

Most cervical erosion does not cause any symptoms and the cells will naturally be replaced over time. On rare occasions it is slow to be transformed and may lead to inflammation. Your doctor may decide to use laser therapy or diathermy to speed the healing process. This redness

of the cervix is not associated with abnormal Pap smear results or cancer of the cervix.

Homoeopathy Hamamelis can be useful for treating cervical erosion.

Cervical polyps

Cervical polyps grow from the endometrial lining or from the cervical canal. They are rarely malignant and are caused by an overgrowth of the lining. They are usually attached by a narrow stalk. If it is long, it may protrude through the external os or opening to the cervix and cause intermittent bleeding or bleeding after intercourse.

Herbal medicine BETH ROOT, *Trillium erectum*: an astringent and balancing herb that helps stop intermittent bleeding.

GOLDEN SEAL, *Hydrastis canadensis*: a nutritive herb with an astringent action. It can help to prevent intermittent bleeding.

RED CLOVER, *Trifolium pratense*: useful for the treatment of cysts and polyps.

Homoeopathy Two useful remedies are phosphorous or thuja which are both specific for polyps.

Medical approach Cervical polyps are easily removed and are tested for malignancy.

Cervicitis

Occasionally the cervix becomes inflamed and this may be referred to as cervicitis. When it is severe, it can cause a vaginal discharge. Mild spotting can occur after intercourse or vaginal examination. This is because the tissue is very sensitive and can bleed if it is bumped or scraped.

Cervicitis can be caused by sexually transmitted bacteria, so if you have any tenderness or discharge it is wise to see a health practitioner who can determine if it is caused by bacterial invasion. Ongoing inflammation can change the cervical mucus and cause problems with fertility.

If there is no infection but it does cause discomfort try acupuncture as an effective form of therapy.

Self-help If the inflammation is caused by physical trauma rather than bacteria you could try a douche that contains calendula or apply an ointment made from vitamin E cream and calendula.

You can break open a vitamin E capsule and apply to the cervix using a cotton bud.

Aloe vera gel can also be helpful and is non-irritating to the vagina.

Emotional trauma can contribute to inflammation of the cervix so it is important to practise some form of stress management. Yoga or meditation can be a good choice.

Medical approach This will depend on the cause of the inflammation. Antibiotic therapy may be required for infection and laser therapy or diathermy may be also recommended.

Dysmenorrhoea

Dysmenorrhoea is the term used to describe painful periods. The intensity and the nature of the pain will vary from woman to woman and also from month to month. Many women experience pain in varying degrees and often consider this to be normal, however while it may be normal for many, it is a signal from your body that something is wrong. It is important to tune into the pain and observe the physical signs that indicate possible causes. Once the cause has been

determined, steps can be taken to eliminate it altogether.

Approximately two days before the beginning of menstrual bleeding, oestrogen and progesterone secretions from the ovaries decrease sharply to a very low level and reduce the stimulation to the endometrial cells in the uterus. In the 24 hours before menstruation, the coiled blood vessels in the walls of the uterus constrict and cut off the blood supply to the endometrium. Approximately 65 per cent of the surface tissue dies and gradually separates from the remaining endometrial tissue in the uterus. The dead tissue breaks down and combines with about 35 ml of blood to form the menstrual fluid, which is then released from the body with the aid of mild muscular contractions, down through the cervix and out of the vagina as our menstrual bleed.

Just before menstruation begins, prostaglandins are released from the lining of the uterus. These stimulate the muscular contractions that control the release of our menses. Sometimes these contractions are too intense and they may be felt as painful cramps. Some prostaglandins cause inflammation and when they are released into surrounding tissues, they can cause nausea, vomiting, diarrhoea and bowel spasm. The hormone progesterone creates the changes in the lining of the uterus that allows the release of prostaglandins. If we fail to ovulate, we do not produce progesterone and the uterus does not release prostaglandins.

The oral contraceptive pill inhibits ovulation and this explains why women taking the pill rarely have period pain.

Pregnancy makes the muscles of the uterus less sensitive to prostaglandins because the density of nerve fibres is reduced once you have a child. This is why some women often overcome period pain after having a child.

Sometimes pain occurs because the os or opening in the cervix is tight and unyielding. Normally our hormonal changes at the end of our cycle tend to soften the cervix, so the menstrual blood can escape freely through the cervical canal. Spasmodic pain can occur because the menstrual flow is not being released. This type of pain can be quite intense before your period but usually stops when the flow starts.

Some women experience a great deal of spasm and cramping when their uterus is trying to expel a clot or large piece of tissue. The cervical canal is fairly narrow and the passage of large particles of tissue can create quite intense contractions that only pass when the tissue is forced through. This type of pain is usually felt during the period and it is quite spasmodic.

If pain comes on after many years of pain-free periods it is probably due to some underlying cause. Varicose conditions in the pelvic area can create a deep throbbing pain at menstruation.

The presence of uterine fibroids, endometriosis, tumour growths, polyps, pelvic inflammation or an infection are among some of the other possible causes. Infections, endometriosis and inflammation tend to create a very congestive type pain. Symptoms often start in the days leading up to the menstrual bleed and continue into the first few days of the cycle.

Structural problems can also increase period pain. It is not unusual for women with lower back problems to experience period pain. As the endometrial lining thickens, the uterus becomes heavier and can place added

pressure on sensitive nerve endings. There can also be extra fluid and prostaglandin release which generally creates congestion and swelling of tissues and blood vessels in the surrounding area. This pain can vary from dull, aching pain to deep stabbing pain and it is highly dependent on which nerves are affected. The sciatic nerve attached to your lower back, just below your waistline, is the thickest nerve in the body and it travels down through the buttocks all the way to your heel. Pressure on this nerve can create pain right down the back of your leg to the heel. If you have this type of pain you would probably need to see a physiotherapist, osteopath, chiropractor or remedial massage therapist.

It is important to prevent constipation if you suffer period pain. An impacted bowel can release toxins into the surrounding tissues and create greater congestion. If the menstrual flow is particularly heavy the pain can be more intense. Herbal medicine is highly effective in controlling excessive flow.

Having an IUD fitted can also make your period more painful. Some of the larger devices can cause the uterus to contract and if the contractions are strong, may even expel the device.

All these factors and more can create pain. It can vary from mild cramping that comes on for an hour or two when the period begins or it can be intense shooting pain that is incapacitating. Pain may be felt in the lower abdomen or it may radiate down the inside of the thighs or through to the lower back. If you regularly experience menstrual pain, observe it closely and keep a record of when it comes on, where it was felt, what it was like and how long it lasted. This information will greatly assist your health practitioner in determining the cause.

Dysmenorrhoea is not to be seen as a disease in itself but a symptom of hormonal imbalance and/or another underlying health problem.

Dietary advice Nutrients required are vitamins B6, C, E, bioflavanoids, calcium, potassium, magnesium and essential fatty acids.

Be sure to include some raw food in your diet, in the form of fresh fruit, salad and green vegetables. This will lighten digestion and avoid bowel congestion due to constipation.

Keep up your water intake despite any possible fluid retention; drinking fresh water will assist your kidney function and help to eliminate fluid.

Eat less sodium in the two weeks before your period. Sodium can deplete potassium levels in the blood and potassium helps to ease muscular contraction. Good potassium foods are bananas, potatoes, green leafy vegetables, oranges and mint leaves.

A lack of calcium in the body can increase the pain of cramping. Eat some calcium foods every day and drink chamomile tea which is a great source. Calcium foods include low-fat dairy products, nuts and seeds, salmon, sardines, hommos and egg yolk.

Magnesium is beneficial for any cramping in the body, including headaches. Foods rich in this mineral are almonds, wheat germ, soy beans, figs, corn and apples.

There can be a need to strengthen blood capillaries and vitamin E, C and the bioflavanoids are helpful. Vitamin C and the bioflavanoids are found in citrus fruits and skins, capsicum, tomato, pineapple, strawberries and rosehips. Vitamin E is found in corn,

almonds, egg yolk, wheat germ, nuts and seeds.

Essential oils can reduce the inflammation caused by prostaglandins. Good sources are linseed oil, fish oils, sunflower seeds, tofu, walnut oil and fish oils.

Vitamin B6 can help you to utilise essential fatty acids. Foods rich in B6 are salmon, egg yolk, tuna, walnuts, legumes and oats.

Have more fish and legumes as a protein source rather than chicken, pork or beef. Hormones in food can have a negative influence on menstruation.

Ginger is a great herb for cramps so use it in your cooking and drink ginger tea.

Try to keep your diet very close to nature and eat more organically-grown food. If your uterus is congested or irritable you may make things worse if you eat too many highly refined foods and chemical additives. Avoid fried foods, animal fats, white flour and white sugar products.

Keep coffee and tea to an absolute minimum and drink the recommended herbal teas instead.

Self-help Cold conditions sometimes makes pain worse, so try to keep your lower back and abdomen warm if you are prone to period pain. A hot compress or hot water bottle may bring some relief. It has been suggested that women should not go about in bare feet at period time because your body will draw the warmth away from the abdomen to try to keep the feet warm. A hot foot bath containing geranium or lavender oil can be helpful.

Soaking in a hot bath that contains lavender oil will help you to relax and may reduce the pain. Some women are helped by having sitz baths. This

Lavender

involves having two shallow tubs of water that are large enough to sit in. One should be hot and can contain a few drops of an essential oil such as lavender or rosemary, and the other one should be cold. Start by sitting in the hot tub for ten minutes and then try the cold for a few minutes (or as long as you can). Alternate between the hot and cold to relieve pelvic congestion. If you feel you can't tolerate the cold then just sit in the warm tub.

Put your feet up and drink some herbal tea to relieve cramps. Try yarrow, valerian, peppermint, chamomile, raspberry leaf, rosemary or ginger tea. Use them alone or in combination.

Some women recommend orgasm for clearing congestion and helping to facilitate the removal of clots.

Herbal medicine BLACK COHOSH, *Cimicifuga racemosa*: a tonic to the uterus, this herb is specific for painful periods and cramping. Black cohosh contains anti-prostaglandin substances that help to prevent spasm. It is also a sedative herb that is effective for the treatment of a menstrual headache.

CHAMOMILE, *Chamaemelum nobile*: has a mild sedative action. Specific for nausea associated with period pain. It is rich in calcium which can help to prevent cramping.

CRAMP BARK, *Viburnum opulus*: as the name suggests, this herb is specific for uterine cramping.

GINGER, *Zingiber officinale*: a warming herb that helps prevent painful cramps and spasms.

PULSATILLA; PASQUE FLOWER, *Anemone pulsatilla*: for dysmenorrhoea with scanty menses. May be useful for an unyielding cervix. It has a sedative action, relieves pain and prevents spasm.

VALERIAN, *Valeriana officinalis*: a sedative herb that also helps with muscular cramping. This is also a good herb for menstrual headaches.

Bach Flower remedies Some helpful remedies are hornbeam, mustard, star of Bethlehem, willow and sweet chestnut.

Homoeopathy Like herbs, homoeopathic remedies will be selected according to an individual's constitution and symptom picture. There are many remedies to choose from so I will include just a few.

Caulophyllum: for spasmodic pain associated with rigidity of the cervical os.

Hamamelis: for pain that extends to the lower back and down the thighs. It is specific for dysmenorrhoea associated with varicose congestion.

Sepia: for a dragging and heavy sensation in the uterus. A feeling that everything is going to be expelled.

199

Cell salts Ferrum phos: for painful menstruation with a bright red flow. It can be useful if there is pain with vomiting. A good remedy for pelvic congestion.

Mag phos: relieves crampy pain. A specific remedy to prevent spasm. Think of this remedy for an unyielding cervix.

Kali phos: for when the menstrual bleeding comes early and the flow is quite dark. This remedy suits women who are sensitive and irritable around menstruation.

Exercise Period pain usually influences the muscles in our pelvic region, including the uterine muscle. When a muscle is in spasm the blood supply to it is reduced and so proper circulation needs to be restored in order to relieve the spasm. Oxygen and other essential nutrients are transported in the blood to the surrounding muscles and tissues to overcome congestion and possible disease. Exercise is an excellent way of improving circulation. A good form of exercise for menstrual pain is yoga. As well as improving circulation, yoga can help to stretch and tone internal organs and muscles. It can also have a wonderful balancing and relaxing effect on the whole body.

Bodywork Massage can greatly improve circulation and provide relief from period pain. There are many different types available so find a therapist and style that suites you. Shiatsu can be highly beneficial for menstrual irregularities. Foot reflexology can also be beneficial.

See your chiropractor or osteopath first to make sure there are no underlying structural problems.

Other Acupuncture or acupressure (without needles) is highly effective for pain relief and clearing any blockages or obstructions that may exist.

Medical approach Painkillers and drugs that block prostaglandins are often prescribed and will significantly reduce pain and inflammation associated with menstrual bleeding.

Sometimes the oral contraceptive pill is prescribed to prevent ovulation and therefore block prostaglandin release.

If pain is associated with excessive bleeding, progesterone may be given to try to arrest the bleeding.

These methods can effectively treat the symptoms of dysmenorrhoea but not the cause. Ask your doctor about any possible unpleasant side effects before commencing treatment.

Your doctor may decide to refer you to a gynaecologist who can investigate the source of your menstrual pain. This may involve having an ultrasound scan or a laparoscopy which will show if you have any growths or physical abnormalities that may be contributing to pain.

Most types of dysmenorrhoea respond well to natural and traditional therapies and I feel it is certainly worth trying these methods before surgical intervention. I must stress however that there are some instances when surgical intervention is necessary. The surgeon may need to physically remove any abnormal growths and/or fibrous tissue that may be interfering with normal reproductive function and contributing to your dysmenorrhoea. If you do require surgery, your herbalist can still work in a complementary way to assist your recovery and wellbeing.

OVULATION PAIN

Some women notice pain in mid-cycle during ovulation when the ovarian follicle ruptures. This is referred to as *mittelschmerz* (German for middle pain) or more simply, ovulation pain. When the egg is released from the follicle there is a small amount of fluid that escapes as well. It can irritate the surrounding tissues and cause tenderness and a tight feeling in the lower abdomen.

In general, the advice given for the treatment of dysmenorrhoea can be applied to ovulation pain as well. There are however, a few specific remedies.

Herbal medicine Cramp bark is a herb that is specific for the treatment of ovarian pain.

Homoeopathy Lycopodium, iodum and apis are good remedies for pain over the right ovary. For pain over the left ovary try lachesis, lilium or xanthoxylum.

Cell salts Calc phos: restores tissue health and can be helpful for ovulation pain.

Ectopic pregnancy

Sometimes an ovum is fertilised while it is free in the pelvic cavity and this leads to a foetus developing in the fallopian tube or the abdominal cavity instead of inside the uterus, and it is referred to as an ectopic pregnancy. These types of implantations will usually fail because the developing ovum cannot make a connection with the maternal blood supply.

Ectopic pregnancy can occur in women who have an IUD because the uterus is already occupied by this device. It can also occur in women who may have a blockage in one or both fallopian tubes due to a build-up of scar tissue from previous infections, endometriosis or surgery.

They tend to occur in the first three months of pregnancy and usually lead to surgical termination and removal of the developing foetus. In some cases

the fallopian tube must be removed as well.

You can expect initially to have all the symptoms of pregnancy but unfortunately you will eventually develop severe pain and possible bleeding. It is not possible for an ectopic pregnancy to develop normally and you will require hospitalisation and surgery. Providing the other fallopian tube is in good condition you may still be able to conceive normally and become pregnant again without future complications.

Having an ectopic pregnancy can be extremely distressing even if you weren't planning a pregnancy. Remember that this can occur with women who have an IUD fitted. Although nursing staff and doctors may tell women that it does not develop like a normal foetus, it is still common to experience feelings of grief and loss afterwards, just as women do after a miscarriage or an abortion. For this reason some Bach Flower remedies will be very helpful and some specific homoeopathic remedies as well.

Dietary advice Nutritious foods are important to assist healing and recovery after an anaesthetic. All the antioxidant nutrients are beneficial and will speed your recovery.

Nutrients required are vitamins A, C, E, zinc and essential fatty acids.

Try to eat some garlic and onions every day to prevent infection.

Vitamin C is a natural anti-inflammatory substance and foods rich in this nutrient will improve your ability to heal well. Your adrenal glands can be affected by anaesthetic and they require vitamin C to function well.

Vitamin A will benefit the health of body tissues and help your immune system.

Zinc, essential fatty acids and vitamin E are highly beneficial for wound healing.

Herbal medicine After surgery these herbs can be beneficial:

CALENDULA, *Calendula officianalis*: a natural antiseptic and nutrient rich herb.

GOLDEN SEAL, *Hydrastis canadensis*: antibacterial nutritive herb to assist healing and prevent infection after surgery.

RED CLOVER, *Trifollium pratense*: for the prevention of adhesions and to assist healing.

WILD YAM, *Dioscorea villosa*: to reduce pelvic inflammation and congestion.

YARROW, *Achillea millefolium*: a wound herb that will assist with healing and it has an affinity with the female reproductive organs.

Bach Flower remedies Some helpful remedies are mustard, aspen, sweet chestnut, star of Bethlehem and Rescue Remedy.

Homoeopathy The two specific remedies that I would use are—

Arnica 200: for shock and assistance with healing and reducing soreness after surgery.

Silicea 200: to discourage adhesive tissue and assist healing.

Cell salts Wounds created by surgical incision are repaired by the blood. Cell salts can assist our ability to heal more rapidly and prevent infection and they are good self-help remedies.

Calc sulph: to assist wound healing.

Ferrum phos: to relieve pain and congestion and assist in repair.

Kali mur: if there is a great deal of swelling.

Silicea and calc sulph: to be used in combination if infection is setting in.

Endometriosis

Endometriosis is a condition in which fragments of endometrial tissue, that normally grows *inside* the uterus, develops in other areas. The tissue grows most commonly around the ovaries as well as the fallopian tubes, in the muscle tissue, the outer lining of the uterus, the outside wall of the intestine and in the pelvic cavity. It forms adhesive fibrous tissue that may affect the function of the organs it attaches to, including the bowel. This endometrial tissue under the influence of hormones will bleed every month, just like the lining of your uterus, into the pelvic cavity. Because the fluid has nowhere to drain from your body it can irritate the surrounding tissue with which it comes into contact. The blood and fluid can pool under the fibrous tissue and form small cysts that we refer to as 'chocolate cysts', because of their texture and colour. Endometriosis is not malignant or cancerous but it can form a large solid mass that will interfere with normal reproductive function.

Women are more prone to endometriosis between the ages of 25 to 40, and its incidence is more common in women who have not had children. This is because hormonal peaks and flows have occurred every month since they started menstruating. During pregnancy and breastfeeding we have no menstrual bleeding and our hormones remain steady.

If you started menstruation at an early age you may be more prone to endometriosis due to an increase in the amount of menstrual periods before age 25, which means many more peaks and flows of hormones. Endometriosis is rarely seen in girls under twenty and when it is, it is always accompanied by extremely painful periods.

The cause of endometriosis is not clearly understood, however we know it is strongly influenced by oestrogen because it tends to improve after menopause when oestrogen levels are low. It can also regrow in women who undergo oestrogen therapy. Failure to ovulate can be an added problem because when this occurs our progesterone may be low and oestrogen can be out of balance.

Endometriosis can occur after surgical procedures that involve endometrial tissue. If tissue from the uterus is accidentally relocated into other tissue by surgical instruments, it can grow outside the uterus in the pelvic cavity.

Some women experience 'retrograde menstruation' where menstrual fluid can flow back into the fallopian tubes and the pelvic cavity, and this is thought to be one of the reasons some women develop endometriosis. Another theory is that the tissue is carried in the blood or lymph to other parts of the body. Regardless of these theories it still needs hormonal triggers to influence its growth.

It seems to occur more commonly in women with a shorter cycle and longer duration of flow. This again indicates an imbalance in oestrogen and progesterone levels. It is possible though, that the short cycle is created by endometriosis itself, stifling normal ovarian function.

It can be difficult to diagnose because many of the symptoms may be due to other causes. Signs and symptoms will vary according to where the tissue has attached itself, how much tissue is there and hormonal activity. Some women have very little discomfort and may not be aware they have it.

Others may experience a great deal of discomfort and become quite distressed during the premenstrual and menstrual phases of their cycle. Common symptoms are a sharp, stabbing pain with strong, thrusting movements during intercourse and a deep pain may continue afterwards. Although this may also be directly caused by the sex act itself or other factors such as infection, trauma, damage to ligaments during childbirth or other physiological abnormalities.

There may be lower back pain and menstrual cramping in the abdominal and pelvic region. The pain can sometimes extend into the groin area and run down the inner thighs. It differs from normal menstrual cramping in that it often starts a couple of days before your period and lasts for the duration of the flow. In some instances pain can be experienced at any time and may not be related to your period.

Due to the inflammation and high prostaglandin build-up you may have headaches, a swollen, bloated abdomen with lots of wind. Some women who have endometrial tissue attached to their colon can experience pain with bowel evacuation. Intestinal upsets commonly occur with endometriosis.

In treating endometriosis we need to control the output of high levels of oestrogen so the endometrial tissue has no stimulation to grow. We can achieve this by introducing weaker plant oestrogens in herbal medicine and through the diet. These are called phytoestrogens, and they will compete with our natural stronger oestrogens for connection with cell receptors. In doing so, they dilute the high oestrogen effect. We also need to reduce the production of inflammatory prostaglandins, which are hormone-like substances that are released into the surrounding area and make symptoms worse.

In some instances the endometriosis can lead to subfertility due to lack of ovulation, hormonal imbalance or blocked tubes. However, it is possible to improve fertility in many women who have not been able to conceive.

Women with endometriosis can also have impaired immunity and may be prone to other illness. It is not known whether endometriosis weakens our immune system or if having a poor immune response makes us more prone to it.

Emotionally endometriosis is seen as a creativity block. If you have endometriosis, it is important to take the time to do something creative, something you enjoy.

Diagnosis It is possible to diagnose endometriosis through consultation and iridology. Symptomatic relief using appropriate natural therapies can be commenced straightaway and quite often women will experience some improvement within two to four weeks. Women must be aware that the treatment of endometriosis is slow however, as we have to breakdown adhesive tissue and cysts, balance the hormones and sometimes restore fertility.

Treatment must continue for at least three months in order to create change at an organ level so that symptoms do not recur when therapy is stopped. Some women may need to continue their treatment for a year, although they will gain relief from symptoms well before they stop treatment.

The symptoms of endometriosis can be similar to other gynaecological disorders and because our bodies are not transparent, the only certain way to make an absolutely correct diagnosis is by laparoscopy. It is considerably more invasive than iridology but if you feel you would prefer this method of diagnosis, discuss it with your doctor who may refer you to a gynaecologist for laparoscopic investigation. You will be anaesthetised and your abdomen filled with air, two small incisions are made and the laparoscope inserted through which the surgeon can view the abdominal cavity and take a tissue sample for examination under a microscope. Endometriosis does not show on an ultrasound or X-ray.

Dietary advice Endometriosis has been linked to high blood oestrogen levels. For this reason it would be beneficial to include foods that are naturally high in plant oestrogens. Current research shows that these plant oestrogens dampen the effects of excessive blood oestrogens by competing with them for access to receptor sites. The weaker plant oestrogens can block the uptake of the more powerful oestrogens and in doing so may prevent or reduce the formation of endometriosis.

Foods that contain plant oestrogens are sprouts, soy beans and soy products such as tofu, linseeds, pumpkin, olives, parsley, corn, wheat, apples, carrots, cabbage, garlic, split peas, olive oil, chick peas, oats, rice, beetroot, green beans, squash, marrow, rhubarb, barley, peas, plums, potato, red beans, cow peas, cherries, rye, sesame and sunflower seeds. These foods are also nutrient-dense foods that are low in fat. Eat them on a regular basis.

Essential nutrients are vitamins A, C, E, B6, bioflavanoids, essential fatty acids, calcium, magnesium, phosphorous and zinc.

Calcium, magnesium, phosphorus

Chickweed

and zinc are minerals that will help to eliminate cramping and maintain tissue health. These minerals are found in chamomile tea, vegetables, eggs, whole grains, nuts and seeds.

Vitamin B6 can assist with mood swings or emotional distress. Foods rich in vitamin B6 are bananas, brewer's yeast, chicken, currants, dried apricots, liver, potatoes, prunes, salmon, soy beans, sunflower seeds, sweet potato, tuna, turkey, walnuts and wholegrains.

The antioxidant nutrients will help to reduce congestion and inflammation. Eat foods containing vitamin A, E, C and the bioflavanoid nutrients every day. Vitamin A is found in yellow and dark green vegetables and fruit. Vitamin E is found in nuts, seeds, dandelion, corn and wheat germ. Vitamin C and the bioflavanoids are in fresh fruits (especially citrus), vegetables and rosehips.

The essential fatty acids have a good anti-inflammatory action and because

endometriosis can be slow and difficult to treat, supplementation may be necessary. Evening primrose oil contains anti-inflammatory prostaglandins to counteract inflammation. Taking a supplement that contains 10 per cent GLA (Gammalinoleic acid) you would commence dosage at 3000 iu each day but may be reduced to 1000 iu after six weeks. Some supplements contain 17 per cent GLA so it is possible to reduce the dose accordingly—read the labels carefully.

Other oils that contain essential fatty acids are linseed oil (store it in the refrigerator to prevent it going rancid in warm weather). You could take this off a spoon daily and it is less expensive than evening primrose oil. Borage oil, starflower oil and fish oils are also very effective at reducing inflammatory prostaglandin activity. Some supplements contain combinations of marine lipid oils and other oils that contain GLA so shop around to find one that suits your body and your budget.

Herbal medicine BETH ROOT, *Trillium erectum*: an astringent uterine tonic.
CHASTE TREE, *Vitex agnes castus*: Progestogenic action to balance hormones.
CRAMP BARK, *Viburnum opulus*: specific uterine herb to prevent pain and spasm.
LICORICE, *Glycorrhiza glabra*: a useful anti-inflammatory herb that is mildly laxative. It can be of great benefit for the intestinal tract and for hormonal regulation.
RED CLOVER, *Trifolium pratense*: nutritive alkalising herb that helps break down cysts and adhesions.
SLIPPERY ELM, *Ulmus fulva*: if there is bowel involvement slippery elm will

always help. It can be used for both constipation and diarrhoea. It is anti-inflammatory and contains mucilage to soothe and protect the delicate tissues that line the intestines and bowel.

Bach Flower remedies Rescue Remedy is a good self-help remedy for endometriosis and also consider hornbeam, sweet chestnut, crab apple, olive and elm.

Homoeopathy Homoeopathic treatment for endometriosis can be very effective. There are many remedies and it is best to let your homoeopath select the appropriate one for you, for example, you could try kali carb for pain with intercourse or sepia for uterine congestion and pain. Silicea 200 can be good to help break down adhesions.

Cell salts Calc fluor: for displaced uterus, dragging pain.

Calc phos: restores tissue health.

Ferrum phos: for pelvic congestion and pain with intercourse.

Kali mur: for congestion in the uterus.

Mag phos: for painful cramping; menstrual flow can be stringy and fibrous.

Nat mur: for spasm and cramping; menstrual flow thin and watery.

Other Acupuncture is wonderful for balancing the hormones and reducing pain.

Exercise can be highly beneficial to improve the circulation and can help to lower high levels of oestrogen. There are a number of yoga postures that can relieve menstrual pain and assist reproductive and emotional health.

Meditation is always beneficial in managing stress and painful conditions.

For some women, the symptoms of endometriosis can be difficult to cope with. As well as causing monthly pain and distress, it can interfere with sexual pleasure and prevent fertility. When you know that your treatment may be slow, with no guarantee of a cure, it can also be emotionally distressing.

Medical approach This will depend on your age and whether or not you want to be pregnant. Your doctor may advise you to take an oral contraceptive pill that contains progestogens. These reduce oestrogen production in the hope that the endometriosis will become inactive and die back. Examples are Duphaston, Primolut N, Provera, Depo-Provera, Danocrine and Azol. Some combined oral contraceptive pills can be taken continuously to prevent menstruation occurring, that is, you do not take the sugar pills or stop your pill for seven days. It can be a good idea to have a bleed after three to four months to eliminate any lining that may be there, although this is not essential. The rationale behind this therapy is to stop your body producing hormones so that the endometriosis will shrivel up.

Danazol is another drug that inhibits ovulation to give your body time to reabsorb the fibrous tissue.

Be prepared that all conventional drug treatments have side effects and there is no guarantee you will be cured. Discuss possible side effects with your health practitioner.

Pain relief or anti-inflammatory drugs may be suggested for treatment particularly if you are approaching menopause because your symptoms will naturally reduce with a drop in oestrogen.

In severe cases, surgical intervention to remove adhesions and cysts may be necessary, especially in women who have been unable to achieve fertility. This can be done by burning off fragments with a laser or cutting them with a scalpel. Be prepared that hysterectomy may be suggested if there is a lot of scarring and be sure to discuss this with your doctor prior to surgery.

If your symptoms are severe and you decide to use conventional drug therapy, it can be advantageous to use traditional therapy in a complementary way and speed the healing process. While you are taking the drug therapy, you can also take some traditional and nutritional medicines to help breakdown the cysts and adhesive tissue, assist bowel function and reduce inflammation.

Fatigue

There are many reasons for feeling unusually tired. The causes can be physical, psychological or environmental.

Dietary advice When you are suffering from fatigue it is not uncommon to try to keep yourself going with stimulants such as tea, coffee, cola, sugary foods or chocolate. Low blood sugar can be a major contributing factor and if you have low blood sugar it is not unusual to crave for sweet foods. Although these cravings can be quite strong, your body really needs starchy foods, such as rice, potatoes, pasta and bread, which will provide a slow release of blood glucose for energy, over a longer period of time. Sugary foods and refined foods provide you with a quick fix but it is not lasting and you can feel more tired after these types of foods than before. Avoid foods that have a high fat intake because they overload digestion and contribute to sluggishness and overweight conditions. It has been shown that eating fatty or fried foods cause us to crave sweet foods

immediately after we eat them.

In cases of chronic fatigue, the immune system can be severely depleted, particularly if you have had a serious illness, allergies or recurring infections. If you are prone to recurring infections or allergies it is important to look at the triggers; it is possible that you are not maintaining good nutrition or are under a great deal of stress. Perhaps you are taking on too much strenuous exercise which is leaving you severely depleted of nutrients. Physical problems, such as anaemia or an underlying infection, must be overcome before you can hope to feel better.

If you feel so weak you can hardly lift your arms, you could be lacking in potassium. Eat a banana every day or make a potassium broth from potato skins and vegetables.

If you do not take salt in your cooking or on your food, it is possible that a lack of sodium is contributing to your fatigue. Try having a small amount of iodised salt and see if it makes a difference. This can indirectly help your thyroid gland as well. The thyroid controls your metabolic rate. If thyroid function is poor due to a lack of iodine then your metabolic rate can also be slow.

Many women who are under a lot of stress have adrenal fatigue. The adrenals rely on vitamin C for proper function so eat plenty of fresh fruit and salads every day.

Self-help Being overweight can contribute to fatigue. Start a good nutritional program for weight loss.

If you are a smoker you can never expect to maintain optimum health. You will be prone to recurring infections and are likely to feel unusually tired. Most smokers who consult with me complain that they always wake unrefreshed. This is hardly surprising given that the lungs are designed to be filled with oxygen and instead, smokers constantly fill them with the toxins that are contained in cigarette smoke. Seek assistance to give up smoking and before long your energy will return.

Herbal medicine The tonic herbs are required in all situations where there is fatigue. There is no point using stimulants in chronic cases of fatigue because there is nothing to stimulate.

ALFALFA, *Medicago sativa*: an alkalising herb that is high in nutrients. It contains vitamins A, D, E and K as well as the minerals calcium, phosphorus, potassium and iron. A great herb for low energy and anaemia caused by excessive menstruation.

GINGKO, *Gingko biloba*: assists by improving circulation.

GOLDEN SEAL, *Hydrastis canadensis*: an antimicrobial, antibacterial herb that is also a wonderful tonic.

LICORICE, *Glycorrhiza glabra*: supports the adrenal glands.

OATS, *Avena sativa*: tonic to the nervous system. Good for convalescence.

SIBERIAN GINSENG, *Eleuthericoccus senticosus*: can be used to treat symptoms related to prolonged stress such as exhaustion, insomnia, mild depression and chronic fatigue. It improves both mental and physical endurance due to its mild anabolic effect which improves strength and fitness. It will also counter the debilitating effects of chemotherapy, radiation and surgery. It seems to exert its effect by improving the health of the individual rather than any direct action on disease.

Bach Flower remedies There are many remedies to choose from in treating fatigue but three specific remedies are hornbeam, vervain and olive.

Essential oils Some oils that can be useful for fatigue may be used as a massage oil, a therapeutic bath or burnt in an oil burner. Try juniper, rosemary, geranium or clary sage.

Homoeopathy Phosphoric acid can be particularly useful for nervous exhaustion and carbo veg for general sluggishness, especially good for those who are overweight.

Cell salts Ferrum phos: for tiredness from anaemic conditions.

Kali phos: is a nerve nutrient.

Fibroids

Fibroids are non-malignant tumours made of fibrous connective tissue and muscle tissue that start growing in the wall of the uterus. They can occur in the lining or the outer surface and they are very common, generally cause no problems and possibly go undetected in many women. Usually fibroids occur in women from age 25 to menopause. After menopause they shrink, due to a natural reduction of hormones.

They start when some fibrous or muscle cells start to grow and divide more quickly than the surrounding tissue. This forms small nodules, or fibroids, within the wall of the uterus, which grow very slowly and can often stop growing before reaching any significant size. It is extremely rare for fibroids to grow as large as a football although people love to tell those stories.

As they grow they enlarge the uterus and change its shape. On examination the uterus will feel bulky and heavy. If the fibroid is quite big it may be felt as a firm lump behind the pubic bone. A woman with a fibroid may feel that her

Sage

uterus is heavy or it can feel as if she has a prolapse; as if her reproductive organs are protruding out of her vagina.

The growth of a fibroid is dependent on hormones, particularly oestrogen, so I would discourage synthetic hormone therapy if you have fibroids.

Fibroids can put pressure on the bladder, reducing its capacity and increasing urinary frequency. Pressure on the bowel may lead to incomplete evacuation and constipation and pressure on the spine can create back pain or sciatica.

They can cause heavy and prolonged menstrual bleeding because they increase the surface area of the endometrium. There are often problems with profuse flooding and the presence of blood clots.

They occasionally push through the cervical canal leading to intermittent bleeding and/or bleeding after intercourse.

Pain may be felt if the fibroid is attached to a stalk and it twists. This leads to a disturbance in its blood supply. Pain can also be felt if the fibroid presses on a nerve.

They rarely cause problems in pregnancy, although occasionally a large tumour may cause miscarriage or premature delivery. A tumour near the cervix could possibly obstruct labour. They seldom cause problems with fertility unless they block the entrance to the fallopian tubes.

Dietary advice This is the same as for other growths in the reproductive area. See dietary advice for endometriosis. If you have bleeding problems associated with having fibroids, see dietary advice for menorrhagia.

Herbal medicine BETH ROOT, *Trillium erectum*: an astringent uterine tonic that prevents excessive bleeding.

BLACK COHOSH, *Cimicifuga racemosa*: a tonic to the uterus, this herb is helpful for painful periods and cramping. It prevents spasm and is also a sedative herb. It is effective for the treatment of a menstrual headache.

FALSE UNICORN ROOT, *Chamaelirium luteum*: a useful uterine tonic that prevents painful periods and helps correct hormonal imbalance.

GOLDEN SEAL, *Hydrastis canadensis*: a tonic herb that arrests bleeding. It contains the alkaloid hydrastine that has vasoconstrictive properties, which means that it tightens blood vessels. Good results can be achieved when this herb is combined with shepherds purse.

RED CLOVER, *Trifolium pratense*: a nutritive alkalising herb that is useful for the treatment of fibroids.

SHEPHERDS PURSE, *Capsella bursa*: an astringent herb that contains vitamin K. Very effective for improving a short cycle with heavy menstrual bleeding.

This herb is specific for uterine haemorrhage.

Bach Flower remedies Consider such remedies as aspen, crab apple, hornbeam, mustard, sweet chestnut and Rescue Remedy.

Homoeopathy Fibroid growths will often respond to thuja or phosphorus which are good general remedies.

Cell Salts Calc fluor: for any situation where there is tumour growth.

Other Acupuncture or acupressure can be helpful.

Yoga exercises can help to ease feelings of heaviness and discomfort.

Medical Approach A pelvic ultrasound will often confirm the presence of fibroids. Your doctor may decide to simply leave them alone and check them again in a few months to see if they have altered in size.

A hysterectomy may be recommended if the fibroids are causing serious problems. However myomectomy may be possible for some women and this involves the removal of the fibroids only. This is a matter for discussion with your health practitioner.

Menorrhagia

Menorrhagia is the medical term used for profuse or excessive menstrual bleeding. It is more commonly called flooding.

During menstruation women will have an average loss of up to 60 ml per period. A loss of more than 80 ml is considered abnormal and apart from being inconvenient it can lead to iron deficiency anaemia. It can be very difficult to determine how much menstrual blood you are losing. The flow is considered excessive if you have soaked through a regular pad or tampon in less than an hour, for more than three to four times on any given day of your cycle. Other indicators are a bright red blood loss, that is excessive, lasting for more than two days and certainly if your period lasts for more than seven days this would also be unusual.

If any of these things are occurring, it is likely that there is a hormonal imbalance, a uterine problem or a possible disorder in your blood clotting. High levels of inflammatory prostaglandins in the uterine lining can be a major contributor to heavy bleeding. These hormone-like substances cause the blood vessels to dilate and they can inhibit blood clotting. Blood clotting disorders often have distinctive symptoms such as excessive bruising, small haemorrhages under the skin and prolonged bleeding time from wounds.

Medical investigation may be required before the cause of heavy bleeding can be determined.

Note: Abnormal bleeding can indicate miscarriage, ectopic pregnancy or the presence of a pelvic infection, fibroids or a malignancy. Therefore, it is important to report any unusual bleeding to your health practitioner for an accurate diagnosis. This will enable them to act promptly to correct any serious health risks, place the problem into perspective or to put your mind at ease if none exist.

Dietary advice Nutritional deficiencies of vitamin K and vitamin C with the bioflavanoids can affect your natural ability to reduce bleeding. Foods that contain vitamin K are broccoli, cabbage, chestnuts, liver, peanuts, pork, spinach, soy beans and sunflower seeds. Try to eat yoghurt every day because it will improve your body's ability to manufacture vitamin K. If you do not tolerate cow's products, try sheep or goat's yoghurt.

Vitamin C and the bioflavanoids are easily obtained by drinking citrus juices with a small amount of the grated rind added.

If inflammatory prostaglandin release is a cause of bleeding, the bioflavanoids with essential fatty acids can be helpful. I recommend the essential fatty acids come into the diet in the form of ground linseeds or linseed oil, wheat germ oil or fish oils. Some women prefer to supplement with evening primrose oil, however high doses can have an adverse effect.

Some drugs and nutrients can interfere with blood clotting. A very high intake of essential fatty acids such as evening primrose oil or borage oil can reduce the stickiness of your blood platelets and interfere with clotting. This can prolong bleeding time and interfere with your body's ability to repair itself, particularly during some medical procedures. Some antibiotics, excessive aspirin intake or long-term use of mineral oils such as agarol can also be a problem.

Vitamins A and E in conjunction with vitamin C and the bioflavanoids will help to strengthen blood capillaries. Vitamin A foods are all yellow fruits and vegetables. Vitamin E is found in nuts and seeds, corn and wheat germ.

Be sure to include foods rich in B vitamins and zinc which help to maintain adequate levels of sex hormones. B vitamins are in all dark green leafy vegetables, egg yolks and wholegrains. Zinc is in pumpkin seeds, oysters and wholegrains.

Iron-rich foods are needed to overcome or prevent anaemic conditions caused by excessive blood loss. These are oysters, parsley, soy beans, lean meats and apricots.

Try to include some vegetarian meals in your weekly regime. It has been observed that excessively high levels of animal proteins in the diet can lead to a heavier bleed while a vegetarian diet tends to produce a lighter flow.

Herbal medicine Many of the herbs that we use to treat uterine bleeding will have an astringent action. When a mixture is dispensed for menorrhagia the herbs are carefully selected so they will also treat the cause of the bleeding. Listed below are a small selection of herbs that I have found to be effective.

AMERICAN CRANESBILL, *Geranium maculatum*: highly astringent and is used in the treatment of haemorrhage. It can also be used to treat bleeding in the gastrointestinal tract.

BETH ROOT, *Trillium erectum*: another powerful astringent herb that has a nice affinity with the uterus. Great for heavy bleeding associated with menopause.

GOLDEN SEAL, *Hydrastis canadensis*: a tonic herb that arrests bleeding. It contains the alkaloid hydrastine that has vasoconstrictive properties which means that it tightens blood vessels. Good results can be achieved when this herb is combined with shepherds purse.

GREATER PERIWINKLE, *Vinca major*: an astringent herb that can be highly effective when used in combination with beth root for the treatment of menorrhagia.

SHEPHERDS PURSE, *Capsella bursa*: an astringent herb that contains vitamin K. Very effective for improving a short cycle with heavy menstrual bleeding. This herb is specific for uterine haemorrhage.

STINGING NETTLE, *Urtica dioica*: a very

211

nutritive herb that is highly effective in the treatment of uterine haemorrhage.

Bach Flower remedies Rescue Remedy, hornbeam, olive, agrimony, walnut or sweet chestnut may be helpful.

Homeopathy Belladonna: periods too frequent with clotting and bright red blood.

Secale: profuse menstruation of a long duration that is worse when moving around.

Trillium: for flooding when there is bright red blood and back pain.

Cell salts Calc fluor: to tone the uterus and prevent flooding.

Ferrum phos: to be taken between periods to prevent the engorgement of blood in the uterus and to improve the uptake of iron after excessive blood loss.

Kali phos: for displaced uterus. Dark, blackish red menses that is profuse and smells offensive. Specific for uterine haemorrhage.

Medical approach I will outline a few procedures here, however the medical approach to the treatment of excessive bleeding will vary from woman to woman according to her circumstances.

Hormonal therapy using progestogens or anti-prostaglandin drugs can relieve heavy menstrual bleeding in many women. Your doctor may also recommend taking an iron tablet if you are anaemic.

Some women will need to be referred to a specialist doctor, such as a gynaecologist or endocrinologist, for further investigation. Abnormal uterine bleeding is usually taken very seriously because it can indicate a serious health problem. Your doctor may suggest an exploratory operation called Dilatation and Curettage (D & C), in order to determine the cause of the bleeding. It

is a diagnostic procedure that is performed under a general anaesthetic and it involves scraping off the lining of the uterus. The tissue can then be observed under a microscope.

Another diagnostic procedure is the hysteroscopy. An instrument called a hysteroscope is inserted through the cervical canal into the uterus under a local or general anaesthetic. This instrument is a bit like a tiny telescope and it enables the doctor to view the cavity of your uterus. It can be used to detect polyps, fibroids or abnormal thickenings, take biopsies and divide scar tissue.

If these methods fail to resolve the bleeding or if there is a serious abnormality, a hysterectomy or endometrial ablation may be suggested to eliminate menstrual bleeding. Hysterectomy is the surgical removal of the uterus. Endometrial ablation involves burning off the lining of the uterus which usually prevents it from regrowing. Today, these treatments are usually considered to be a last resort unless medical investigation has revealed there is a malignancy.

Other treatment options may be considered and this is a matter for discussion with your gynaecologist.

Menstrual headache

Some women experience headaches just before their menstrual bleeding and occasionally during their period. This is usually due to low levels of hormones in the blood or prostaglandin release. A hormonal headache is often felt as a constant dull ache however some women develop a severe migraine attack.

I have observed that some women develop these headaches from low blood sugar levels just before the menstrual bleeding. Those who are prone to this will often crave chocolate or sweet foods prior to their period. Chocolate can be a headache trigger so it can be difficult to ascertain whether the headache is due simply to low hormones or whether the foods that are consumed at this time are the major contributing factors.

Your doctor may advise you to take oestrogen to prevent your headache and for some women this will be highly effective. On the other hand, if you are taking hormone therapy or the oral contraceptive pill you may be experiencing headaches as a side effect of your drug therapy. Some women are highly sensitive to synthetic oestrogen and will suffer headaches as a consequence.

Headaches can have a number of triggers such as muscular tension or structural problems with the spine or cranial bones. If you suffer from headaches consult a good osteopath who can correct any structural problems you may have. Cranial osteopathy can be highly effective in the treatment and prevention of headache. There are many other forms of therapy to correct postural problems and muscular tension that can also cause headaches. Some of these are Alexander technique, Feldenkrais, Shiatsu, acupuncture and massage therapy.

Dehydration and constipation can be contributing factors to headaches, so drink six to eight glasses of water every day.

Some foods, chemical additives and alcohol can cause headaches in sensitive individuals. Common food triggers can be cheese, chocolate, oranges, ice-cream, over-ripe bananas and offal. MSG, which is preservative number 621, is renowned for causing headaches that commence with tension in the neck and shoulders and then seat themselves over one eye.

While food can be a primary trigger, I feel that headaches are rarely caused by one single factor. For instance, if your period is due *and* you eat chocolate or if you are under a lot of stress *and* your oestrogen is low, you are more likely to get a headache.

Apart from the usual drug therapy for the prevention and treatment of hormonal headaches, there are some useful naturopathic remedies. For effective dietary advice see 'Dysmenorrhoea'.

Herbal medicine BLACK COHOSH, *Cimicifuga racemosa*: contains anti-prostaglandin substances that help to prevent spasm. It contains plant oestrogens and it is also a sedative herb. This plant is highly effective for the treatment of a menstrual headache.

HOPS, *Humulus lupulus*: an oestrogenic herb that is good for tension headaches.

ROSEMARY, *Rosmarinus officinalis*: effective in the treatment of pain and is very useful for treating menstrual headaches.

VALERIAN, *Valeriana officinalis*: a sedative herb that also helps with muscular cramping. This is a useful herb for menstrual headaches.

WILD YAM, *Dioscorea villosa*: has a good anti-prostaglandin action.

Bach Flower remedies Some Bach Flowers worth considering are hornbeam, mustard, willow and Rescue Remedy.

Essential oils Lavender is specific for the treatment of headache. Try rubbing a little on your temples or put a few drops on your pillowcase.

Homoeopathy Cimicifuga: for shooting throbbing pain in the head.

Hypericum: for shooting nerve pain.

Lachesis: for when you wake with a headache.

Lycopodium: for headaches that come on late in the afternoon.

Cell salts Ferrum phos: can be useful if there is pain with nausea.

Mag phos: relieves cramps. A specific remedy to prevent or treat headache.

Metrorrhagia

Metrorrhagia is the medical term used to describe spotting of menstrual blood that occurs at irregular intervals.

There are some natural causes of bleeding that can be inconvenient but not dangerous, for instance, it is not unusual for some women to have a slight amount of spotting around ovulation. However any bleeding that occurs outside menstruation should still be investigated.

Hormonal imbalance is a common cause of abnormal bleeding. If your progesterone levels drop too low, the endometrial lining in the uterus is shed erratically which can lead to spotting. This can occur a few days before your actual menstrual bleed or it can cause prolonged bleeding that may last for weeks. Spotting caused by a lack of progesterone can be swiftly and easily corrected using herbal medicine, however correct diagnosis is critical.

Other more serious causes of bleeding can be: cervical cancer or cancer of the endometrium; infections; inflammatory conditions of the cervix and uterus; fibroids, cysts or polyps in the uterus or cervix; endometriosis; and miscarriage, abortion or ectopic pregnancy.

A regular Pap smear is an excellent way to detect abnormal cells at the entrance to your uterus. Under normal circumstances women have a Pap smear when they are not having their period and therefore some women who have erratic bleeding may be deterred from having a Pap smear because they are waiting to be checked when they are not bleeding. However, women with irregular bleeding need a thorough gynaecological assessment done *without delay* to rule out the possibility of malignancy. Early detection is critical and may save your life.

Note: The nutritional information and naturopathic treatments for menorrhagia can also be helpful with metrorrhagia.

Homoeopathy There are many homoeopathic remedies that are quite specific for the treatment of metrorrhagia. I have listed just a few for your interest.

Hamamelis: for bleeding mid cycle with ovarian pain.

Phosphorus: frequent and profuse spotting.

Sabina: for discharge of blood between periods.

Ovarian cysts

A cyst is a small sac or pouch that is filled with fluid or semi-solid material. It is quite common for women to develop cysts on the ovaries. Most cysts tend to remain quite small and usually cause no problems whatsoever. In fact, they will often drain away with minimal or no intervention. There are several types of cysts that can form around the ovaries.

Follicular cysts are formed when an ovarian follicle fails to release its ovum or egg. Instead it continues to fill with clear fluid and enlarges. The follicle then becomes a fluid filled cyst. Small cysts like these are often found unexpectedly during a pelvic ultrasound or a routine pelvic examination. If the cysts are less than 7 cm they will often disappear of their own accord within a couple of months. If you have ovarian cysts, your menstrual blood will often have a strong smell and be quite dark in colour. Clots are often present when there are ovarian problems.

Occasionally cysts will continue to increase in size and grow quite large, although this is rare. Large cysts can cause dull pelvic aching and sometimes they put pressure on other nearby organs. For example, they can cause urinary frequency if they put pressure on the bladder, giving it less space to expand. If you have no symptoms and your cycle is regular, you can safely decide not to use treatment and let nature take its course.

Corpus luteum cysts occur after the follicle releases its ovum. It seals itself off and fills with fluid forming a cyst. Normally the corpus luteum produces progesterone in the second half of the cycle and then shrinks away at the end of the menstrual cycle. If you have a corpus luteum cyst it can interfere with the normal production of progesterone, which can lead to menstrual irregularities like intermittent bleeding (spotting) and an irregular cycle. Like follicular cysts they often disappear without treatment.

Dermoid cysts are another type of ovarian cyst that are quite peculiar. They are stimulated to progress toward foetal development in a disorganised way, and often contain teeth, hair, bone and body tissues. This type of cyst produces an oily substance and if it ruptures, will cause severe irritation to the surrounding area.

Cystadenomas are cystic growths made of cells that secrete jelly-like fluid. They can grow to an enormous size and are actually multiple cysts within an outer capsule.

Problems with cysts Both follicular cysts and corpus luteum cysts rarely cause problems unless they grow quite large. When they grow large there is a danger that they can rupture or if the cyst is attached to the ovary by a narrow stem it may twist. The large cysts do occasionally rupture and if this happens you will feel strong pain and will probably need surgical intervention.

Occasionally a cyst may slowly leak into the abdominal cavity and the pain will be less acute which can make a diagnosis difficult. The symptoms can be similar to appendicitis or pelvic inflammatory disease.

Dermoid and cystadenomas are not reabsorbed by the body and can twist or rupture causing problems. They can be detected by an ultrasound or laparoscopy and removal of these cysts is usually advisable.

Naturopathic treatment Cysts respond very well to traditional therapy, which will cause them to gently implode, drain and be reabsorbed by the body. It does not cause the cyst to rupture and should not have any untoward effects. The fluid in the cyst needs to be drained and reabsorbed and astringent herbs that have an affinity with the ovaries will assist and encourage this process. It is a natural process because this is how cysts disappear by themselves without any therapy or intervention.

Herbal medicine While the astringent properties of the herbs encourage drainage of cysts, hormonal substances in the plants will also balance your menstrual cycle. This will do much towards preventing the recurrence and

215

formation of the cysts in the future. I include some herbs used to treat ovarian cysts for your interest.

BETH ROOT, *Trillium erectum*: an astringent herb that arrests bleeding.

CRAMP BARK, *Viburnum opulus*: an astringent herb that relieves pain and spasm. It has a good affinity with the ovaries.

FALSE UNICORN ROOT, *Chamaelirium luteum*: a good tonic herb that will help to balance hormones. It has a good affinity with the ovaries.

GOLDEN SEAL, *Hydrastis canadensis*: an antibacterial herb with a very powerful effect on tissue secretions.

PULSATILLA; PASQUE FLOWER, *Anemone pulsatilla*: useful for the treatment of ovarian pain and menstrual irregularity.

RED CLOVER, *Trifolium pratense*: a purifying herb, specific for cysts, that has a nice affinity with the ovaries.

Bach Flower remedies some useful Bach Flowers are agrimony, crab apple, honeysuckle and wild oat.

Homoeopathy Apis: for cysts on the right ovary with tenderness and 'stinging' pain.

Thuja: for cysts on the left ovary.

Cell salts Calc fluor: to help the body reabsorb cyst contents.

Kali mur: the chief remedy for ovarian cysts; reduces swelling.

Silicea: for cystic growths and enlarged glands.

Other Acupuncture or acupressure (without needles) is often used successfully to treat ovarian cysts and associated pain.

Medical approach The oral contraceptive pill prevents ovulation and follicular development so if you are on the pill you will not be prone to the development of cysts.

Doctors will sometimes suggest the removal of ovarian cysts and this is only required if they are large or are interfering with your fertility.

Pelvic inflammatory disease

Pelvic inflammatory disease or PID is the term given for any inflammation in the fallopian tubes and surrounding tissues of the pelvis. This name is an umbrella term and is not really an accurate description of what the disease is as it indicates that it is simply tissue inflammation. In fact, it is often a bacterial infection that may have been passed on through sexual transmission. It can also be caused by vaginal bacteria infecting tubes that were previously damaged by a sexually transmitted disease or pelvic surgery.

It is more commonly seen in women who have multiple sexual partners or whose sexual partner has multiple sexual partners. Barrier methods of contraception, such as condoms, will reduce the risk of PID.

Symptoms can range from mild discomfort to acute pelvic pain. Some women simply feel unwell, with a temperature and mild lower abdominal or back pain. Others notice bleeding after sexual intercourse or intermittent bleeding between periods. There is often an abnormal vaginal discharge that may have an unpleasant smell. Gastro-intestinal symptoms can include diarrhoea, abdominal bloating and wind. Other symptoms of PID can be tiredness, backache, pain on urination and weight loss.

Pelvic pain should never be ignored and pelvic inflammatory disease should be diagnosed and treated as quickly as possible because it can lead to pus formation and scarring. Tubal damage can occur before symptoms are noticed and if it is left untreated it can cause permanent scarring of the fallopian tubes. Scarring caused by PID is considered to be a major contributing factor to infertility in women. When the fallopian tubes are blocked, there is also an increased risk of ectopic pregnancy (pregnancy that occurs outside the uterus).

Sometimes PID is caused by an induced or spontaneous abortion. It is also seen in some women who have an IUD.

It is very important for your sexual partner to have a medical check-up in case they also have the infection. If you have pelvic inflammatory disease do not have unprotected intercourse as it is possible that you will pass on an infection to someone else.

Dietary approach Vitamins A, C, E and zinc will all boost your immune system and help your body fight infection and improve tissue health. So eat plenty of yellow and dark green vegetables for vitamin A; fresh salads and fruit for vitamin C; wheat germ, nuts, seeds and cold-pressed vegetable oils for vitamin E; zinc is found in wholegrains, pumpkin seeds and oysters.

Essential fatty acids will help to reduce inflammation. These are found naturally in fish oils, linseeds, sunflower seeds, evening primrose oil and starflower oil.

Try to eat garlic and onions every day to prevent recurring infections.

It is important to eliminate processed and fatty foods. Try to stay close to nature and eat lots of fresh fruit and vegetables, wholegrains, legumes, nuts and seeds. Drink fresh pure water every day and reduce tea and coffee intake.

Protein is important to help your body repair itself after illness. If you are a meat eater, choose lean cuts and try to eat fish two or three times a week.

Eat some legumes such as lentils, soy beans, chickpeas and other dried beans as a vegetarian protein source.

Include some grains such as rice and barley with meals. They are a good source of carbohydrate for energy, provide adequate fibre and are easy to digest.

Herbal medicine If your pelvic inflammation is being caused by some particularly nasty bacteria then medical intervention will be necessary as naturopathic treatment is not effective in destroying some sexually transmitted bacteria. If, however, no organisms are detected or you are unable to tolerate drug therapy, traditional medicine may help you. Some herbs used to treat pelvic inflammation and congestion are listed below.

CALENDULA, *Calendula officinalis*: a nutritive anti-inflammatory herb that prevents muscular spasm.

ECHINACEA, *Echinacea purpurea* or *echinacea perforlatum*: boosts the immune system and is referred to as nature's antibiotic.

GARLIC, *Allium sativum*: contains natural antiviral and antibacterial substances.

GOLDEN SEAL, *Hydrastis canadensis*: is antimicrobial and antibacterial in its action. It also contains vitamin A that improves immunity and tissue health.

RED CLOVER, *Trifolium pratense*: a nutritive herb that has an alkalising action on the tissues in the reproductive area.

WILD YAM, *Dioscorea villosa*: is a good anti-inflammatory herb that is specific for pelvic congestion.

Calendula, red clover and American cranesbill can be used in a douche.

217

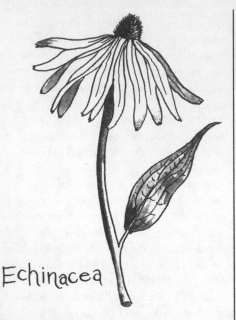

Echinacea

Homoeopathy Apis: for abdominal tenderness with swelling.

Bryonia: for intense abdominal and pelvic soreness.

Silicea 200: to prevent or break down scar tissue.

Cell salts Ferrum phos: for fever.

Kali mur: a general remedy for diseases of the fallopian tubes.

Medical approach Your doctor will usually do a pelvic examination that may reveal tenderness and enlarged tubes and ovaries. A swab may then be taken from any areas that may be infected through contact with a penis, such as the cervix, throat or rectum. This will be sent to a laboratory or it may be examined straightaway under a microscope if you attend a sexual health clinic.

The treatment for this disease will depend on whether bacteria is found to be present and what type it is. Specific antibiotic therapy will be given and the choice of the drug may depend on where the infection is and how widespread it has become. Other considerations will be whether a woman is pregnant or allergic to the drugs. In some cases, for accuracy, your doctor may need to examine the pelvic area using a laparoscope.

In severe cases that do not respond to treatment, surgery may be necessary.

If your doctor fails to isolate bacteria and there appears to be no medical reason for your discomfort, don't despair. Alternative therapy never dismisses symptoms as simply being psychological.

Polycystic ovaries

Sometimes the ovaries become full of tiny cysts that prevent normal ovarian function. This is referred to as Stein Levanthal syndrome or polycystic ovary syndrome (PCO).

In women who have PCO, the follicles that are stimulated to maturity in the first half of the cycle, fail to release an ovum or egg. Ovulation does not occur and the follicles remain active. The pituitary gland continues to stimulate more and more follicles which results in the ovaries being filled with small cysts. This causes the ovarian capsule to thicken, making ovulation more and more unlikely.

The cells around the walls of the follicles continue to produce oestrogen but because there are more follicles, the levels released into the blood are much higher than normal. This can cause the endometrial lining of the uterus to become much thicker due to an increase in oestrogen, which will also lead to heavier menstrual bleeding. When ovulation does not occur there will be a lack of progesterone in the second half of the cycle, which makes bleeding irregular.

If this process continues unchecked it will eventually lead to complete ovarian dysfunction and when the ovary cannot function oestrogen output is also reduced. When oestrogen levels fall, we can then develop the completely opposite effect: oestrogen levels drop and no endometrial lining is formed so menstrual bleeding does not occur. Without oestrogen women can develop subfertility and signs of masculinisation, due to progesterone being out of balance. These symptoms can be acne, increased facial and body hair (hirsutism), oily skin, deepening of the voice, baldness, irritability and sometimes weight gain in the upper body.

Dietary advice Polycystic ovary syndrome is made worse when women are overweight. If you have been diagnosed with this condition and you are overweight, your treatment program must include a weight-reducing diet. Studies have indicated that normal ovarian function can be restored in subfertile women when excess weight is shed. Research results at Queen Elizabeth Hospital in Adelaide suggests that when subfertile overweight women lose between 6 and 10 kilograms they ovulate more regularly and are more likely to conceive.

In the *Body Shaping Diet* book that I co-authored, you will find a suitable weight-loss program in detail, with recipes designed to assist women with polycystic ovary syndrome.

If you still have a period and need to reduce oestrogen levels, eat more soy products, sprouts, legumes, fresh fruit and vegetables. If your period has ceased and progesterone is high, eat more fish and legumes, low-fat milk and yoghurt, fresh fruit and vegetables. Eat no fats, this includes cheese and fried foods, and keep salt intake to a minimum. Drink lots of pure water and

exercise for a half an hour every day.

Medical approach Polycystic ovary syndrome is diagnosed by pelvic ultrasound. The treatment program will be determined after discussions with your health practitioner and will probably be dependent on fertility issues.

Some medical treatments include hormonal therapy with fertility drugs or the oral contraceptive pill.

Sometimes a wedge resection of ovaries is performed and this involves the removal of the thickened capsule in the ovary.

Once polycystic ovary syndrome has been corrected it rarely recurs.

See 'Ovarian cysts' for naturopathic treatment.

Prolapse

If the muscles and ligaments that support your vagina and pelvic organs lose tone and become weak, your uterus may bulge into your vagina and put pressure onto your bladder or rectum. This is referred to as a prolapse and it can be quite common, especially in women who have had a large number of children.

It is understandable that as we become older our internal organs may drop a little due to the downward pressure of gravity and a reduction in muscle tone. However, regular exercise and good dietary habits will do much towards preventing this.

Prolapse can also occur in reasonably young women during childbirth. The cause is mostly due to a rapid labour or a forceps delivery that may have weakened the ligaments. Normal vaginal delivery rarely leads to prolapse.

Other contributing factors can be habitual constipation which leads to straining and pressure. An ongoing

219

chronic cough or being overweight can also weaken the body's support structures.

Prolapse does not usually occur straightaway and it tends to develop over a period of time. This is why pelvic floor exercises should be part of every woman's daily exercise routine regardless of her age. For women who have experienced childbirth, these exercises should be commenced as soon as possible after delivery.

The signs of a prolapsed uterus will vary according to whether it is a partial or a complete prolapse. The symptoms of a partial prolapse may start with a dull, heavy sensation in your vagina, as if everything would escape or is falling out towards the vaginal opening. This is often more noticeable as you approach menstrual bleeding when your uterus is thicker and heavier. Prolapse can cause vaginal discharge and some women will have difficulty passing urine or emptying their bowels if there is pressure on these organs.

If a partial prolapse is not addressed through preventative measures, over time it can develop into a complete prolapse. When this occurs, part of the vaginal wall or uterus can protrude through the vaginal entrance, leading to increased risk of infection and a great deal of soreness or discomfort. As the uterus sags downwards it can pull on the front wall of the vagina and drag the bladder with it. This is referred to as a cystocoele. If it drags on the back wall of the vagina and pulls on the rectum, it is called a rectocoele.

One of the most distressing symptoms for women is stress incontinence or the leakage of urine when coughing, laughing or sneezing. In chronic cases women may experience the discomfort of urine leaking out simply from a postural change, like standing up from a chair, and they may need to wear a sanitary napkin continuously. These women are consequently prone to soreness and rashes due to being continually damp, from irritation of the napkins or burning from ammonia in their urine. They often feel self-conscious too, because they notice the smell of the urine and are concerned that they have an offensive body odour. If this is happening, let me reassure you that as long as napkins are changed regularly, the odour should not be noticeable to others. Understandably, it can undermine your self-esteem, particularly if you are sexually active.

Women with severe prolapse often express a desire to be touched but they avoid intercourse and foreplay because it may be uncomfortable or they worry that their partners will find them undesirable.

Treatment The best way to treat prolapse is first to eliminate any contributing factors such as constipation. Increase the amount of insoluble fibre in your diet and drink plenty of fresh water, even if you have stress incontinence. If you are above a healthy weight range please go on a sensible weight reduction diet. In the *Body Shaping Diet* you will find nutritionally sound weight reducing diets that will help you lose weight and help to keep your hormones in balance.

Overcoming constipation When the bowel is impacted it places a lot of pressure on the bladder so this must be corrected before prolapse and the stress incontinence can improve.

Foods that help with constipation are those that contain insoluble fibre, for example, bran, the husks on whole-grains (eat wholemeal bread), the skin on apples, the fibres in whole fruit and vegetables. This type of fibre does not break down in our gastro-intestinal tract and it adds bulk to our faeces and they absorb water. This makes faeces heavier and moist, so they will move through the intestines quickly and will be soft enough to pass without discomfort.

Avoid highly refined, processed foods and only have small serves of meat with large amounts of salad and vegetables.

Eat three to five serves of fruit every day and drink six to eight glasses of water.

If you still have problems with constipation try taking a non-chemical laxative such as psyllium husks or ground linseed every day until it is corrected.

Self-help It is important to strengthen abdominal muscles as well as pelvic floor muscles to counter prolapse.

This muscle exercise can be done anywhere and it doesn't really matter if you are standing, sitting down or lying on the floor. Squeeze the muscles in your vagina and draw them up; as if you are trying to hold something inside yourself or prevent yourself urinating. Imagine you are going up five levels in a lift, pausing briefly at each floor. Take your time and count slowly as you go. First floor, second floor, third floor, fourth floor. . . hold at the fifth floor for as long as possible and slowly come back down. Do this as often as possible during the day.

Do this next exercise every night just before going to sleep. Lie on your back in bed with your knees together, bent upwards and your feet flat. Tip your pelvis up slightly and squeeze your buttocks as tight as possible, at the same time draw vaginal muscles in.

Hold this for as long as possible, remembering to breath at the same time. You will find that it doesn't take long before you can hold this for around five minutes.

To strengthen abdominal muscles without placing stress on your lower back or neck, try doing crunches with your feet up. Lie on your back in front of a straight backed chair (student's chair or kitchen chair is good). Wriggle forward until the back of your calves and heels are resting on the seat of the chair and the front edge of the seat is at the crease in the back of your knees. The angle of your knees and hips must both be at 90 degrees and the small of your back must be flat on the floor. Place your fingertips at your temples (not behind your neck), elbows out, inhale deeply and as you exhale, *slowly* bring your upper body up from the floor toward your knees. You do not have to strain or attempt to put your head to your knees because you will find that even moving your shoulders up slightly from the floor, will tighten and exercise both upper and lower abdominal muscles. As you exhale, *slowly* return your upper body to the floor. Start with five to ten every day and increase them as you become fitter and your muscles tighten. If you do this correctly you will not place any stress on your back or neck, and if you have a sore back it is very important to strengthen your abdominal muscles as they help to support your lower back.

Yoga poses can be beneficial, and for those who are reasonably agile, head stands and leg raises will help. If you have access to an inversion machine, that passively tips you upside down, strap yourself in and hang upside down. This is a great way to defy gravity.

Herbal medicine In treating prolapse I recommend using herbs that are astringent uterine tonics. These will act on the muscle to tighten and improve the tone of the pelvic organs. Any secondary problems such as incontinence or constipation will also need attention with herbs to strengthen and tone the bladder and perhaps an aperient or laxative for the bowel. Some useful uterine tonics are listed here.

AMERICAN CRANESBILL, *Geranium maculatum*: is highly astringent and it is used in the treatment of prolapse.

BETH ROOT, *Trillium erectum*: another powerful astringent herb that has a nice affinity with the uterus.

BLACK COHOSH, *Cimicifuga racemosa*: an oestrogenic uterine tonic that also prevents pain and cramping.

FALSE UNICORN ROOT, *Chamaelirium luteum*: a great female corrective herb that is a uterine tonic.

HORSETAIL, *Equisetum arvense*: an astringent urinary herb that is a good natural source of silicea. It is useful when prolapse is causing urine leakage.

LICORICE, *Glycorrhiza glabra*: reduces inflammation and is a mild laxative.

Homoeopathy This treatment is dependent on symptom picture, however one of the following remedies may be helpful.

Belladonna: for the sensation of downward pressure as if uterus is protruding through the vagina.

Nux vomica: for prolapse with pain, frequent urination and irregular menstruation.

Sepia: specific for uterine prolapse with a desire to cross the legs to prevent protrusion.

Cell salts Calc fluor: for relaxed conditions of tissue and poor muscular tone.

Liquorice

Calc phos: for displaced uterus with a sense of weakness.

Kali phos: for prolapse with corrosive discharge and back pain.

Nat mur: for prolapse with urinary incontinence.

Nat phos: for prolapse with sinking feeling after a bowel motion.

Medical approach It is not always possible to overcome a serious prolapse with self-help measures and I would not expect any women to put up with the distressing symptoms that some have to endure. If necessary you should discuss options with your gynaecologist and find out what can be done. The first step may be to have a retaining vaginal ring pessary fitted, which sits behind the pubic bone and supports your uterus. If this fails it may be advisable to consider surgical repair. Having surgery to correct a prolapsed uterus does not necessarily mean a hysterectomy as well. This is usually the last resort, however there will be some instances where hysterectomy may be recommended in order to resolve the problem and make the surgery more successful. This is a very personal decision and as long as you are well-informed and have good communication with your surgeon it is not necessarily the wrong one.

Sexually transmitted disease

The term STDs is given for sexually transmitted diseases and they range from mild to life threatening. Unfortunately, our society has associated these infections with being immoral and despite education to the contrary, some individuals still see them as punishment for promiscuity.

Feel comfortable with your sexuality and help eradicate the spread of these infections by using barrier methods to prevent them. Talk to your lover about risks before having sex and always use a condom, which is the best barrier method. A diaphragm will not be as effective, however it may slightly lower the incidence of STDs that primarily affect the cervix, such as chlamydia.

Not all STDs have obvious physical symptoms but some do, so look at your sexual partner's body for signs of infections such as bad odours and discharges. They might have redness, itching or blemishes that may indicate an infection. If you have any suspicions at all, don't have sex with them and don't touch their sores.

If you are unfortunate enough to have been infected with an STD please seek treatment immediately and inform any sexual partners you may have been in contact with. Even someone who is comfortable with themselves and their sexuality can find it very difficult to talk about their disease. They may feel depressed and possibly angry at their partner, particularly if they thought their relationship was monogamous.

Correct and prompt diagnosis is important. There are many clinics where you will be assured of confidentiality. Swabs may need to be taken from the cervix, or other possible areas of infection, such as from the rectum or the throat if there has been anal or oral sex. The swabs are then wiped onto a glass slide and examined under a microscope.

This will indicate the type of infection present so treatment can begin immediately. The slide is then used to culture or grow any germs that may be causing the infection. The results of cultures will be ready two to fourteen days later to confirm which bacteria it is. The lab may also use the culture to test which treatment will be most effective in destroying the bacteria. STDs may take a couple of days or a number of weeks to be detected in the laboratory.

Never douche before a swab as you may wash away bacteria, resulting in a false negative.

If you have no symptoms you may have to rely on your sexual partner to inform you if they have any symptoms.

STDs, once they are outside the body, usually die within minutes because the organisms that cause them need a warm, moist environment to survive. You cannot catch them from toilet seats or door knobs. They are sexually transmitted, and your only protection against them is a condom or other latex barrier.

I do not recommend treating serious STDs with herbal medicine. You will need to treat them with specific antibacterial medications often in high doses. Herbs can be used, however, to boost the immune function and to

223

assist in the healing process. If you are allergic to penicillin or you have bad reactions to antibiotics and you prefer treatment with herbal medicine, please follow up with pathology tests to ensure the treatment has been effective.

Do not have any sexual contact until you are cleared of the infection.

AIDS AND HIV

AIDS is caused by infection with a virus called Human Immunodeficiency Virus or HIV. The virus is found in the blood (including menstrual blood), semen and vaginal fluids of people who have been infected. HIV attacks the body's immune system that is its defence against infections and prevents it from forming antibodies against disease. Most people infected with this virus will develop AIDS in seven to fifteen years.

AIDS stands for Acquired Immune Deficiency Syndrome and it is the most serious form of HIV infection. It is diagnosed when your body has certain illnesses which indicate that your immune system isn't working.

How the virus is contracted The virus does not discriminate and it can infect any woman including lesbian women. The spread of the virus is increasing among heterosexual women and they need to be guarded against possible risks. If you are in a relationship where you are having unprotected sex, you should discuss HIV risks with your partner and set some guidelines for the relationship. Trust and honesty is very important, your life may depend on it.

The virus can be passed on through unprotected oral, anal and vaginal sex as well as from sharing sexual toys, needles or syringes. It can also be passed from a mother to her baby during pregnancy or childbirth and through breastfeeding.

For infection to occur, the virus must enter the blood stream. It can enter the body through cuts, sores and abrasions (including herpes lesions).

Symptoms of HIV About two to four weeks after being infected, about 50 per cent of people can experience mild to severe flu-like symptoms. The glands may swell for a short time and then it will pass like any other flu. They can then remain well for many years although the virus is still in their system.

Without intervention about 35 per cent will develop some symptoms that are associated with immune suppression within the following five to seven years. The severity and the nature of the symptoms will differ from person to person.

Noticeable symptoms will be *persistently* enlarged lymph glands in the neck, armpits and groin, known as lymphadenopathy. This does not mean occasional swollen glands; it means swollen glands in two or more places that last for more than three months. Other symptoms are recurring fevers, night sweats, recurring thrush, unexplained weight loss, diarrhoea, persistent cough, fatigue, loss of appetite, memory loss, pneumonia and some forms of cancer.

Testing There is a specific blood test for HIV that will either be positive or negative. It is a voluntary test which means no-one can force you to have it. You can be tested at any doctor's surgery, sexual health clinic, family planning clinic, some women's health centres and medical centres.

HIV infection will not show in the blood until one to three months after infection. So if you feel you are at risk, you will need to wait to be tested. In the meantime it is crucial that you do not have unprotected sex or share needles. Of course, in the interest of your own health and the health of others you should always avoid having unprotected sex and should never share needles. It takes about two weeks to get the result and a positive result means you have antibodies to the virus in your blood and a negative result means you do not.

You will receive counselling before the test and if the results are positive, the test will be repeated. Counselling is also advised after the test to put you in touch with support groups and information networks if necessary.

If you do test positive it is very important for you to tell your lover and any sexual partner you may have had contact with. If your partner does not have HIV but you have tested positive, you can still have sex provided it is safe. **What is safe sex?** Safe sex is any sex that does not allow semen, vaginal fluid or blood to pass from one person into the body of another. This means using latex barriers to protect yourself from infection. Condoms offer good protection, so do latex gloves during finger penetration or fisting (inserting the fist or hand into the vagina or anus). Latex 'dams' are also available for safe oral sex. These are squares of latex rubber that you can stretch over the vagina or anus for safe oral–vaginal and oral–anal sex. Using plenty of water-based lubricant can make these practices more enjoyable.

HIV has never been spread through saliva (kissing is safe), tears or body sweat but it can be spread in faeces and urine if there is blood in it.

Do not share toothbrushes or razors. **Treatment** If you have HIV infection or AIDS, you will need to help your immune system as much as you possibly can. This means giving up drugs (including smoking) and alcohol, eating a nutrient-dense and protein-rich diet and practising some form of relaxation or meditation.

Herbal remedies and nutritional supplements can greatly assist your immune system and lymphatic drainage massage may help to improve your overall health.

There is no cure for AIDS but there are drugs that can treat the infections associated with the disease. Treatment with the antiviral drug AZT has been shown to slow the progression of AIDS. You will need to be in the care of a doctor who can monitor your health accurately and provide assistance as required.

Boosting the immune system The ability of our immune system to seek out and destroy specific viruses in our bloodstream is totally dependent on it being strong and healthy. Women are more prone to illness and infection if their immune system is being undermined by currently having or previously having been exposed to other viruses that further weaken immunity. It is also possible to be born with a weakness in immunity and so be more prone to recurring infections. Cigarette smoking further weakens the immune system.

Dietary advice The nutrients required to improve the immune system are:

B complex vitamins + B6: 100 mg per day

Vitamin A or betacarotene

Vitamin C and bioflavanoids: 1000–2000 mg per day

Vitamin E: 500–1000 iu per day

Selenium, your doctor can prescribe Selemite B: 50 micrograms (mcg) per day

Magnesium: 400–800 mg per day

225

Zinc: 25 mg per day

Garlic: fresh is best so incorporate it in your cooking.

Lysine: an amino acid found in good quality protein foods such as fish, chicken, lamb and mung bean sprouts.

Improve bowel flora by eating yoghurt every day or supplement with acidophilus and bifida.

Herbal medicine ECHINACEA, *Echinacea angustifolia*: has powerful immune enhancing activity.

GARLIC, *Allium sativum*: an excellent herb for the immune system. This herb has been shown to decrease cancer risk.

GOLDEN SEAL, *Hydrastis canadensis*: a nutritive antibacterial tonic that aids digestion.

MYRRH, *Commifora molmol*: is an antiseptic and antimicrobial herb.

PICRORRHIZA, *Picrorrhiza kurroa*: a prominent Ayurvedic herb that is fairly new to the West. Research has revealed that it is capable of producing a broad spectrum immune response. When

combined with the herb St Mary's thistle they provide an effective immune stimulating formula. There are no major adverse side effects associated with these herbs.

SIBERIAN GINSENG, *Eleutherococcus senticosis*: double blind studies have revealed strong enhancement of immune function. Populations of Natural Killer cells and T-helper cells significantly increased in healthy volunteers. This indicates that it may be very useful for boosting the immune system.

ST MARY'S THISTLE, *Silybum marianum*: an excellent tonic herb for the liver.

CHLAMYDIA,
CHLAMYDIA TRACHOMATIS

Chlamydia is a very common and serious sexually transmitted disease caused by bacteria.

In women, it can infect the cervix causing cervicitis which leaves the cervix raw, sore and inflamed. It can easily spread to the urethra and cause painful infections there as well. This disease can cause long-term effects such as infertility and it can lead to complications during pregnancy and childbirth. It can be passed on to babies during birth causing eye and ear infection and pneumonia. Also, it has been linked in some cases to an arthritic condition called Reiters syndrome.

If you practise anal sex, this organism can cause inflammation of the rectum (proctitis). It may spread up into uterus and fallopian tubes causing pelvic inflammatory disease and it is estimated that chlamydia causes about half of the cases of pelvic inflammatory disease. You may experience a fever, abnormal vaginal discharge and/or painful intercourse.

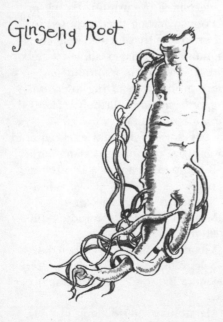

Ginseng Root

It is possible to have chlamydia and show no symptoms, which can make this bacteria difficult to detect. The danger is that it can silently cause harmful changes to your body and you are unaware of this damage. Chlamydia can live in the cervix undetected for many months and the infection may flare up at any time.

Chlamydia is passed on during intercourse, so in order to reduce the risk of infection please use a condom.

The bacteria cannot live outside the body so it cannot be caught in swimming pools or on toilet seats etc. **Medical approach** You must have a specific chlamydia swab and if detected you will need specific drug therapy to eradicate it.

The chlamydia organism will not be detected in a routine vaginal examination or Pap smear. It commonly occurs with other STDs, so tests for these should be done at the same time.

If your infection is severe you may need intravenous treatment in hospital. Your sexual partner will also require treatment. Avoid intercourse during the treatment.

Ask your doctor for a chlamydia test if: you have signs of genital infection; you are diagnosed with another STD; your partner has chlamydia or another STD; your Pap smear suggests you have an infection; you have more than one sexual partner or have recently changed partners; your sexual partner has had sex with another person.

Please back up your treatment program with pathology to make sure the infection has not returned.

The chlamydia epidemic went undetected for so long because it usually occurred with gonorrhoea.

Penicillin cleared up the gonorrhoea but not the chlamydia.

GENITAL WARTS
The medical term for genital warts is Condylomata accuminata and they are caused by infection with the Human Papilloma Virus (HPV).

Genital warts are very common, in fact it is estimated that they are three times more common than genital herpes. They often appear in clumps anywhere on the female pubic area, around the anus or in the vagina. Some women may not be aware that they have them until they are alerted through their Pap smear result or by a health worker whilst performing a vaginal examination. The warts are usually visible but occasionally are not and can cause changes in moist membranes. Genital warts grow well in a moist warm environment, which is why they are so easily spread in women. They should not be neglected as they are easily transmitted to your sexual partner and spread through cross-infection. Intercourse is an ideal means of transfer, as cells from the surface of the wart that are loaded with the virus are easily rubbed off. Using condoms during intercourse is a good barrier method to help prevent the spread of this virus.

The virus can also be carried in body secretions and so it is possible to contaminate your hands or anal region if body fluids are spread to those areas. Any tiny break in the skin is all the virus needs to get in and once you are contaminated, it can rapidly spread. The warts can be spread by towels and not necessarily from direct skin to skin contact.

If you have some genital warts don't panic as there are about a dozen

227

different types of warts that can be associated with the genital area and of these very few have been linked to malignancy.

Genital warts can differ in appearance with some having a flat surface and these are called plane warts. Others are pimple shaped and we call these papular warts. They occur individually or in a clump and may have a cauliflower appearance. They tend to feel softer than the warts that occur in other parts of the body and seldom grow larger than about one centimetre across. Warts themselves have not been incriminated with genital cancer but some subclinical wart virus infections have been associated with it. These tend to be flat warts not the lumpy warts usually seen. Most genital warts will cause no problems and occasionally will simply drop off or disappear without treatment.

Recent evidence suggests that the incidence of genital warts occurring in women is closely linked with their immune system. The ability of our immune system to seek out and destroy specific viruses in our bloodstream is dependent on it being strong and healthy. Women are more prone if their immune system is being undermined by currently having or having previously been exposed to other viruses that further weaken immunity, such as the Ross River virus, Que fever, the Epstein Barr Virus or HIV/AIDS. It is also possible to be born with a weakness in immunity and so be more prone. Babies may be infected during birth if the mother has genital warts. The warts can take weeks or years to grow big enough to be seen or felt but they can grow quite large during pregnancy and most people want to get rid of them.

They do not cause problems for everyone and this is probably dependent on your immune system.

Men can have the warts inside the urethral opening at the tip of the penis. Look for them before having intercourse. It is also possible to detect warts on a penis by wrapping it in a cloth soaked in vinegar. The warts will appear white when the cloth is removed.

Condoms offer limited protection against genital warts.

Herbal medicine Herbs to boost the immune system should be given (*see* 'AIDS and HIV').

You can try a local application of the herbs celandine, thuja and golden seal in equal parts. I have found it is most successful to wash the area, dry with a hairdryer and then paint the mixture on with a small paintbrush. Otherwise the area is too moist due to natural secretions and it is not possible to apply the mixture effectively. Constant moisture helps this virus to multiply.

Bach Flower remedies Crab apple can act as a good emotional cleanser, for when you feel ashamed of your ailments.

Rescue Remedy is a general remedy for anxiety associated with this condition.

Homoeopathy Thuja 200: is often a constitutional remedy for wart removal.

Cell salts Nat sulph: for warts caused by exposure to dampness.

Medical approach Your health practitioner will apply a chemical called podophyllin paint to the warts twice a week. This originates from the resin of American mandrake or podophyllum, which is a herb that is a topical irritant. It can be absorbed through the skin and damage healthy tissue so it is best not to treat yourself. The paint is washed off after six hours.

Some people are sensitive and get a burning sensation from podophyllin. If this occurs wash it off straight away and inform clinic staff.

It is not to be used if you are pregnant because it can cause abnormalities.

If the warts have not gone in four treatments it is unlikely it will work. Your next form of treatment will be for a gynaecologist to freeze or burn them off with laser or diathermy under local or general anaesthetic. Recurrence is common.

Avoid sex during treatment and while the tissue is healing. It would be painful anyway.

GONORRHOEA

This is also commonly known as 'the clap' and it is caused by bacteria called neisseria gonorrhoeae. Like chlamydia, it attacks the cells of the cervix, uterus, fallopian tubes, urethra and rectum in women.

Symptoms include pus formation, scarring, pain, a smelly, yellow discharge, urinary frequency and discomfort with urination. The Bartholins glands can become infected, causing them to swell on one side or both sides of the vaginal entrance.

Women with gonorrhoea can experience abdominal pain, pain with intercourse, lower back pain, fever and a general feeling of being unwell. They can have heavier periods or intermittent bleeding.

In rare instances it spreads from the fallopian tubes to the abdominal cavity. This can cause inflammation on the surface of the liver which in turn causes upper abdominal pain on the right side of the body. The pain will be worse when coughing or breathing deeply. Occasionally pain will be felt in the right shoulder. This is referred to as the Fitz-Hugh-Cuttis syndrome. If women engage in anal sex they may experience rectal pain, pain when defaecating and a discharge from the back passage.

Gonorrhoea can spread in the bloodstream and cause fever and skin rashes. It can also cause multiple joint infection with redness, swelling and pain in the joints of the fingers, wrists, elbows, ankles and knees.

Engaging in oral sex with an infected partner can lead to throat infection which may cause no symptoms but can transmit the STD. This is called pharyngeal gonorrhoea. If it spreads to the eyes it may cause severe conjunctivitis that can result in blindness.

Strict hygiene is essential because gonorrhoea can be easily passed on. It can be spread to others if they use a towel that is contaminated with fresh discharge. Also, it can be passed on to babies during childbirth if the mother has the infection.

Like all infectious diseases it is very important to use preventative measures to avoid this bacteria.

HEPATITIS B AND C

The hepatitis virus is spread by body fluids including blood, semen, vaginal secretions and saliva.

Both hepatitis B and C affect the liver and symptoms can include fatigue, nausea, vomiting, skin rashes, tenderness in the upper right side of your abdomen (over your liver), loss of appetite, dark urine, pale faeces, and yellow skin (jaundice). Jaundice is not always present with hepatitis C. Some carriers of this disease will develop

229

cirrhosis of the liver or liver cancer.

Women who have hepatitis B or C can become carriers of the virus without feeling sick. This means there is a possibility they can pass on the virus to someone else through unsafe sex, sharing needles and other personal items such as toothbrushes and razors.

There is currently a vaccine for hepatitis B but not for type C.

Some women have been exposed to hepatitis C during surgical procedures and blood transfusions. If you suspect you may have been in contact with the virus, you will need to have a specific blood test for identifying hepatitis C. It will not show up on a normal liver function test.

Dandelion

It is important to determine whether you have this virus so you can take good care of your liver and avoid the onset of liver disease.

Naturopathic treatment There are some very good herbs for the liver including St Mary's thistle and dandelion. St Mary's thistle is available in a tablet form and dandelion root can be made into a pleasant beverage as a substitute for tea and coffee.

Some good foods for the liver are beetroot, carrots, garlic, onions, chicory, chives and watercress.

HERPES

Herpes is a recurring viral infection that enters the body through the skin and mucous membranes and is caused by the Herpes Simplex Virus. There are two types of herpes virus which are referred to as Herpes Simplex Virus 1 (HSV1) and Herpes Simplex Virus 2 (HSV2). Both are caused by the same virus and apart from the site affected, the infections are essentially the same.

HSV1 mostly causes cold sores around the mouth and chin, although it can also cause corneal ulcers if the virus is crossinfected to the eyes. Herpes can be transferred by touching moist or broken skin on another part of your body or someone else's, immediately after touching an infectious lesion. It is sometimes contracted in the early phase of an infection, before the actual lesion has broken out.

Most people with HSV1 have picked up the infection during childhood, often before age five. HSV1 is not a sexually transmitted disease, however like HSV2 it is contagious and can be spread to the genital area through crossinfection.

HSV2 occurs mostly in the genital region and is usually sexually transmitted. The risk of clinical herpes infection after sexual contact with an individual with one or more active lesions is estimated to be around 75 per cent.

Either type can infect any part of the body containing the type of cell formation that the virus favours. Because this virus is a primitive form of life, it is completely dependent on the cells it invades for survival. Specifically these are the stratified squamous epithelium cells found in the skin, buttocks, thighs, neck and hand.

The virus can penetrate moist membranes such as those around the eyes, inside the mouth, genitalia or rectum. It can also infect you through a break in the skin that may be so small you failed to notice it. This is why it is commonly spread during sexual intercourse and kissing. Both practices can often cause small tears in the body tissue allowing the virus to penetrate. Skin to skin contact is ideal for herpes transmission, with the mouth and genital area being the most common sites.

Regrettably, once you have contracted either strain of the virus, it stays in your body forever because after the virus has invaded the cell, some of its particles enter a sensory nerve fibre close to the site of invasion. The virus then moves up the sensory nerve fibre to the nerve source, which is a small cluster of cells called the sensory ganglion. Two common sites are the Trigeminal ganglion in the face and the Sacral ganglion near the tail of the spinal chord. Here, the virus has found its niche and this is where it will live for the rest of your life. Fortunately, the virus will remain in a latent or inactive form most of the time and it rarely poses any long-term risks to your health.

The first attack of herpes is usually the most severe and we call it the *initial infection*. Once you have been initially infected, an outbreak will occur after a period of two days to three weeks. The incubation period for herpes is generally two to twelve days and the outbreak averages six to seven days, however an initial infection can last twenty days.

After the virus has invaded your body, it uses the material inside the cell to reproduce or replicate. During this process, the cell is destroyed which leads to the appearance of the common symptoms and characteristics of the herpes virus. The sensations felt initially are itching, tingling and soreness, building in intensity as the surrounding tissue starts to swell. The area will become quite red and painful in the first four days, which we call the *prodrome*, followed by the appearance of a single or multiple clusters of small vesicles or watery, blistery sores that we refer to as *lesions*. They generally appear on the body near the mouth, lips, genitals or eyes, however they may also be around the lower back or buttocks. Sometimes the blisters will merge together and become quite large and extremely tender and sore. When the blisters burst, they leave painful ulcers that dry and scab over, while the skin underneath heals. When the lesion has completely healed, the scab will drop off, usually revealing healthy skin underneath. Sometimes you will notice it has left a slight scar which should eventually fade. It is not unusual to notice that glands near the site of infection have also become swollen and tender.

Genital herpes in women can cause a discharge and urination can be quite painful and difficult if the lesions are close to the urethral opening. During the initial infection, it is also possible to experience fever, aches and pains and it is not unusual to feel depressed and run down. Try not to feel guilty or ashamed and keep in mind that after your lesion has healed, you are no longer contagious despite the virus still being present in your body. So you can maintain a normal sex life most of the time. You are only contagious when you have an active lesion, and if you are a healthy individual with a good diet and you manage your stress well you may remain completely free of herpes outbreaks. Some people never have another outbreak after the initial infection, while others with poor immunity may experience an outbreak every month. Maintaining a strong immune system is the best defence against the herpes virus. Your body's immune system does produce antibodies to the virus which tends to lessen the frequency and severity of future attacks.

It is possible to have antibodies in your blood even though you may be unaware of having any herpes infection. The episode may have been so mild it went unnoticed. Some people genuinely do not know they have had the virus because symptoms can differ in severity from person to person. Keep in mind that it is possible for an initial outbreak to occur unnoticed and the second outbreak may not appear until a few years later. This can explain a sudden herpes attack in a supposedly monogamous relationship. Neither partner may genuinely know how it happened and both may have remained faithful to each other. This is important to remember to avoid confusion and confrontation in your relationship should one of you have an outbreak of the herpes virus.

A recurrence of herpes can occur when the virus is reactivated by various forms of emotional and physical stress. Emotional stresses include anxiety, constant worry, emotional trauma such as grief, as well as positive stresses like finishing work or going overseas. Physical stresses which lead to outbreaks are minor infections, direct trauma from hard pressure or a blow, nutritional stress caused by a deficiency or poor dietary patterns and environmental stress like too much sun exposure or getting burnt and dry cracked lips from windy weather. Localised physical stress can also be caused by vaginal dryness or friction from tight clothing.

It is not uncommon for some women to experience a herpes attack that comes on premenstrually or with a period. If this occurs with frequency it may be due to hormonal imbalance, nutritional deficiency, extreme physical or emotional stress or anxiety and/or a suppressed immune system. Some women find they may have recurring herpes attacks during a stressful pregnancy. If you have herpes and you are pregnant, your midwife or obstetrician should be informed because a severe attack in early pregnancy can lead to miscarriage. It is also possible for babies to be infected with the herpes virus during childbirth if their mother has an active lesion or by cross-infection during the early months of life. A herpes attack in the final stages of pregnancy may prevent a normal delivery because of the risk of cross-infection in the birth canal, however if the lesion has healed prior to delivery it should not be necessary to deliver by caesarean section because the risk of a baby contacting herpes in utero is low, due to it gaining some immunity from its mother.

Chronic herpes is commonly seen in immune suppressed individuals, therefore in treating this disorder it is important to support the immune system. This can be achieved by maintaining optimum nutrition through dietary intake and possibly taking nutritional supplements when required. Learn a deep-body relaxation technique, and practise it often. This will keep you physically relaxed and emotionally balanced. It will help to alleviate negative stresses in your life and persistent unwanted thoughts that can undermine your health.

Self-help Apply ice to the lesion during the prodrome phase. Bathe the area with salty water and practise good hygiene.

The amino acid lysine prevents herpes attacks. It is found in high quality protein foods such as fish, chicken, lamb, milk and mung bean sprouts. Include them in your diet.

Foods that contain the amino acid arginine, can bring on an attack as argenine is required by the virus to make viral proteins. A diet that is high in arginine and low in lysine can facilitate an infection. Avoid having a high intake of chocolate, peanuts, pecan nuts, cashews, garlic, wheat and almonds because they are high in arginine. Ginseng also contains arginine.

Herbal medicine Specific herbal medicines can be dispensed by an accredited herbalist as a medicinal formula that will meet your individual needs. It is best not to self-medicate, instead talk to someone who is well trained and can dispense with safety and correctly advise you about dosage.

Homoeopathy Borax: for herpes outbreaks in anxious individuals.

Nat mur: for herpes eruptions in people who have either too much or too little salt.

Rhus tox: for herpes in restless individuals.

Medical approach A good diagnosis is important if you suspect you have herpes. If you have an active lesion, a swab can be taken of the fluid in the sore to verify if it is herpes virus. Blistery sores can occur from other reasons.

Your doctor can prescribe creams to assist healing. If you have recurring outbreaks drug therapy can be given to reduce the frequency.

Prevention of herpes It is always difficult to tell your partner you have herpes but it is very important that you do. Remember, herpes is quite common and your partner will not be at risk of catching it from you if you remain watchful for its presence and take the necessary precautions.

Reassure your partner that you will be responsible and always let them know if you have an active lesion or if you suspect you may be getting one. Condoms will definitely reduce the risk of infection from a herpes lesion on the penis, however if the lesion is around the testes you may still be infected.

Please make an effort not to infect anyone. Do not kiss anyone when you have an active HSV1, and make sure you don't have sex with anyone when you have an active HSV2.

TRICHOMONIASIS VAGINALIS

This vaginal infection is caused by a single-celled trichomonas parasite called Aemelia organism. It can infect the vagina, urethra, bladder and occasionally the glands just inside the entrance to the vagina and the urethra.

You will usually know if you have this infection because the organism produces a profuse discharge that has a distinct fishy smell, not unlike the smell of your local fish market. If you wear slacks or jeans you will notice it is even strong enough to penetrate your clothing. The discharge itself can be yellowish but tends to be grey to green in colour and may be frothy. At times the symptoms can be similar to thrush, causing severe irritation, itching and soreness and on examination you may notice that the tissue in the vagina appears to have pinpoint red spots.

Trichomoniasis is usually sexually transmitted but it can also be caused through poor genital hygiene. In men it can live under the foreskin of the penis but it is more commonly found in women. Some women are unaware that they have trichomoniasis, perhaps because like many different organisms there is a possibility of it always being present in the body and flaring up only when situations allow it to thrive, such as during times of stress or poor nutrition.

It is easily diagnosed due to the nature of the symptom picture, however to be certain, a swab can be taken for examination under a microscope where the organism will be seen quite distinctly.

Self-help I have treated trichomoniasis very successfully using the following garlic treatment.

Make several small drawstring bags from fabric that has an open weave, such as surgical gauze or muslin cloth. One end should remain open with a drawstring top, like a little dillybag. Place into this a peeled clove of garlic that has not been scored with a knife, and insert it into your vagina. Allow the string to hang down so it can be retrieved, much like a tampon. Change this three or four times each day replacing the garlic with a fresh clove and discard the contaminated bag. After a few days the infection should be gone and it is a good idea to follow up with a vaginal swab to check that the organism has gone.

Although it is rare, some women may find they are sensitive to the garlic so if you notice any irritation from this method please discontinue the treatment.

Maintain good personal hygiene and wear cotton close to your skin.

Try to have showers rather than a bath.

You may need to restore vaginal acidity with a vinegar douche (for this and dietary advice see 'Thrush').

Herbal medicine Boost your immune system with herbs such as garlic, echinacea, picrorrhiza or golden seal.

You can add calendula tincture to a douche.

Homoeopathy Bovista: for greenish discharge.

Carbo veg: for thick, greenish, milky discharge that is corrosive.

Mercurious: for greenish discharge causing itching and rawness.

Sulphur: discharge causing redness and burning in the vagina.

Medical approach Your doctor will usually prescribe an antibiotic such as tinidazole or metronidazole. These drugs are contraindicated during the first trimester of pregnancy and also during breastfeeding. Your sexual partner should be checked and treated for the organism as well.

UREAPLASMA UNREALYTICUM AND MYCOPLASMA HOMINIS

You may carry these bacteria within the genital tract without symptoms or disease. They can occur quite commonly. Often there is no need to be treated but occasionally they overgrow and cause inflammation.

If you feel discomfort, swelling and pain and only these organisms are detected it may be advisable to treat them with antibiotics to eliminate your symptoms.

Alternatively you can use the garlic treatment recommended for trichomoniasis and boost your immune system with herbal and nutritional therapy.

Toxic shock syndrome

This is a very rare but serious illness which can occur in women and is caused by a toxin produced by 'golden staph' bacteria (staphylococcus aureus). It occurs most commonly in young women who are menstruating and using tampons. The tampons can scratch the lining of the vagina and allow the organism to release toxins into the blood. Super-absorbent tampons containing fibres other than cotton tend to create the problem more often than regular tampons. In some instances toxic shock from these tampons has proved fatal.

Symptoms include a sudden, high fever, vomitting and/or diarrhoea, shock and a rash resembling sunburn that progresses to peeling skin. If you develop these symptoms stop using tampons and see your doctor immediately.

Treatment will require antibiotic therapy. Prevention is the best approach so only use tampons if you really need to, such as when you go swimming. Wash your hands before you insert tampons and throw away any that have damaged wrappers. Change your tampon regularly and avoid using the super-absorbent types. On heavy days it is best to use a napkin.

Urinary incontinence

Many women suffer unnecessarily from urinary incontinence. This term describes the involuntary escape of urine that can be difficult to control. Women with this problem often pass urine quite frequently and often with urgency. When they feel the urge to go, it happens very suddenly, so they often don't make it to the bathroom and wet pants are a consequence. When there is a need to go very frequently the problem is made worse because only small amounts of urine are passed each time.

The most common cause is weakness in the muscles that keep the bladder outlet closed tight and those that cause the bladder to empty. There may also be irritation to the nerve endings and tissue lining the bladder causing frequent and involuntary urination. Sometimes there is an underlying infection, allergy or inflammation that is causing the problem.

Stress incontinence is another problem caused by weakened or damaged pelvic floor muscles. There may also be damage to the sphincter or urinary outlet, which can occur during childbirth. Urine is released involuntarily when a woman coughs, sneezes, laughs, jumps, lifts objects or strains. In some instances, this type of incontinence may require surgical repair.

With urge incontinence there is a loss of control. As soon as you feel the urge to urinate there is extreme urgency and it usually leads to dribbling of urine or it can cause uncontrollable flooding. If you have this problem you will need to retrain your bladder. This involves improving the bladder's ability to stretch and hold more. Some women have both types of incontinence.

Other causes of stress incontinence can be low oestrogen levels that can weaken the pelvic floor, overweight conditions and chronic constipation.

Urinary incontinence can also occur

235

due to stroke, spinal injury, Parkinson's disease or multiple sclerosis. Some medications for the treatment of high blood pressure can also affect the urinary sphincter.

The hormone relaxin is secreted during pregnancy and just prior to a menstrual period. This hormone can relax the muscles of the urinary area and can lead to an involuntary release of urine in some women.

Self-help Coffee weakens the muscles of the bladder so drink dandelion beverage or herbal teas instead.

Drinking two litres of water a day can help to retrain your bladder and will take some stress off your kidneys. Continue to drink water even though you have a bladder weakness.

Pelvic floor exercises must be done along with bladder retraining (*see* 'Prolapse').

Try pulling in the anus and tightening the muscles at the base of your tail bone without using your abdominal muscles. Do this as often as possible any time of the day or night.

Avoid constipation and maintain a healthy weight range.

Take care to use a lubricant during intercourse to avoid irritation and tissue damage.

Keep a bucket of cold water next to the toilet with a plastic dish or cup in it. After urinating you can scoop out the water and wash your genital area rather than using toilet paper. The cold water works as a good astringent to tighten the urinary sphincter.

Ask your doctor if your medication is possibly a problem.

If your bladder feels irritated you could have tissue inflammation that may be leading to irritation and incontinence. Avoid foods that may cause irritation such as white pepper, mustard, curry, tomatoes, capsicum or orange juice.

Herbal medicine There is a need to improve muscular tone and also maintain the health of the tissue that lines the urinary tract and bladder.

AGRIMONY, *Agrimonia eupatoria*: a mildly astringent herb that is specific for urinary incontinence.

AMERICAN CRANESBILL, *Geranium Maculatum*: highly astringent and it is useful where incontinence is caused through lack of muscular tone and prolapse.

GOLDEN SEAL, *Hydrastis canadensis*: astringent and highly nutritive to the tissues.

HORSETAIL, *Equisetum arvense*: urinary astringent herb. Highly effective where there is leakage of urine.

Bach Flower remedies Try using agrimony, aspen, impatiens, mimulus, scleranthus or walnut.

Homoeopathy Causticum: for when urine escapes when coughing or sneezing.

Equisetum: for involuntary urination.

Nat mur: for involuntary passing of urine when walking.

Nux vomica: for frequency of urination from an irritable bladder.

Pulsatilla: for increased desire to urinate that is worse when lying down.

Cell salts Calc fluor: for relaxed conditions of the urinary sphincter.

Calc phos: for frequent urgency to urinate.

Kali phos: for nervousness.

Nat mur: to regulate your fluid balance.

Other There are special incontinence clinics for women that will teach you how to retrain your bladder and strengthen your pelvic floor. The Continence Foundation of Australia can provide you with more information.

Their phone number is listed in the white pages of your phone book.

Urinary tract infection
CYSTITIS

Cystitis is inflammation of the bladder. It is rarely caused by bacteria, however it can pave the way for infection to occur.

Inflammation of tissue is usually a result of some type of irritation. It can be caused through trauma at the entrance of the urinary tract caused by bruising after a heavy bump or damage from friction or rubbing during intercourse. 'Honeymoon cystitis' is not unusual in women who develop inflammation from frequent sexual intercourse without sufficient lubrication.

The most common symptoms of cystitis are frequency of urination with extreme urgency. When you try to pass urine, very little is voided and there can be a severe, painful drawing sensation at the end of urination. There can also be low abdominal pain and burning. Sometimes blood will be present giving the urine a pink colour. You may also notice the urine has a strong smell and it can be very cloudy. If there is an infection the urine can become quite dark and you can experience pain over the kidneys in your loins. Whenever there is an infection or inflammation, you will feel very tired and may develop a fever.

There are always lots of bacteria around the opening of the urethra, including those from the bowel. Some germs live there constantly and generally do no harm, however it is very easy for bacteria to travel up into the bladder and cause an infection. Some sexually transmitted diseases can infect the bladder.

Kidney stones can damage the lining of the urinary tract as they travel through and pave the way for infection. Herbal medicines that contain mucilage are of great benefit in these circumstances.

URETHRAL SYNDROME

Some women experience recurring pain and frequency of urination without the presence of a bacterial infection. This is usually related to sex, however it can be caused by damage from a catheter, previous surgery or childbirth. Sometimes allergies or chemicals can cause tissue irritation and pressure from a diaphragm can also lead to inflammation.

It is not uncommon for women with low oestrogen levels to become more prone to infections because this can cause the tissue to become more fragile.

If your urine is highly acidic you may be prone to bladder inflammation. Avoid high intakes of vitamin C and citric acid in cordials and tinned tomatoes or fruit.

If you experience symptoms immediately after sexual intercourse, there may not be an infection present and inflammation should respond well to self-help measures. Antibiotics are not necessary for this type of cystitis. If symptoms develop several hours after intercourse, it usually indicates an infection and antibiotic therapy may be required. It can take about eight hours for an infection to establish itself in the bladder.

Self-help Drink two litres of water every day to take the stress off your kidneys.

Barley water is a great remedy for cystitis or kidney infections. To make your own, boil barley in water, strain off the liquid and set the boiled barley

237

aside. (You can eat the barley or add it to soup.) Add some lemon juice to the barley water and sweeten it with a little honey. Store it in the refrigerator and drink it regularly. It is a wonderful drink for the kidneys and bladder.

Drink a glass of cranberry juice every day as it will prevent bacterial invasion in the urinary tract. It does this by altering the tissue that lines the bladder so that bacteria cannot take hold. Avoid cola, chocolate, coffee and tea because they contain caffeine and therefore can irritate the bladder. Alcohol should be kept to a minimum and completely avoided while the inflammation is present.

Take a urinary alkaliser such as one teaspoon of bicarbonate of soda in a glass of water.

Try to have showers rather than baths and do not use bubble bath, talc, harsh soaps or vaginal deodorants.

Some women find tampons can irritate while others can be sensitive to deodorants in some napkins.

You may need to change your washing powder to check if it is causing chemical irritation.

Keep a bucket of cold water next to the toilet with a plastic dish or cup in it. After urinating you can scoop out the water and wash your genital area rather than using toilet paper. The cold water works as a good astringent to tighten the urinary sphincter and lessens the risk of urinary infection.

Sexual self-help Empty your bladder before and after intercourse.

Try to relax during intercourse and always use a lubricant that is designed for the vagina. This will prevent friction and tissue damage caused by dryness.

Women with recurring infections from intercourse may need to experiment with positions to try to prevent pressure and friction on the urethral opening.

Herbal medicine BUCHU, *Agathosma betulina*: a very soothing urinary herb. CORNSILK, *Zea mays*: a very soothing herb for chronic inflammation in the urinary tract. COUCH GRASS, *Agropyron repens*: for cystitis with irritation and inflammation. GOLDEN SEAL, *Hydrastis canadensis*: a good anti-microbial and anti-bacterial herb. MARSHMALLOW, *Althaea officinalis*: a soothing herb rich in mucilage that coats and protects the urinary tract. UVA URSI, *Arctocstaphylos uva-ursi*: a good anti-inflammatory herb for highly acid urine.

Bach Flower remedies Consider such remedies as aspen, hornbeam, impatiens and mimulus.

Homoeopathy Berberis: for burning sensation while not urinating.

Cantharis: for urgency to urinate with severe drawing after.

Thuja: a good remedy for non-specific urinary infections.

Cell salts Calc phos: for frequency and increased urinary output.

MaRShmallow

Calc sulph: for chronic cystitis with pus present.

Ferrum phos: for cystitis with feverishness and frequency of urination.

Kali mur: for acute bladder and kidney inflammation with dark acidic urine.

Kali phos: for frequent scalding urination.

Kali sulph: for chronic cystitis associated with bacterial infection.

Medical approach Your doctor will take a mid-stream sample of urine to determine if there is an infection. A specific antibiotic will be given and the urine sent to a lab to determine which bacteria may be present. A follow-up urine analysis is usually done to check that the infection has gone.

Diabetes causes an increased incidence of urinary tract infection so your doctor may check to see if you have any blood sugar irregularities.

Vaginal discharge

By observing our vaginal secretions we develop a better understanding of our menstrual cycle, our fertility, our hormones and our sexual health. In consultation with women I have observed that many are not clear about natural vaginal secretions produced throughout their monthly cycle. At times, some women are concerned they may have an abnormal discharge and are relieved to find the secretions are simply related to their ovulation. So, before I discuss abnormal discharges let's look at what is normal.

Day 1 of our menstrual cycle is the first day of bleeding. Bleeding generally occurs for three to seven days for most women. After it stops you may notice that you produce a slightly sticky mucus or none at all for a few days. Then you will produce what is called 'fertile

mucus'. It resembles the white of an egg and it has a slippery texture. This is the mucus produced a few days before we ovulate and it is the medium which sperm require for increased survival time. They swim through this mucus to fertilise the egg that is produced at ovulation.

It is unlikely that this mucus would be noticeable on your underwear. You are more likely to notice it when you wipe after you have been to the toilet or by feeling inside your vagina. During ovulation you will notice a thicker discharge on your underwear around Day 10 to Day 14, although this will vary according to your menstrual cycle. Some women with a short cycle of 21 days, sometimes ovulate close to the end of their menstrual bleed.

This heavier ovulation mucus can differ significantly among women. The colour may vary from white to pale yellow and the texture can be creamy or thick and gelatinous. Some women have a very slight amount while others may need a pantyliner at this time. The secretion is actually a thick plug of mucus that is inside the cervical canal. When it comes away it enables any fertile sperm to swim up into the uterus and fallopian tubes for fertilisation to occur.

After ovulation women continue to produce fertile mucus for a few days and then sticky mucus or no mucus until bleeding commences again around Day 28 and once again the cycle continues.

During sexual arousal women also produce natural secretions which may be noticeable at the entrance of their vagina. These are completely normal and indicate good sexual health.

LEUKORRHEA

Quantities of vaginal secretions can vary considerably from woman to woman. They are influenced by our hormones, our diet and our physical and emotional health.

Sometimes women notice an increase in vaginal secretions that concerns them. When natural secretions become copious and do not follow a natural mucous cycle, they may be referred to as a discharge. Some excessive discharges are non-irritating and may clear up without any intervention while others can cause irritation and distress and require treatment. The medical term for vaginal and uterine discharges is sometimes referred to as leukorrhea or 'the whites'.

Most unpleasant vaginal discharges result from vaginitis or inflammation in the vagina.

Herbal medicine AMERICAN CRANESBILL, *Geranium maculatum*: an astringent herb that stops bleeding. Can be used as a douche for leukorrhea in combination with beth root.

BETH ROOT, *Trillium erectum*: can be used in a douche for leukorrhea.

BISTORT, *Polygonum bistorta*: a soothing anti-inflammatory and astringent herb. It contains natural mucilage which is very healing and protective to inflamed tissue. It can be used as a douche, particularly if there are fissures or cracks in the skin.

GREATER PERIWINKLE, *Vinca Major*: can be a highly effective astringent for the treatment of leukorrhea.

LADIES MANTLE, *Alchemilla alpina*: is an astringent herb that is also anti-inflammatory. It is helpful for reducing excessive menstruation.

WHITE POND LILY, *Nymphaea odorata*: an astringent herb that is also quite mucilaginous. This herb will be soothing to inflamed tissue and particularly useful in combination with beth root and geranium as a douche for leukorrhea.

Bach Flower remedies Try using such things as chestnut bud, crab apple, elm, scleranthus and white chestnut.

Essential oils Lavender: soothes rashes and skin irritation so add some to your bath water.

Sandalwood: added to your bath water it can provide temporary relief from burning and soreness.

Homoeopathy Calc carb: for milky leukorrhea and heavy menstruation that lasts too long.

Helonias: leukorrhea associated with prolapse and lower back pain.

Hydrastis: for acrid, corrosive leukorrhea that is worse after menstruation.

Pulsatilla: discharge is thick, yellow and non-irritating.

Cell salts Calc phos: for discharges that are worse in the mornings.

Kali mur: for white, thick, irritating discharges.

Kali phos: for yellow or orange coloured discharge.

Kali sulph: for slimy, watery, yellow discharge.

Nat mur: for watery discharge that burns the tissues.

Silicea: for when discharge is profuse.

GENITAL ODOUR

It is perfectly natural and healthy for women to have certain body odours. Providing we maintain good genital hygiene, these odours are not unpleasant and there is absolutely no reason to feel embarrassed or uncomfortable about them.

Most women at some time have some concern about their body odour and will often apologise for not taking a shower before a vaginal examination or sexual contact. There is no need for concern as these odours are usually more noticeable to ourselves than to others.

Healthy vaginal secretions often have a slightly sweet, musky smell and these aromas act like pheromones and often enhance sexual arousal in our partners.

Be comfortable with your body, the way it smells, the way it feels and the way it looks. There is no need to stifle your sexuality and spontaneity by refraining from sexual activity unless you have taken a shower. Equally, there is no need to cover up your natural body odour with deodorants, perfumes and talcs. These substances are likely to lead to irritation or vaginitis.

Observing body odours and understanding where they come from can teach you a lot about your body. It will help you to be more comfortable with yourself and you will learn to detect changes in odours and secretions that may indicate health problems.

Where do odours come from? Several types of glands in our skin produce oil and perspiration and body odour develops from the action of bacteria on these secretions.

The sebaceous glands, located in our pubic mound and on the labia majora and minora, produce an oily liquid called sebum.

Other tiny glands called eccrine glands, found in the skin, produce the watery perspiration that comes on from heat and exercise.

From puberty, women also produce a milky fluid from their apocrine glands, through the hair follicles onto the surface of the skin. These secretions are emitted during stress, excitement, fear

or pain and produce the fluid that helps to form pheromones. Women have 75 per cent more apocrine glands than men.

Other natural odours are produced by the action of bacteria on vaginal mucus or pubic hair. There is also the smell of semen which will leak out from the vagina after intercourse.

Menstruation will also produce a mild odour, which is not offensive providing we change tampons and napkins regularly. However, if you leave a tampon inside your vagina without realising, it will definitely become quite rank after a few days, making you aware of the problem.

Any other unpleasant odour will only come from bacterial infections or sexually transmitted disease.

Genital hygiene Good sexual hygiene simply involves these few basic steps:

Always wipe from front to back after toileting to prevent bringing bacteria from the anus into the vagina.

Wash your anal area with a mild, non-perfumed soap, using clean hands rather than a cloth or flannel which may harbour bacteria.

Rinse with water until all traces of soap are gone.

Use fresh water to clean between the folds of the labia and pat dry with a clean soft towel.

Vaginal pH

The chemical term for describing levels of acidity or alkalinity is pH. The environment of a healthy woman's vagina has a pH of 4 to 4.5, which makes it reasonably acidic. Most bacteria will not thrive in an acidic environment and so in maintaining vaginal acidity the body keeps the vagina naturally healthy, clean and free of germs.

The vagina maintains acidity through a friendly bacteria called Doderlains bacilli which feeds on glycogen that is produced in the cells of the vaginal lining under the influence of oestrogen. This in turn produces lactic acid which favours the growth of this particular bacteria. Lactic acid is unfavourable to other bacteria. As a result the Doderlains bacilli flourish and so another body cycle continues and the vagina maintains its acidity.

Destruction of Doderlains bacilli will therefore result in the vagina becoming too alkaline. Harmful bacteria will thrive in an alkaline environment, making the vagina prone to infection, discharge and irritation. This is a good reason why it is not desirable to regularly douche your vagina. You risk flushing away the very bacteria that keep your vagina in good health. There are times however, when douching may be beneficial, for instance, when an imbalance or infection has already occurred.

Never use products that contain chemicals or perfumes inside or at the entrance of your vagina. Vaginal sprays, deodorants, perfumed soaps, moisturisers and bubble baths can all interfere with this delicate environment.

Broad spectrum antibiotic therapy can destroy the Doderlains bacilli and disturb the normal vaginal environment. This then allows other bacteria and micro-organisms to thrive. Unfortunately some women become prone to developing vaginal problems such as candidiasis or gardnerella as a consequence of taking these drugs. You can reduce this risk with a daily supplement of acidophilus with bifida.

VAGINAL THRUSH

Many women suffer the discomfort of thrush, which may also be called Candida albicans or Monilia. It is very common and women usually know when they have it.

The signs and symptoms include genital itching, soreness, vulval swelling and intercourse is usually painful. There may also be a discharge and on examination it looks like small white curds around the entrance and walls of the vagina. The tissue inside and around the vagina is red and inflamed. The vagina is slightly alkaline and this allows bacteria to flourish. We all carry the thrush organism in our bodies and it is normal for it to erupt in times of stress or during pregnancy. Hormonal changes can also influence the growth of this organism and some oral contraceptive pills that are high in oestrogen can actually make the body more prone to thrush. Oestrogen leads to a greater amount of glycogen in the vagina which is a form of sugar. This provides nourishment for the organism. Diabetic women and those on antibiotic therapy are more prone. If you are prone to thrush and need to take an antibiotic, be sure to use an antifungal substance and take acidophilus at the same time. If the vagina becomes excessively dry or irritated through a lack of oestrogen you may also be prone to thrush.

Thrush is not generally a sexually transmitted disease although you can cause cross infection from sexual activity.

The treatments listed below are not usually needed for long-term use, however dietary changes should be strictly adhered to for stubborn recurring cases.

Dietary advice Dietary changes are

needed, particularly if you tend to have low-grade thrush most of the time.

Eat acidophilus yoghurt every day or take acidophilus tablets to restore a healthy balance to the intestinal flora. It is a good idea to take acidophilus during or after antibiotic treatment because while the antibiotics destroy the nasty bacteria they can also deplete the good ones that maintain the health of the intestine.

Avoid alcohol and all foods containing sugar or yeast. Absolutely no cakes, yeasted bread, biscuits, sweets, honey, glucose or sugar.

Eliminate all fruit except lemon, lime and grapefruit for the first two weeks of this diet. Fruit is rich in sugar and can feed the candida.

You can have all legumes, vegetables and vegetable juices, but you should avoid mushrooms.

Vitamin A is important at a tissue level so eat plenty of cooked yellow vegetables.

Garlic is a natural antifungal herb so include it in your daily eating regime.

Wheat can be a problem so eat foods made from other grains such as corn, barley, rice and oats. Rice cakes, rice cruskits, corn chips, taco shells, pumpernickel, Ryvita or Kavli crackers can be eaten freely. If you miss bread, try making your own damper or buy yeast- and wheat-free bread.

Avoid sauces and spreads, although you can have some almond paste or cashew butter.

Nuts and seeds can be eaten if they are put in the microwave for twenty seconds to kill moulds.

You can have a little olive oil and butter.

To eliminate thrush you may also need to eliminate all dairy products (except butter) and replace them with goat's, sheep's and soy milks. Goat and sheep's milks, cheeses and yoghurts are available at health and bulk stores and delicatessens. It is also possible to buy calcium-enriched soy milk that does not contain added sugar. By replacing cow's milk with this product, your calcium needs can still be met without the need for supplementation.

Reduce high levels of chicken or red meats and instead eat more fish (not fried, please). White meats only are to be eaten during the first two weeks. Tinned fish products such as tuna, sardines or salmon are fine.

Rely on water to quench your thirst, and satisfy your sugar cravings by eating lots of starchy vegetables, barley, rice or rolled oats.

Do not eat leftovers more than three-days old or foods that may harbour moulds such as dried fruits or cheeses.

Eat lots of fresh raw and cooked vegetables, legumes and fish, rice and barley and home made soups.

Some people will lose weight on this diet. Keep in mind there are no restrictions on the quantity of food you can eat.

Self-help Use the following douche mixture to restore acidity in the vagina.

Mix 1 tablespoon of lemon juice or cider vinegar with 1 cup of cooled, boiled water.

You can either purchase a douche from a pharmacy or simply use a soft, plastic container that has a nozzle. Fill this with the liquid and lie or squat in a bath or shower recess. Squeeze the contents into your vagina and try to hold it there for a short time using muscular contractions. Then just let it naturally run out and pat yourself dry. Alternatively, heavily moisten some cotton wool with the liquid. Wipe around and just inside the entrance of your vagina with the wet cotton wool. Discard the cotton wool after each time you wipe and use a fresh piece. This is best done in the bath because it doesn't matter if you make a mess. Although it can initially sting a little, relief from itching happens immediately.

Do this twice a day and within a few days you can stop douching. Long-term douching is not recommended. In chronic thrush you may need to douche with an acidifying agent once a month. Douching is contraindicated during menstruation or pregnancy.

Simply putting vinegar in bathwater can be enough to provide relief from low-grade thrush.

If your discomfort persists then seek further advice from your naturopath or doctor.

Herbal medicine I would recommend a local application of a herbal genital wash for irritation. This can be made by a herbalist and can also be used to treat your sexual partner. It should contain antifungal and anti-inflammatory herbs.

Tea-tree oil has a natural anti-fungal action and can be purchased as a cream or douche solution. Although, I have found it can be a bit harsh for many women as the vagina is a sensitive area for such a powerful substance. Full strength tea-tree may cause irritation if the skin is raw or inflamed. You can dilute tea-tree oil with a light oil like jojoba or vitamin E.

CALENDULA, *Calendula officinalis:* application of this herb to the genital area will heal inflamed tissue and prevent itching.

GARLIC, *Allium sativum:* a good antifungal herb that is useful for treating thrush.

THUJA, *Thuja occidentalis:* a very good herb to mix in a genital wash because it

reduces irritation and itching.

THYME, *Thymus vulgaris:* an antifungal and antibacterial herb.

WHITE POND LILY, *Nymphaea odorata:* very useful for local application because it is antimicrobial, astringent and very soothing to the tissue because of a high content of mucilage.

YARROW, *Achillea millefolium:* antiseptic herb that will also help to heal raw tissue.

White Water Lily

Bach Flower remedies Try using crab apple, impatiens and sweet chestnut.

Homoeopathy Calc carb: for thrush that is worse before the menstrual period.

Nettle: for discharge that is corrosive and itchy.

Rhus tox: for itchy red skin.

Sulphur: for burning, red, swollen inflamed skin.

Cell salts Kali mur: for thick, white, irritating discharge.

Silicea: for when discharge is profuse.

Other Thrush loves a moist, warm environment so do not wear restrictive clothing. Avoid wearing nylon tights, nylon underwear or tight jeans. Try wearing stockings rather than pantyhose and wear natural fibres such as cotton or silk close to your skin.

Personal hygiene is important so always wash your groin and genital area well every day.

After toileting always wipe from the front to the back, otherwise you may bring infection producing bacteria from the anus to the vagina or urethra.

Use a condom during intercourse if you have thrush and be careful not to cross-infect. The anus and vaginal entrance are quite close. If there is any anal contact with hands, sex aids or a penis you must be sure to wash them before vaginal contact resumes.

Medical approach Thrush is normally easy to diagnose, however your doctor may decide to take a vaginal swab to see if candida can be cultured in the laboratory for confirmation.

Pessaries or antifungal creams are often prescribed for you and your sexual partner.

Your doctor may also prescribe special antifungal tablets for some women with chronic thrush, although they can have side effects. They cannot be used during pregnancy or lactation.

Vaginismus

Vaginismus is the term used when the muscles around the entrance to the vagina go into spasm, making sexual penetration or vaginal examination painful or impossible. It begins as soon as any penetration is anticipated and the muscular spasm can be so intense that any form of penetration is impossible.

Usually psychological and sexual therapy or counselling are required to determine the cause and to provide assistance to overcome it. It can be a physical problem.

Bach Flower remedies Try Rescue Remedy as a good general remedy for fear and anxiety. Select others to suit your individual needs and consider using aspen, mimulus, star of Bethlehem, elm, pine and sweet chestnut.

Homoeopathy Aurum metallicum: for vaginal sensitivity; self condemnation and a feeling of worthlessness.

Cactus: for vaginal constriction.

Hamamelis: for vaginal tenderness.

Plumbum met: for nerve pain with a feeling of constriction in the vagina.

Cell salts Ferrum phos: for vaginal spasm with dryness.

Mag phos: for muscular spasm.

Nat mur: For pain with intercourse and vaginal dryness.

Vaginitis

Vaginitis is a term that simply means inflammation of the vagina. When the vagina becomes inflamed it usually feels irritated and sore; there may be swelling, itching and tenderness. Almost always there will be an abnormal discharge and a change in vaginal odour.

Vaginal inflammation is not always caused by an infection and is not necessarily sexually transmitted. It may be caused by taking certain antibiotics, having extremely low oestrogen levels, from direct irritation and sometimes allergies.

Herbal medicine WHITE POND LILY, *Nymphaea odorata:* is astringent, soothing and antimicrobial. It can be used as a douche for vaginitis in combination with beth root and American cranesbill.

Homoeopathy Specific remedies are listed under Leukorrhea.

Cell salts Ferrum phos: for heat, dryness and inflammation in the vagina.

245

Kali phos: for acrid, corrosive discharge and vaginal itching.

Nat mur: for burning and soreness in the vagina.

Silicea: for sensitive vagina with a profuse discharge.

ALLERGIC VAGINITIS

If your vagina feels raw and irritated and a vaginal swab fails to detect any infection, it is quite possible you have allergic vaginitis caused by a chemical irritant or allergy.

The discharge is usually thin, watery and non-irritating, however it can at times be corrosive, causing a burning or chaffing of the skin leaving it quite sore. This type of non-infectious vaginitis can be caused by the use of vaginal sprays and deodorants, talcum powder, bubble baths, perfumed soaps and some washing powders.

If you are particularly sensitive you can occasionally develop vaginitis from products that are designed for the genital area such as spermicides, douches, condoms, deodorised sanitary napkins, tampons and tea-tree oil products. Another cause may be from using moisturisers or body lotions as lubricants, particularly those that are perfumed.

In rare cases vaginitis may be caused from sensitivity to moulds or food chemicals but usually there will be additional health problems associated with it.

The best treatment for allergic vaginitis is to recognise the substance that is causing the problem and stop using it.

GARDNERELLA VAGINALIS

In the past this has also been known as non-specific vaginitis and it is a very common cause of abnormal vaginal discharge.

Gardnerella bacterium along with other micro-organisms live in the vagina but are normally present in very small amounts. Like thrush and trichomoniasis, they can flourish if the vagina becomes too alkaline or if your immune system is depressed.

There is usually no itching or soreness because gardnerella does not inflame the vagina it just produces a discharge that can vary from being thin and frothy or thick and gelatinous. Like trichomoniasis, it usually has a distinct smell that can be fishy or sour. An internal examination will often reveal a whitish, frothy discharge on the cervix.

At times gardnerella is detected by Pap smear and included in the results as being seen on the slide. If you have no symptoms there is no need to undergo treatment because it is part of normal vaginal micro-organisms.

If you have symptoms of gardnerella both you and your sexual partner must undergo treatment.

Dietary advice Women who are run down and/or have low immunity can be prone to these infections. For this reason it is very important to have yoghurt, fresh fruits and vegetables in your diet every day. Include garlic and onions in your cooking or take garlic as a supplement.

Avoid all refined foods and eat no foods that are fried or high in fat.

Self-help Check the acidity of your vagina with litmus paper by holding it against the moist tissue inside the vagina. It should be acidic, which means the paper will turn yellow/orange. If it is alkaline the litmus paper will turn blue/green and you will need to restore vaginal acidity with a cider vinegar or lemon juice douche (*see* page 243).

This organism responds to the garlic

treatment recommended for Trichomoniasis.

Cell salts Kali mur: for thick discharge.
Nat mur: for thin discharge.
Nat phos: for sour smelling discharge.

Medical approach Sometimes specific antibiotics and/or a sulpha cream is prescribed.

Varicose ulcers

If varicose conditions are not treated it is possible to develop leg ulcers because when circulation is poor, there is a lack of fresh blood to heal any cuts or injuries to the skin, making them slow to heal. This can cause the site to become ulcerated. Varicose ulcers are usually found around and above the ankles or on the lower parts of the legs. The centre of the ulcer will be weepy and the surrounding skin is often red and itchy.

Herbal medicine A drawing poultice can be made from comfrey, yarrow and mullein. These herbs can be added to some rolled oats or slippery elm that is mixed to a thick paste using boiled water. Always apply the poultice hot, cover with a gauze bandage and leave on overnight. In the morning it should be removed and discarded. This is useful if the ulcer has become swollen and inflamed and you wish to draw out any rubbish from the sore.

Local application of a herbal mixture containing equal quantities of comfrey, golden seal, chickweed and yellow dock extracts, will heal sores and ulcers very effectively. An accredited herbalist can prepare this combination for you and it will be inexpensive and safe to use.

I find that you need to dry out these types of sores in order to heal them because they are often quite raw and infected. Ointments usually keep them moist and sloppy so I prefer to use a tincture that contains a little alcohol. Be prepared that it will sting a little after application for a few seconds but painting it on regularly will heal the ulcer very quickly. If the surrounding skin is too dry and inelastic you can rub some vitamin E cream around the border of the ulcer, after you apply the liquid herbs. The vitamin E and the herbs will both reduce the risk of unsightly scars.

HAEMORRHOIDS

When varicose veins are in the anal area they are called haemorrhoids. These are usually attributed to low-fibre diets and chronic constipation. Repeated straining can force blood down into the veins around the anus which increases pressure in the veins leading to haemorrhoids. Constant lifting of heavy objects and bearing down during childbirth will have the same effect on the veins.

Avoid and prevent constipation by drinking six to eight glasses of water every day and following a diet that is rich in fibre and low in highly refined processed foods.

Dietary advice Generally follow the same dietary guidelines as those for varicose conditions with added emphasis on fibre-rich foods to improve elimination. Foods that contain moisture and are enzyme rich will assist with digestion and provide adequate fibre, examples are green vegetables, salads and fruits such as pineapple, kiwi fruit, pawpaw and citrus.

Good digestion is very important because the longer it takes for food to move through the alimentary canal the more likely that your stool will become impacted and dry and constipation will result. Include some prunes, dates, figs, licorice, molasses and rhubarb in your diet to achieve a natural laxative action.

In order to improve elimination we sometimes need to improve the function of the liver. Good liver foods are beetroot, dandelion greens, garlic, onion, chives, watercress, carrots, olives and lemon juice. Try to include them in your diet and drink dandelion beverage as a self-help measure to enhance the flow of bile. Bile insufficiency can be an added problem with constipation and by avoiding fried and fatty foods you will prevent the formation of gall stones, which can block the flow of bile.

Generally, the avoidance of fats, cigarettes and alcohol can greatly improve liver and gall bladder dysfunction.

If you feel bloated and full after a meal, you may benefit from taking digestive enzymes. These do not stop your body from producing enzymes, they simply add a few extra to help breakdown food. Take one or two immediately after finishing a meal. Do not chew them, just swallow them whole. You may not need to take them if your meal is simple and includes foods that are rich in enzymes but take them if you have a particularly rich meal. Another option is to drink a teaspoonful of cider vinegar in a glass of water to improve digestion.

Be sure to balance your meals well by only eating small amounts of animal products and large amounts of vegetables, fruits, grains, cereals and legumes.

Self-help Apply a paste made from bicarbonate of soda and water to take away the itch.

Lemon juice is naturally astringent and can be applied to help tighten protruding veins.

Try taking Sitz baths to reduce pain and inflammation (*see* 'Dysmenorrhoea').

The essential oils of cypress, chamomile, lavender or juniper can be added to a hip bath.

A combination of lavender and geranium can be diluted with jojoba oil and applied directly to the haemorrhoids.

Herbal medicine AMERICAN CRANESBILL, *Geranium maculatum:* an astringent, anti-inflammatory and healing herb that can be taken as a medicine.

CALENDULA, *Calendula officinalis:* an anti-inflammatory herb that also prevents bleeding. Use for topical application.

GERMAN CHAMOMILE, *Matricaria recutita:* antiseptic and anti-inflammatory for topical application.

OAK BARK, *Quercus robur:* can be taken internally and also used for topical application. This herb is astringent,

Calendula

antiseptic and also helps to stop bleeding.

PILEWORT, *Ranunculus ficaria:* can be used for topical application with witch hazel and calendula. This is an astringent herb that is specific for haemorrhoids.

WITCH HAZEL, *Hamamelis virginiana:* specific for varicose conditions including haemorrhoids. It can be used internally in combination with other herbs and topically as an ointment or tincture.

Cell salts Calcium fluoride: specific for relaxed conditions of veins.

Varicose veins

Varicose veins are created when the walls of the veins weaken and dilate causing them to lose elasticity and bulge unnaturally. This usually occurs in the superficial veins of the legs but can also take place within the pelvic and anal region.

In varicose conditions, the walls of the veins lose their ability to offer resistance to the force of the blood. This results in blood accumulating and pooling in the vein causing it to swell and force fluid into the surrounding tissue, leading to a feeling of heaviness and sometimes pain.

Occupations that require standing for long periods of time greatly increase the risk of developing varicose veins. This is because the blood is pumped through the arteries and veins away from the heart and out to the extremities; when you stand, there is barely enough upward pressure to balance the force of gravity which is also forcing blood downwards.

Women are more prone to varicose conditions than men due to a variety of causes. High levels of progesterone make us more prone and this hormone is released in large amounts during pregnancy. This combined with added pressure of the baby in the abdominal cavity can put increased pressure on the veins of the pelvis, causing them to become stretched and flabby. When the veins are distended for long periods they can become permanently stretched. The valves inside the veins no longer seal properly and the blood pressure is further increased, which can completely destroy the function of the valves and cause serious varicose conditions.

Other contributing factors are obesity and constipation, so it is important to exercise and maintain a healthy diet to provide adequate fibre and stay within a healthy weight range. A general lack of exercise or being immobilised through injury or illness will result in poor venous return. We rely on the contraction of muscles around the veins to help open valves and propel the blood back to the heart and inactivity leads to poor muscle tone.

I cannot stress enough the importance of making dietary changes and getting regular exercise if you have varicose veins because they can increase the risk of embolism or clot, thrombophlebitis (vein inflammation) and stroke.

In the natural processes of clot formation, platelets—tiny cells produced in our bone marrow—are released into the blood. They have an ability to become sticky and this can be very useful for repairing damaged tissue in our body. When they come into contact with a damaged surface, such as from a cut or laceration, they swell and stick together to form a plug which usually prevents blood loss. Another substance, fibrin, attaches to the platelets making the plug tighter and

249

stronger and with the help of some other substances in the blood, effectively form a clot.

If a clot has formed to plug a hole, it will then be invaded by other substances called fibroblasts which form connective tissue through the clot, in order to repair the damage. If a clot has been formed from leaking blood, it will eventually be dissolved over a few days by natural anticoagulants in our blood. This is part of our natural blood clotting mechanism to prevent blood loss and repair damaged tissue.

Some people develop an abnormal clot in unbroken blood vessels called a thrombus. A thrombus can be formed if the blood is flowing very slowly and this is common in varicose conditions and atherosclerosis (thickened arteries). If a thrombus is not dissolved it can break away from its attachment and it can cut off the oxygen supply or block circulation to a vital organ. This condition is known as thrombosis.

An embolus is any foreign or abnormal particle such as a piece of fat, bubble of air or other debris transported in the blood. If it becomes lodged it is called an embolism.

If you are at risk of developing abnormal clots, you may wish to take nutritional supplements to reduce the stickiness of blood platelets and assist in maintaining tissue health and elasticity of the veins. Once again dietary changes should be made to help prevent further deterioration.

Some individuals have abnormalities that can lead to excessive bleeding due to an inability to form clots. Three common causes are vitamin K deficiency, haemophilia (not usually found in women) and platelet deficiency (Thrombocytopenia). Most blood clotting factors are formed in the liver and some disorders of the liver can also create a tendency to bleed.

People with these abnormalities should not supplement with nutrients that can further reduce the stickiness of their platelets, such as evening primrose oil, starflower oil or borage oil. If you are having any surgery it is important to stop supplementation with the essential fatty acids beforehand. Your surgeon will not want you to take anything that can interfere with your ability to prevent bleeding.

Dietary advice Maintain a balanced diet with lots of fibre-rich foods such as fresh fruit, fresh vegetables (scrubbed not peeled), wholegrains, cereals, bread, oat bran, rice bran and legumes.

Eat onions and garlic every day because they are rich in fibre, prevent infections and naturally lower blood pressure. Garlic, onion, ginger and capsicum also reduce platelet accumulation and break down fibrin (a clotting agent) in the blood.

Lecithin helps to lower cholesterol and it occurs naturally in soy beans and corn.

Rutin is part of the bioflavanoid group that is specific for varicose conditions. Buckwheat is naturally high in rutin and will help to strengthen the walls of the veins and also helps to prevent aching.

Essential fatty acids such as fish oils, borage oil, starflower oil or evening primrose oil reduce the risk of blood clotting by reducing the stickiness of platelets in our blood.

Bromelain is an enzyme contained in fresh pineapple and it also reduces your risk of forming dangerous blood clots.

Zinc will help to strengthen blood vessel walls and it is found in wholegrains, oysters and pumpkin seeds.

Foods rich in the antioxidant vitamins A, B, C and E are fresh fruits, green leafy and yellow vegetables, nuts, seeds and wheat germ.

Nutritional supplements that can be beneficial are magnesium, vitamin C with bioflavanoids, vitamin B6, vitamin E, vitamin A, zinc and essential fatty acids.

Self-help Exercise every day by going for a half hour walk. Women don't need to go power walking or jogging, just walking at a good pace will be extremely beneficial.

Yoga stretches are superb for improving flexibility and blood flow. They do not place added stress on the body and are never meant to be forced.

Always wear comfortable footwear that provides good arch and heel support. Throw away those high heel shoes that are no longer a necessary fashion accessory because attractive flat shoes are now readily available.

Do not stand or sit for long periods of time.

Avoid tight clothing such as tight jeans or knee-high stockings or socks as they can interfere with circulation.

Try not to cross your legs or ankles and elevate your legs as much as possible to improve venous return.

Wear good quality support stockings if your legs ache.

Herbal medicine PRICKLY ASH, *Zanthoxylum americanum:* a herb to improve poor circulation.
WITCH HAZEL, *Hamamelis virginia:* is specific for varicose conditions.
STINGING NETTLES, *Urtica dioica:* a nutritious herb that is good for the vascular system.

Essential oils Some useful essential oils to add to a bath or blended into massage oil are cypress, hypericum, juniper and lavender.

Homoeopathy Witch hazel and bellis are two remedies that can be very helpful for varicose conditions.

Cell salts Calcium fluoride is a cell salt specific for relaxed conditions of veins.

Other Massage therapy is an excellent way to exercise muscles and improve circulation, especially for people who find it difficult to walk or exercise. Make sure you see a well-qualified therapist though, because it must be done with care in varicose conditions. All movements must encourage the blood back towards the heart instead of increasing the blood in the extremities.

For tired aching legs you could relax in a bath that contains Epsom salts, which are rich in magnesium.

Understanding Nutrients and their Sources

T HE most important factor that influences and maintains health is good nutrition. Always try to ensure that food is your first choice as a source of nutrients because not only does it contain important balances of macro and micronutrients, but it also provides us with bulk and fibre for elimination as well as water and mucilage to soothe and protect the lining of our gut.

On an emotional level, the experiences and joys of growing, preparing and eating food can be highly therapeutic. Food does not simply provide relief from hunger or calm a nervous stomach, we have many important rituals that surround its preparation and eating. We often make mealtimes social occasions where we prepare and share food with others in a display of friendship. To celebrate special events and successes we may prepare a feast or share an intimate dinner.

Food can be used for sexual pleasure and it can enhance sexual responsiveness, depending on what you eat and how you eat it! There are some wonderful textures in food and many exquisite flavours. Aromas produced while food is cooking can awaken memories of places, people and our past.

When we eat in a relaxed environment and take the time to chew our food well, we can actually reduce our stress level and improve our body's ability to absorb nutrients. Chewing promotes salivation and the secretion of enzymes. It triggers our body into a number of responses that prepare it for the digestion, absorption and the utilisation of food.

As a traditional therapist, I prefer to work as close to nature as possible and I often use food as medicine. There are times however, when I need to prescribe vitamin supplements and this can be necessary for a number of reasons.

* Some people refuse to change their diet or simply don't like certain foods.
* Many people have food intolerances and allergies and if they eat specific foods or groups of foods they may have unpleasant and sometimes serious reactions.
* There are illnesses that interfere with the absorption of nutrients and/ or place greater nutritional demands on the body, such as immune suppressive disorders and gastrointestinal diseases.
* Drug use, including cigarette and alcohol addiction, can lead to destruction or depletion of essential nutrients.
* Ongoing emotional and physical stress places a greater demand for nutrients in our bodies.
* Despite nutritional education, most people do not eat a balanced diet and do not take the time to prepare and eat nutritious food.
* Some people simply like to take vitamins. They find it a convenient and effortless way to ensure they meet their daily nutritional needs.

I would like to stress though, that nutritional supplements must never be used as substitutes for food. They will not make up for the negative effects of ongoing poor dietary habits and there are many things we will never obtain from a vitamin pill.

Nutritional deficiencies

In this chapter I present an overview of nutrients and their sources and provide information on deficiency signs. I also explain some of the traditional diagnostic techniques that I use to determine health problems, for instance, the use of tongue analysis and monitoring changes in the eyes and fingernails.

Learn to read your body closely, it can tell you a great deal. If you suspect you have a deficiency and you identify with the symptoms, look at the list of food sources for that particular nutrient. Do you include these foods in your daily diet? If the answer is no, it is reasonable to assume that you may have a deficiency. Keep in mind that your body does not manufacture the essential nutrients required for the maintenance of health and they need to be replenished daily. When you bring a variety of these foods back into your diet your symptoms may disappear altogether without any further therapy.

Recommended daily allowances

Recommended daily allowances (RDAs) are standards set by a panel from the National Research Council's Food and Nutrition Board. They are determined according to recommendations for healthy individuals based on age and gender and are reviewed every five years.

If you do decide to take over-the-counter preparations of supplements, follow the dosage recommendations written on the packet. They are given for your safety and may provide you with adequate levels of nutrients.

Therapeutic doses of nutritional supplements are often much higher than the recommended daily allowances. There are times when these higher doses are needed to correct nutritional deficiencies or to assist a healing process. While a therapeutic dose is still within limits of safety, it should only be prescribed by a qualified therapist who has the knowledge to accurately determine when it is required, when it is no longer needed, and to provide the necessary supervision in between.

If people notice an improvement from taking supplements they are sometimes tempted to take higher doses. Taking more is not always better. Excesses of nutrients are not always flushed from the body; some are stored in the body and excesses can accumulate to undesirable levels. Self-prescribing megadoses of nutrients for a long time is often unnecessary and can be very costly to your health as well as your wallet.

If you have a health problem or if you simply want to remain in good health and are considering taking nutritional supplements, it is generally worth a visit to a qualified natural therapist. They are trained to assess your level of health and your treatment program will be tailored to meet your individual needs.

Foods and herbs as nutrient sources

While it is important to know what nutrients are provided in the food we eat, it can be very difficult to provide this information accurately. Nutrient levels in food are highly dependent on growing conditions, harvesting, freshness, preparation and cooking methods.

Recommended daily allowances are only estimates of a person's needs for the maintenance of good health and it is impossible to accurately assess

how much of the nutrients provided from a food source will be assimilated. For this reason I have not provided you with the nutritional information of individual foods. Instead I have listed foods that are known to contain moderate to high levels of the specific nutrients. Many of these foods are referred to as being 'nutrient dense' and they play an important role in maintaining good health.

There are also many herbal remedies that are rich in nutrients and can provide essential vitamins and minerals. The preparation methods of herbs will determine which nutrients become available to our bodies. Herbal teas provide us with the water-soluble nutrients contained in the herb. For instance, rosehip tea usually contains vitamins A, C, B2 and B3 and some mineral salts.

To extract the fat-soluble nutrients of a plant we have to prepare them in a different way. A good example is fenugreek seed which contains iron as well as vitamins A and D and lecithin. These seeds have a chemical composition that closely resembles cod liver oil. It yields fatty acids and

255

the seeds of this plant can be prepared in a variety of ways so as not to deplete the fat-soluble nutrients. They can be steeped in alcohol and made into a medicine; they can also be crushed, ground and used as a spice, sprouted and served as a food, soaked and eaten or made into a paste.

Nutrients are present in many of our medicinal herbs and, although they may appear in low doses, they are often available in a highly desirable form. Alfalfa, for example, contains several mineral salts including calcium phosphate. Research shows that we absorb and utilise this form of calcium much better than when we take calcium alone. Alfalfa also contains vitamin D and silicon which are necessary for effective calcium absorption.

I have included herbs in this chapter because they are often underestimated as a dietary source of nutrients. When nutrients are taken in a botanical form they are generally well balanced, well tolerated and well utilised.

Biochemic cell salts

Biochemistry is the science that deals with the chemistry of living tissue. In 1873 Dr Scheussler analysed human blood and found basic minerals and called them cell salts or tissue salts. He attributed disease to cell-salt deficiency and some symptoms as distress signals indicating the need for certain elements. In order to treat disease, he administered these tissue salts in homoeopathic doses, which are minute doses that are potentised.

An analysis of our blood will reveal that it is composed of both organic matter (sugars, fats and albuminous substances—the physical base of tissue) and inorganic matter (water and certain minerals). This inorganic matter we commonly call cell salts and they unite with and activate organic matter to enable our cells to function in a normal way. Our blood is a marvellous transport system and by supplying the correct tissue salts in a homoeopathic form, they are easily administered and readily taken up in the bloodstream to be made available to our cells. The cells can then select the nutrients they require to restore normal function.

Dr Scheussler's tissue salts are inexpensive and their safety and efficacy are well documented. They can be used in conjunction with other systems of medicine. Just as we need fertile soil in our garden to produce healthy plants, so we need a proper supply of all twelve tissue salts to enable our body to be healthy and strong.

CALCIUM FLUORIDE

This can be used for all relaxed conditions of tissue. Think of it for situations such as varicose conditions, prolapsed or displaced uterus and lack of uterine muscle tone. Calcium fluoride helps to maintain elasticity in the fibres of the skin, muscle tissue and blood vessels. It is a component of the hard surface of bones and tooth enamel.

Tongue indicator: swollen and cracked tongue.

CALCIUM PHOSPHATE

Calcium phosphate is the tissue builder. It unites with albumen to give strength to our bones and teeth and is also a constituent of blood cells and gastric juices. This cell salt can be used as a general tonic for lowered vitality and to improve digestion and assimilation of nutrients during convalescence. It should be considered for improving bone density or to assist tissue growth. It can also be used for chilblains.

Please note that in treating osteoporosis, cell salts do not provide adequate calcium levels to be used alone. An added supplement containing higher elemental levels of calcium and magnesium are needed in this condition.

Tongue indicator: pimples or blisters on tip; can feel numb and swollen.

CALCIUM SULPHATE

This is the blood cleanser and purifier. Use it to assist the removal of waste products from the blood, tissues and lymph glands. Try this cell salt if you have leucorrhoea and the discharge is thick and yellow. Calcium sulphate is indicated for slow healing wounds, sinus congestion and skin ailments (pimples, acne, boils, ulcers and abscesses).

Tongue indicator: tongue can be inflamed.

IRON PHOSPHATE (FERRUM PHOS)

Iron phosphate can be called the oxygen carrier. Our health cannot be maintained without the proper balance of iron in our blood. We use this cell salt in the treatment of anaemia. It is the initial salt to be considered in first-aid treatment of all conditions where there is inflammation or congestion, such as sore throats, fevers, coughs and colds. Think of it as a treatment for vaginal dryness, uterine congestion and heavy, painful menstruation. Iron phosphate also gives strength to arterial and blood vessel walls.

Tongue indicator: tongue is usually clean and dark red.

MAGNESIUM PHOSPHATE

This is a constituent of nerve tissue considered to be a nerve and muscle relaxant. It should be the first remedy to use in the treatment of muscular cramps and spasm anywhere in the body. Use it for menstrual cramping, headache, neuralgia, hiccups, convulsions, nervous tics and coughing fits. This remedy is best taken with warm water.

Tongue indicator: the tongue is usually clean.

POTASSIUM CHLORIDE (KALI MUR)

This is a glandular tonic that acts as a blood conditioner and liver salt. It is a remedy for sluggish conditions such as dyspepsia, indigestion and constipation. Stools are often pale or clay coloured indicating an insufficiency of bile. This remedy can be used for soft glandular swellings and catarrhal conditions of the middle ear. Think of this remedy if your menstrual blood is very dark and clotted, or if you have constant thick, white, non-irritating leucorrhoea.

Tongue indicators: coated greyish-white, can be dry or slimy.

POTASSIUM PHOSPHATE (KALI PHOS)

Potassium phosphate is known as the nerve nutrient. It is found in the grey matter of the brain and also in nerve tissue. If you are over-worked and feeling stressed, this may be the tissue salt you need. It is indicated for brain fag, nervous or tension headaches, nervous dyspepsia, fatigue, depression, irritability, sensitivity to noise and sleeplessness. It can also be used in the treatment of shingles. Think of it for premenstrual tension and irregular menstruation.

Tongue indicators: thick, yellow coating, dry on waking with offensive breath.

POTASSIUM SULPHATE (KALI SULPH)

Potassium sulphate is used as a skin salt. It helps to form the internal linings on our organs and mucous membranes as well as the layers of our skin. The sulphates are involved with the transfer of oxygen and kali sulph can be referred to as an oxygen carrier. It can be combined with iron phosphate to help with oxygen distribution to the cells. It is indicated for the treatment of rheumatic pain, chilliness, pins and needles, dizziness and bronchial asthma. Symptoms of deficiency can manifest in the skin causing psoriasis, dandruff and eczema. Think of this remedy if your menstrual bleeding is late and you feel heavy and full in your abdomen. It may help leucorrhoea when the discharge is yellow or greenish in colour and slimy.

Tongue indicator: tongue feels slimy with a yellow coating.

SILICEA

This cell salt is a cleanser and conditioner that improves toxic elimination. It is indicated in all conditions where there is suppuration such as recurring boils or abscesses. Silicea can also be used to check offensive perspiration, copious night sweats and is good for sweating, smelly feet. It maintains the health of our hair and skin and is a useful remedy for brittle nails.

Tongue indicator: ulcers on the tongue, hardening of the tongue.

SODIUM CHLORIDE (NAT MUR)

This tissue salt is the water or fluid distributor in the body. It maintains the degree of moisture needed for proper cell division and growth and it is associated with glandular activity and digestion. Sodium chloride can be used for either excessive fluid or dryness and thirst because it corrects fluid imbalances. There may be a craving for salty foods and excessive salivation. The eyes may water excessively and are easily irritated by the wind. Use this remedy for colds that start with sneezing and where the nasal discharge is thin and watery. Deficiencies of sodium chloride can lead to a constant desire to sleep and you wake tired and unrefreshed. Vaginal discharges and menstrual blood may be thin and watery causing itching and soreness. It is a good remedy for skin conditions that start with watery blisters such as herpes.

Tongue indicator: can be frothy with blisters on tip and bubbles on sides, mouth ulcers.

SODIUM PHOSPHATE (NAT PHOS)

This tissue salt is the acid neutraliser and so itn is useful in the treatment of rheumatic conditions, overacid stomach and heartburn. It regulates the consistency of bile and in doing so assists in the breakdown of fats during digestion. Deficiencies can lead to increased uric acid deposits around joints (gout). Think of this remedy for acrid vaginal discharges that smell sour and cause rawness, soreness and itching.

Tongue indicator: moist tongue and the back of the tongue appears creamy yellow.

SODIUM SULPHATE (NAT SULPH)
This tissue salt is the water or fluid eliminator and it is found in the intercellular fluids. A deficiency can prevent elimination leading to fluid retention and increased toxicity. There can also be an excess of bile production causing diarrhoea, biliousness and vomiting.
Tongue indicator: greenish-grey or greenish-brown coating at the root of the tongue. Mouth can feel slimy with a bitter taste.

Vitamins
VITAMIN A
Vitamin A is a fat-soluble vitamin that is essential to maintain the health of our skin, hair and all the mucous membranes in our body, that is, the tissue lining the mouth and throat as well as the entire digestive tract, stomach, lungs, uterus, vagina, bladder, rectum, eyes, ears, nose, sinus cavities etc. Vitamin A is involved in tooth development, bone growth, reproduction and has an important role in maintaining immunity.

There are two forms of vitamin A. One is called retinol, which is easily obtained and absorbed from animal products, such as liver. The other form is betacarotene (also called provitamin A), which is produced in plants.

There is no danger of toxicity from betacarotene because our bodies will only convert and absorb what it needs. Occasionally however, people develop yellow skin from consuming too much of it. This sometimes occurs when people fast on carrot juice. It is not considered dangerous and the symptom will go away when you stop the high intake.
Deficiency The first signs of a vitamin A deficiency will often be problems with your eyes. When there is a vitamin deficiency, they will often become dry, red and sore. You may have difficulty with your vision in low levels of light indicating a condition called night blindness. This is easily prevented and responds well to nutritional therapy to correct deficiencies. Another indicator for vitamin A therapy is a tendency to hayfever or sinus problems. When the tissue lining your sinus and nasal cavities is in poor health due to a vitamin A deficiency, you are more likely to react to airborne irritants such as dust or pollens. You will never get rid of these irritants, however you can make the internal environment of your body less reactive. This is also true for inflammation in the gastrointestinal tract. Wherever there is inflammation, there is redness, swelling and tenderness. In order to soothe and relieve this we need to improve the integrity of the tissue.
Eyes: dry, itchy, red, inflamed; night blindness.
Hair: dry
Mouth: loss of taste; gum disorders.
Nose: dry, scabby; poor smell; sinus.
Skeletal: thickening of bones; slow growth.
Scalp: dry, flaky, itchy, rough.
Skin: dry, rough; acne.
General: allergies; poor growth; susceptibility to infections.
RDA 5000–10,000 iu
During pregnancy: 2500 iu
Herbal sources Cayenne, dandelion, eyebright, golden seal, marshmallow, mint, paprika, parsley, raspberry leaf, violet, yellow dock.
Food sources Vitamin A foods not only provide nutrients, they are also healing foods, rich in natural mucilage to soothe and heal rather than irritate. Foods high in vitamin A tend to be

yellow or deep green because natural carotene is almost orange in colour. The darker the vegetable, the more betacarotene it contains. Vegetables containing betacarotene should be moderately cooked to improve their absorption. This fat-soluble vitamin is locked within the cellulose fibres of the vegetable. We need to soften these fibres in order to unlock this nutrient so yellow vegetables should be cooked while green vegetables can be eaten raw or steamed. Examples of these yellow vegetables are pumpkin, kumara, carrot, squash and sweet potato.

Other good sources of betacarotene are: dried apricots, beetroot, broccoli, kale, lemon grass, mangoes, nectarines, okra, papaya, peaches, red peppers, spinach, sunflower seeds, watercress.

Retinol source: beef liver, chicken liver, fish liver oils, pork liver.

B COMPLEX VITAMINS

The B complex group of vitamins are water-soluble nutrients that have a common source and usually act together. They are closely interrelated in their function and they should always be taken together. The proper absorption and utilisation of an individual B vitamin will usually be dependent on the others being present. For instance, it may be of no therapeutic value to take vitamin B6 alone because it may not be absorbed. However, if it is taken with a B complex formula there is a greater likelihood of it being utilised.

If you are feeling the effects of a high level of stress in your life you may benefit from taking a regular B complex formula. B complex nutrients are recommended for the treatment of the nervous system and its related illnesses, such as insomnia, anxiety and depression. If you are a smoker or you have a high alcohol intake, these nutrients are essential.

While the individual B vitamins can have specific actions, in nature a single vitamin is never isolated from the rest.

VITAMIN B1: THIAMINE

Thiamine is beneficial for the health of our entire nervous system and it is specifically involved with the transmission of nerve impulses. It also has a role in digestion and is part of a co-enzyme that is responsible for over 24 enzyme systems.

Deficiency Thiamine deficiencies are commonly seen in people with a high alcohol intake and anorexic women. The signs are:

Digestive: constipation; loss of appetite; nausea; vomiting.

Mind: inability to concentrate.

Mood: depression; irritability; vague feelings of anxiety and uneasiness.

Muscular: pain in the calf muscles.

General: fatigue; headaches; poor hand–eye co-ordination; laboured breathing; insomnia.

RDA 1–5 mg

Herbal sources Dandelion, fenugreek, kelp, marshmallow, raspberry leaf.

Food sources Asparagus, barley, beef, Brazil nuts, legumes, liver, okra, pecan nuts, pine nuts, pork, walnuts, wheat bran, wheat germ.

Note: Thiamine is heat sensitive; when cooking green vegetables, lightly steam rather than boil.

VITAMIN B2: RIBOFLAVIN

Riboflavin is necessary for all cell reproduction and it is essential for the growth and repair of body tissue, including nerve tissue. It is found in every cell in the body and it is beneficial for maintaining normal

eyesight and healthy skin, nails and hair. It works closely with vitamin A.
Deficiency Eyes: sensitive to light; blurred vision; itchy eyelids; increased tears; blood shot; cataracts.
Lips: red; burning; peeling.
Mouth: cracks and sores in the corners of the mouth.
Nose: scaling around nostrils.
Nails: skin cracking around base of nails.
Scalp: seborrhoea (like cradle cap).
Skin: dermatitis; flaky around nose and eyebrows.
Tongue: geographic (looks like a map); purple colour; sore/inflamed tongue.
Urine: inability to urinate.
General: oversensitive to cold and pain.
RDA 1.5–2 mg
Herbal sources Fenugreek, kelp, marshmallow, rosehips, saffron.
Food sources Almonds, brewer's yeast, eggs, dairy products, liver, okra, pork, wheat germ.

VITAMIN B3: NIACIN

This nutrient is involved in the digestion of macronutrients by stimulating bile and gastric secretions. It also lowers cholesterol and helps to regulate fats in the blood. Niacin is necessary for the manufacture of our hormones. It nourishes our nerves, skin, brain and hair and is required for proper function of the liver. Synthetic forms of niacin are niacinamide, nicotinic acid nicotinamid.
Deficiency Mood: irritability; depression.
Mouth: bad breath; tender gums; ulcers.
Muscular: weakness.
Skin: dermatitis; rough, inflamed skin.
Stomach: indigestion; loss of appetite; nausea; vomiting; inflammation.
Tongue: red; inflamed.
General: fatigue; memory loss;

recurring headaches; tension; tremors.
RDA 13–18 mg
Herbal sources Alfalfa, kelp, fenugreek.
Food sources Almonds, chicken, eggs, legumes, mackerel, okra, peanuts, salmon, sardines, sunflower seeds, wheat germ.

VITAMIN B5: PANTOTHENIC ACID

Pantothenic acid can improve our bodies' ability to withstand ongoing stressful conditions and it is involved in the breakdown and storage of glucose for energy. It helps to increase vitality and is particularly useful for people who use lots of adrenalin, such as athletes. Pantothenic acid is essential for the formation of cholesterol, fatty acids and hormones. Along with other nutrients it can help to prevent premature ageing and wrinkles.
Deficiency A deficiency of this nutrient is extremely rare because it is widely distributed in food, however low dietary intakes of B5 may contribute to a slow metabolic rate.
Bowel: constipation.
Feet: burning; tenderness of heels.
Hair: dry; loss of hair; premature greying.
Immunity: decreased antibody formation.
Mouth: ulcers.
Muscular: cramps.
Nails: split.
Skin: dermatitis.
Stomach: underacidity, vomiting.
General: fatigue; low blood sugar; restlessness.
RDA 5–10 mg
Food sources Avocado, brewer's yeast, egg yolk, green leafy vegetables, liver, molasses, peanuts, royal jelly, wholegrains.
Other sources It is synthesised by bacterial flora in the intestines.

VITAMIN B6: PYRIDOXINE

Vitamin B6 is needed for the production of hydrochloric acid in the stomach and the formation of over 60 enzymes. Pyridoxine has a vital role in many biochemical reactions including the regulation of blood sugar levels and the manufacture of haemoglobin for oxygen transport in the blood. It assists in the formation of hormones and neurotransmitters and helps to maintain the correct balance of sodium and potassium in our body. This regulates fluids and promotes a healthy nervous system. B6 also works with magnesium to help eliminate excess hormones via the liver, which makes it useful in treating side effects of the oral contraceptive pill.

Deficiency Vitamin B6 deficiency can be quite common because pyridoxine is not stored in our body as it is flushed out in the urine within eight hours of ingestion. Women often have an increased need for foods containing B6 and if they follow low-calorie diets for long periods of time they may be prone to deficiency.

Three classic signs of pyridoxine deficiency are cracks in the corners of the mouth, inflammation of the tongue and patches of itchy, scaling skin.
Other deficiency signs are:
Extremities: tingling; numbness; burning feet.
Eyes: cracks at corners; visual disturbance.
Hair: thinning and loss of hair.
Mood: depression; irritability.
Mouth: fissures and cracks at corners.
Muscular: weakness and cramps.
Skin: acne; dermatitis; eczema; psoriasis.
Urine: increased urination.
General: fluid retention; arthritis associated with menopause; low blood sugar.

RDA 1.5–2.6 mg
Note: B6 is an antagonist to the drug Levadopa, which is used to treat Parkinson's disease. Do not take more than 5 mg of B6 per day with this drug or you may render it inactive.

Food sources Bananas, brewer's yeast, chicken, currants, dried apricots, liver, potatoes, prunes, salmon, soy beans, sunflower seeds, sweet potato, tuna, turkey, walnuts, wholegrains.

VITAMIN B12

This is essential for the formation of new blood, normal growth and healthy nerve tissue. Iron functions better in the body with the aid of B12. It is prepared for absorption by gastric secretions and a special enzyme called the 'intrinsic factor' must be present. Failure to produce this enzyme will result in pernicious anaemia.

Deficiency Vitamin B12 is stored in the liver and the body uses it sparingly so deficiencies are rare as long as you eat animal products. Strict vegetarians who eat no eggs or dairy products must watch their diet very closely to avoid deficiencies. Others at risk are those who have gastro-intestinal diseases, such as Crohns Disease or ulcerative colitis, because these illnesses can cause malabsorption problems.

Deficiencies of B12 and folic acid can cause a type of anaemia called megoblastic anaemia. In this condition red blood cells fail to mature properly in the bone marrow and become large and misshapen. Symptoms of this are fatigue and shortness of breath. The symptoms of B12 deficiency can take years to develop and if they remain undetected and untreated, they can cause irreversible nerve damage. They are:
Extremities: numbness and tingling; walking difficulties.
Eyes: double vision.
Muscular: weakness.
Stomach: poor appetite.
Tongue: inflamed, sore.
General: diminished reflex response; hot and cold sensations; memory loss; nervousness; stammering; confusion; unpleasant body odour; weight loss.
Note: Consult your doctor if you suspect B12 deficiency because in order to correct it you may need a series of regular B12 injections that put the nutrient straight into the bloodstream.
RDA 2–5 micrograms (mcg)
Herbal sources Alfalfa, kelp
Food sources Animal protein such as kidney and liver, dairy products (especially non-fat dry milk powder), eggs, fish, molasses, mushrooms, shellfish, tempeh, wheat germ.

BIOTIN
Biotin is an essential nutrient that helps to make fatty acids and is involved in the production of energy in our body.

It helps our body utilise protein, folic acid, B5 and B12 and it is a potent stimulator of cell growth.
Deficiency Deficiencies can arise from eating large amounts of raw egg white as it contains a protein that will bind with biotin and prevent it being absorbed. The same protein is inactivated by heat so cooking the egg will prevent the problem.

Symptoms can be muscular pain, fatigue, poor appetite and sleeplessness. Skin: will also become dry; appear grey in colour; dermatitis can develop.
Hair: baldness can be related to biotin deficiency.
General: a lack of biotin can lead to elevated blood cholesterol levels.
RDA 200 micrograms (mcg)
Food sources Bean sprouts, brewer's yeast, egg yolk, liver, milk, soy beans.
Other sources Can be synthesised by bacteria in the gut.

VITAMIN C: Ascorbic acid
Vitamin C is an antioxidant vitamin that is a water-soluble essential nutrient. An antioxidant prevents substances in our body from breaking down and combining with other substances that may be harmful. Vitamin C produces and maintains collagen which is essential for the formation and repair of connective tissue, muscles, bones, teeth and skin. It also helps to form red blood cells and prevent haemorrhage. It helps to fight infections and is a natural anti-inflammatory. It protects the vitamins B1, B2, folic acid, pantothenic acid A and E from oxidation.
Deficiency Extremities: swollen or painful joints.
Gastrointestinal: poor digestion.
Gums: bleeding.
Mood: depression.

Nose: nosebleeds.
Skin: capillary fragility; easy bruising;
poor wound healing; rough skin.
General: shortness of breath; poor
lactation; susceptibility to infection;
weakened tooth enamel.

RDA 70–150 mg

If you are taking a supplement, it may
be useful to know that very little
vitamin C is absorbed in high doses;
absorption is improved if it is
administered in smaller amounts more
often. For instance, it is better to take
250 mg four times a day than to take
1000 mg once a day. If you take high
levels of vitamin C, you should also
increase your calcium intake.

Note: High doses of vitamin C can
cause headaches. This does not occur
when it is administered by intravenous
methods.

Herbal sources Burdock, calendula,
chervil, elder berries, marshmallow,
paprika, parsley, raspberry leaf,
rosehips, stinging nettles.

Food sources Blackcurrant, broccoli,
cabbage, cantaloupe, capsicum, citrus
fruits, guavas, kale, kiwi fruit, melons,
papaya, strawberries, tomato, watercress.

Note: Vitamin C loses its potency
when it exposed to light, heat and
air. For this reason foods containing
this nutrient should be eaten fresh
and preferably raw. Cooking these
foods at boiling point can destroy this
nutrient.

CHOLINE

Choline assists digestion and helps to
maintain a healthy nervous system. It is
a basic constituent of lecithen and is
involved in breaking up and
transporting fats in our body. This
prevents fatty accumulation in the liver
and it aids in the prevention of gall
stones.

Deficiency Fatty deposits in the liver
accumulate because of prolonged
deficiencies. These can result in poor
digestion, high blood pressure, kidney
and heart problems. Some signs may be
palpitations, dizziness, ear noises,
constipation, headaches and visual
disturbances.

RDA 1 gram

Food sources Brewer's yeast, egg yolk,
lecithen, liver, milk, wheat germ.

VITAMIN D

Vitamin D is a fat-soluble vitamin that
aids in the absorption and utilisation of
calcium and phosphorus for the
formation of bones and teeth.

The relationship it has with these
two minerals makes it a strong
contributor to the maintenance and
stability of our nervous system, normal
heart action and normal blood
clotting. It is also involved in enzyme
reaction and it affects the acidity of
gastric juices.

We obtain vitamin D from food and
also from the sun. Ultraviolet rays
from the sun activate a type of
cholesterol in the skin and converts it
to vitamin D.

Deficiency Vitamin D deficiency is rare
in this country because of the strong
sunlight. We must be careful though, to
keep sun exposure to a minimum to
prevent the development of skin
cancer.

Because deficiencies of vitamin D will
result in incomplete absorption of
calcium and phosphorus, bone
structures will be affected.

Signs of deficiency are softening of
bones (rickets); bone malformation
such as bowed legs and curved spine;
enlarged joints; loss of bone density.
The muscles can also be affected
causing numbness, tingling and spasm.

There can be increased nervous irritability and because vitamin D is involved with the production of thyroid hormones, a deficiency can affect metabolism.

Vitamin D deficiency has also been associated with tooth decay and gum disease.

RDA 400 iu

Vitamin D must be supported with adequate levels of calcium and phosphorus in order for it to be effective.

Herbal sources Alfalfa, dandelion (flower)

Food sources Fish oils, lettuce, milk, sprouted seeds, sunflower seeds, watercress, wheat germ.

Other sources Sun exposure

VITAMIN E: Tocopherol

Vitamin E is a fat-soluble vitamin that is part of the antioxidant group. As an antioxidant it protects against cancer, heart disease, ageing, eye problems, diabetes and arthritis.

Many studies have shown the benefits of vitamin E in the prevention of heart disease and clot formation. It has a beneficial action on all the tissues in our body by maintaining tissue elasticity, assisting healing processes and reducing scar formation.

The addition of vitamin E to the diet can regulate menstrual rhythms and reduce flushing and headache during menopause.

Deficiency One of the first signs of vitamin E deficiency can be ruptured blood vessels due to fragile capillaries.

The vascular and immune system may be weaker so there can be a worsening of varicose veins and varicose ulcers. The skin can become dry and inelastic with an increased risk of infection.

Vitamin E is involved with oxygen transport in the body and deficiencies can cause a myriad of serious health problems.

There is a stronger likelihood of haemorrhage during menstrual bleeding and fertility may be impaired.

Severe vitamin E deficiency may also contribute to an increased risk of miscarriage.

RDA 12–18 mg

Herbal sources Alfalfa, dandelion leaves, kelp, raspberry leaf, rosehips.

Food sources Almonds, brown rice, linseeds, nuts, sunflower seeds, sesame seeds, wheat germ.

FOLIC ACID

Folic acid is a basic compound in a group of water-soluble nutrients that also include Folates and Folacin.

Folic acid plays an important part in cell growth and division. It is necessary in the formation of red blood cells and helps to breakdown and utilise protein.

It can increase the appetite and stimulates hydrochloric acid in the stomach, which is needed for proper digestion. This also helps to prevent intestinal worms and food poisoning.

This nutrient can help to improve liver function and when taken by pregnant women will help prevent neural tube defects in infants.

Deficiency Hair: premature greyness; hair loss (especially after pregnancy).
Mood: Irritability.
Mouth: ulcers.
Nails: flake.
Tongue: inflammation; redness.
General: tiredness; low libido.

RDA 400 microgram (mcg)

Note: While anticonvulsants can deplete folic acid, please note that large doses of this nutrient can increase seizures.

Food sources Avocados, cashews, eggs,

green leafy vegetables, lentils, organ meats, parsnips, soy beans, sunflower seeds, wheat germ.

INOSITOL

Like choline, inositol is found in high concentrations in lecithen and so has a similar function in the body. It breaks down and transports fats and helps to reduce cholesterol. Inositol is beneficial in the cellular nutrition of our brain, bone marrow, eyes and intestines. It helps prevent baldness and thinning hair.

Deficiency High intakes of coffee or cola drinks can deplete inositol and deficiency signs are constipation, skin and eye problems.

RDA 500–1000 mg

Food sources Brewer's yeast, citrus fruits, corn, liver, molasses, nuts and seeds.

Other sources Bacterial synthesis in the gut.

VITAMIN K

Vitamin K is a fat-soluble vitamin that is necessary for the prevention of haemorrhage. It is produced in the intestines by certain intestinal bacteria, mixed with bile and transported to the liver. In the liver it helps to form a chemical called prothrombin that is required for the proper clotting time of blood.

Vitamin K production is improved by including yoghurt, which is rich in acidophilus and bifida organisms, in your diet.

Deficiency Deficiencies can be found in people with inflammatory diseases of the intestines. The symptoms are haemorrhage, bruising, menstrual problems, prolonged blood clotting time, miscarriage, nosebleeds and slow wound healing.

RDA 150 micrograms (mcg)

Herbal sources Alfalfa, kelp, shepherds purse.

Food sources Broccoli, cabbage, chestnuts, liver, peanuts, pork, spinach, soya beans, sunflower seeds, yoghurt.

The following nutrients are not considered to be true vitamins by the Federal Health Department. Nevertheless, they are contained in our foods so I have included a brief summary of each.

BIOFLAVANOIDS

The bioflavanoids are rutin, quercetin, citrin and hesperidin and they are closely associated with vitamin C. They are a component of many fruits and vegetables and were first discovered in the white segments and skin of citrus fruits. They improve the absorption of vitamin C, protect against infection and help to keep collagen (our cellular cement) in a healthy condition.

Bioflavanoids strengthen our blood capillaries, help to prevent haemorrhage and can minimise bruising. They will help to prevent spider veins on cheeks and thighs. One of the bioflavanoids, rutin, is particularly useful in treating varicose veins and haemorrhoids.

Herbal sources Alfalfa, lemon grass, paprika, rosehips.

Food sources Capsicums, black currants, buckwheat, pith and skin of citrus fruits, cherries, rosehips and plums.

A good way to increase bioflavanoids in the diet is to add some of the finely grated skin of citrus fruits into freshly squeezed juices.

PARA-AMINO-BENZOIC ACID: PABA

PABA is a constituent of folic acid and is involved in the formation of red blood cells.

It plays an important role in determining the health of our intestines, skin and hair. It also influences the pigmentation of our skin and hair and has been used in the prevention and treatment of grey hair. It acts as a natural sunscreen and is often a constituent of sunscreen lotions.

Food sources Brewer's yeast, liver, molasses, yoghurt, wheat germ.

PANGAMIC ACID: B15
This is a naturally occurring element in some food. It increases the uptake of oxygen into our tissues and improves circulation. It also assists in the utilisation of fat in our body. Pangamic acid helps to reduce lactic acid build-up in muscle tissue during exercise.

Food sources Brewer's yeast, pumpkin seeds, sesame seeds, wholegrains.

VITAMIN U
This is not considered to be a true vitamin by the Federal Health Department, however it is a property found in cabbage and sauerkraut that has been shown to promote the healing of peptic and duodenal ulcers. Try a small glass of cabbage juice daily.

Minerals
CALCIUM
Calcium is the most abundant mineral in the body. It combines with phosphorus to form calcium phosphate which gives density and hardness to our teeth and bones. It is essential for healthy blood and is involved in regulating our heartbeat. Calcium also maintains the health of our nervous and muscular systems.

Deficiency The increased incidence of osteoporosis in women has alerted women to the need for adequate daily intakes of calcium. Despite this, some women still consume very little and pave the way for deficiencies to occur.

Calcium absorption can be highly inefficient. It requires the presence of vitamins A, C, D, magnesium, phosphorus and silica in order for it to be utilised.

It is possible to have a deficiency for a long time and not notice any symptoms, resulting in serious loss of bone density.

Deficiency signs are:
Extremities: numbness and tingling in the arms and legs; joint pain.
Heart: palpitations; slow pulse rate.
General: tooth decay; muscle cramps; insomnia; irritability of nerves and muscles; slow blood clotting time.

RDA 800–1400 mg
It is not wise to take calcium alone without the buffering effect of magnesium. They should be in a ratio of two parts calcium to one part magnesium.

Herbal sources Alfalfa, chamomile, chives, clivers, dandelion, horsetail, meadowsweet, plantain, raspberry leaf, shepherds purse, sorrel, stinging nettles.

Food sources Almonds, dairy products, egg yolk, hommos, molasses, rhubarb, salmon, sardines.

CHLORINE
This is an essential mineral that is widely distributed in the body in the form of chloride. It helps to regulate the acid/alkali balance in the blood and it stimulates the production of hydrochloric acid in the gut to ensure proper digestion. It helps to distribute hormones and clear toxic waste out of the body.

Deficiency Deficiencies rarely occur because most people obtain this

nutrient from table salt and drinking water. Deficiencies include hair and tooth loss, poor digestion and poor muscular contraction.
RDA Nil
Herbal sources Alfalfa, kelp.
Food sources Potato, beetroot, coconut, figs, olives, radish, rye.

CHROMIUM

Chromium is essential for the metabolism and regulation of blood glucose in our body.
Deficiency Deficiency symptoms can be anxiety, fatigue and weight loss.

Chromium can be difficult to absorb and when a deficiency occurs it usually affects the body in a serious way. This is because it can interfere with our bodies' ability to convert glucose for energy. In severe cases this may cause diabetes.
RDA 50–200 micrograms (mcg)
Food sources Asparagus, brewer's yeast, cheese, egg yolk, liver, molasses, mushrooms, nuts, oysters, prunes, wholegrains.

COBALT

Cobalt is a mineral necessary for normal maintenance and functioning of red blood cells. Our body primarily depends on animal sources for this mineral although ocean vegetation will provide some. Most of the cobalt we absorb is excreted in the urine after it have been used by our body.
Herbal sources Kelp.
Food sources Clams, liver, kidney, oysters, milk.

COPPER

Copper is an essential trace mineral involved with the transport of oxygen in the body. It is a constituent of many enzymes and it functions as an antioxidant.

It is involved in the maintenance of our skin, hair, bones and the proper function of our nerves.

This mineral works closely with vitamin C to maintain the health of body tissues and muscle fibres.
Deficiency Deficiencies symptoms are weakness and skin sores.
RDA 2 mg
Food sources Almonds, green leafy vegetables, legumes, liver, potato, wholegrains.

FLUORIDE

There has been much debate over the issue of fluoride. It is routinely added to the water supply in many cities and towns in the form of sodium fluoride, which is a by-product of aluminium refining. Calcium fluoride is the form that this trace element is found in nature. It is available as a tissue salt, and good natural sources are mackerel, sardines and sunflower seeds.

There is no doubt that fluoride has a protective role for the teeth. Extensive studies have revealed that the addition of fluoride in toothpastes and public water supplies has greatly reduced the amount of tooth decay and cavities. It does this by improving the absorption of calcium, which strengthens teeth, and fluoride also reduces acid in the mouth. Sugary foods, soft drinks and fruit juices all contain acids that soften tooth enamel and increase the risk of cavities.

Excessive levels of fluoride in the body however, can lead to the development of fluorosis. When fluoride reaches a dangerous level, the teeth develop a mottled appearance. Chronic cases of fluoride toxicity have been linked with cancer and bone abnormalities.

If you are concerned that you have a high fluoride intake, you may well decide to drink bottled or filtered water and use a toothpaste that does not contain fluoride. It can be difficult to make a decision about fluoride intake. Some studies reveal that in areas where they add fluoride to the water there is a higher incidence of fluoridosis. Other studies reveal that in areas where it is not added, the incidence of decay is high.

Of course, you can always take a balanced approach, and drink filtered water but still use a fluoridated toothpaste. Your teeth will benefit slightly from the fluoride in the toothpaste but you reduce the risk of overloading your body with fluoride.

There are two types of flouride: sodium fluoride, which is added to drinking water and calcium fluoride, which occurs in nature.

Deficiency Extremely rare.
RDA Not available.
Herbal sources Garlic
Food sources Cabbage, spinach, watercress.

IODINE

Iodine is converted to iodide in our bodies and it assists in the proper function of the thyroid gland. It is involved in the production of the hormone thyroxine. This hormone affects both our physical and mental development. It has an important role in stimulating our metabolic rate and regulating energy production and it helps the body burn excess fat.

Deficiency Deficiencies are related to under-activity of the thyroid gland which causes weight gain, deepening of the voice, general sluggishness, dry hair, slow mental reactions, palpitations, nervousness and irritability. The thyroid gland in the neck can enlarge resulting in a goitre.
RDA 150 mcg
Herbal sources Black walnut, garlic, irish moss, kelp.
Food sources Agar agar, artichoke, beans, cod, iodised salt, mushroom, oysters, sunflower seeds.

IRON

Iron transports oxygen around the body and is responsible for many enzyme reactions.
Deficiency The most common iron deficiency is anaemia which causes pale skin, constipation, fatigue, brittle, spoon shaped nails, sore tongue, blue sclera (whites of the eyes), and shortness of breath. Iron deficiency can also cause absence of menstruation (amenorrhoea) and chronic vaginal infections.
RDA 10–20 mg
Herbal sources Alfalfa, burdock, dandelion, gotu kola, meadowsweet, mullein, parsley, raspberry leaf, red clover, stinging nettles, yellow dock.
Food sources Apricots, asparagus, barley, bran, lentils, lettuce, liver, red meats, spinach, strawberry, watercress.

MAGNESIUM

Magnesium is essential for many biological functions in the body. It is involved with muscular contraction, nerve impulses and the conversion of blood sugar into energy. It has a role in the prevention of heart disease and can reduce pain caused by vascular disorders.

Magnesium helps to form the hard enamel on our teeth and it is found in high concentrations in our bones. It is a very important nutrient to use in the treatment and prevention of osteoporosis and research shows that this mineral has a key role in improving bone density.

It is a highly alkaline substance that acts as an antacid in the body and it also helps to regulate body temperature.

In order to prevent the formation of calcium stones in the kidneys and cholesterol deposits in arteries our diet needs to include some foods that contain magnesium.

The balance between magnesium and calcium is very important. If magnesium levels are high and calcium levels are low, toxic symptoms can develop. On the other hand, if calcium is very high then magnesium intake also needs to be high, in order to buffer the calcium This should be considered if you take a daily calcium supplement that does not contain the correct ratio of magnesium. The ratio of calcium to magnesium should be 2:1. For example, if you are taking 800 mg of calcium in a supplement form then you will also need 400 mg of magnesium.

Deficiency Generally your body will regulate magnesium absorption to meet its needs. Some illnesses such as alcoholism, kidney disease or diabetes and certain drugs can interfere with the absorption of this nutrient.

Deficiency signs are depression, insomnia, restlessness, muscular twitching and tremors, apprehensiveness, confusion and disorientation.

To overcome magnesium deficiency you may need to remove milk from the diet.

RDA 350 mg

Herbal sources Black willow, broom tops, dandelion, gotu kola, kelp, meadowsweet, mullein, parsley, peppermint, walnut leaves, wintergreen.

Food sources Almonds, cashews, citrus fruits, kale, legumes, nuts and seeds, okra, prunes, tofu (bean curd), watercress, wheat bran, wheat germ.

Other sources It is high in a synthetic form of vitamin D (calciferol), which can bind with magnesium and inhibit its absorption.

MANGANESE

Manganese is a trace mineral that has a key role in digestion. It is involved in the activation of enzymes and the metabolism of fats and carbohydrates. Manganese helps to maintain the production of sex hormones and it helps to nourish our nervous system.

Deficiency We only require very small amounts of manganese but we can have difficulty absorbing it if we have a high calcium intake.

Deficiency symptoms can be ear noises, dizziness and loss of hearing.

RDA 2.5–7 mg

Herbal sources Kelp, mint, parsley, nasturtium flowers.

Food sources Almonds, coconut, corn, endive, olives, peanuts, potato, walnuts, watercress, wheat germ.

MOLYBDENUM

This is a trace mineral that is present in almost all plant and animal tissues. It has an essential role in bringing iron out of storage from our liver reserves and helps to prevent dental caries.

Deficiency It is widely found in food so deficiency is extremely rare.

RDA 0.15–5 micrograms (mcg)

Herbal sources Nettles, parsley, raspberry leaf.

Food sources Dark green leafy vegetables, legumes, liver, oats, sunflower seeds, wheat germ, wholegrains.

NICKEL

Nickel is an essential trace mineral found in our body but very little is known about its application in human nutrition.

PHOSPHORUS

Phosphorus is present in every cell in our body and plays a part in almost every chemical reaction. It often functions with calcium and in order for either of them to be used effectively they must occur in the correct balance.

Phosphorus helps to form phospholipids, such as lecithen, to effectively transport fats and fatty acids in our bodies. It is involved in the production of energy, bone and tooth development, kidney function and muscular contractions. Phosphorus helps to keep our nervous systems healthy and our minds sharp.

Deficiency Deficiencies of phosphorus can cause irregular breathing, mental and physical fatigue, nervous disorders, arthritis and poor quality bones and teeth.

RDA 800 mg

Herbal sources Alfalfa, calamus, caraway, calendula, chickweed, garlic, licorice, meadowsweet, oats, raspberry leaf.

Food sources Almonds, barley, cabbage, lentils, okra, peas, sesame seeds, sorrel, watercress.

POTASSIUM: (K)

Potassium is the third most abundant element in our body and it is essential for life. It is often referred to as the muscle mineral because it plays a key role in the function of nerve and muscle tissue, including the heart muscle.

It performs as an electrolyte, carrying a tiny electrical charge to promote muscular contraction. Most of the potassium in our bodies is stored in muscle tissue. Potassium and sodium work together to maintain the fluid volume in our cells, ensuring there is a proper distribution of fluid on either side of our cell walls. It is involved in digestion and helps to regulate the acid/alkali balance in our body.

Both too much and too little potassium can seriously upset the body's delicate metabolic processes.

Deficiency A severe potassium deficiency can lead to heart failure. Sudden death can occur from starvation, fasting, severe and ongoing diarrhoea and low calorie liquid-protein diets.

The first sign of potassium deficiency is a severe lack of energy. You feel so weak you can hardly lift your arms. If you suspect you have a potassium deficiency, talk to your health practitioner before you take supplements. If you are taking a diuretic, check with your doctor that it is potassium sparing, otherwise, supplementation may be necessary.

Circulatory: irregular heartbeat.

Digestive: continuous thirst; constipation.

Mood: irritability; depression.

Muscular: weakness; paralysis; cramps and spasm.

Reproductive: temporary sterility due to loss of Follicle Stimulating Hormone (FSH).

Skeletal: bone fragility due to calcium loss.

Skin: acne; dryness.

General: acidosis; cognitive impairment; insomnia; tiredness; weight loss.

Note: A high intake of licorice, either from a herbal source or from eating too much of the confectionary type, can cause potassium depletion. This is

271

completely reversed without harmful effects, as soon as licorice intake is stopped.

RDA 2–5 gram.

Herbal sources Alfalfa, blackberry, borage, calamus, chamomile, dandelion, eyebright, fennel, mint, mullein, oak bark, parsley, peppermint, plantain, primrose flowers, stinging nettles, summer savory, walnut leaves, yarrow.

Note: Many herbal diuretics contain potassium.

Food sources Almonds, apricots, avocado, banana, brewer's yeast, cashews, citrus fruits, coconut, currants, dates, figs, lentils, lettuce, milk (skim), peaches (dried), pecan nuts, potato (skins), prunes, pumpkin seeds, raisins, sardines, sunflower seeds, turkey, vegetables (all), watercress, wheat germ.

SELENIUM: Se

This trace mineral is an antioxidant, which means it prevents deterioration at a cellular level. It assists chemical detoxification, improves immune function and helps prevent disease.

A healthy level of selenium can improve the action of vitamin E, however a deficiency of selenium can accentuate a deficiency of vitamin E.

Selenium is a micronutrient that is only required in the body in small amounts.

It has been shown to have a role in sex hormone production.

Studies have shown deficiencies of this nutrient in our soils so we cannot be certain we are obtaining adequate amounts in our food.

Nutritional supplements of selenium are only available in Australia on prescription. If you have a serious illness, such as cancer, and would like to include selenium in your nutritional program you will need to ask your doctor to prescribe it. The name of a selenium supplement is Selemite B.

Deficiency Premature ageing; inappropriate bruising; heart disease; infection; liver damage; muscle degeneration.

RDA 50–200 micrograms (mcg)

Herbal sources Garlic.

Food sources Baked beans, Brazil nuts, chicken, cottage cheese, eggs, lean meat, milk, organ meats, oysters, prawns, salmon, tuna, whole wheat cereal.

The above sources yield adequate levels of selenium, however the content in food is highly dependent on where it is grown.

SILICON: Si

This is a major constituent of collagen which is the substance that holds cells together. It is found virtually in all cells of the body and it is like the formwork in cement. It is present in connective tissue, bones, teeth, skin, eyes, glands and nails.

This mineral is required for elasticity in our skin and resilience of connective tissue. Silicon also reduces infiltration of cholesterol into the arterial walls. Dietary deficiency of Silica can reduce our ability to absorb and utilise other nutrients, such as calcium.

Deficiency Nails: soft, splitting or brittle.

Hair: dull, lifeless, split, thinning.

Bones: fragile; osteoporosis.

Teeth: increased cavities; weakened enamel.

Skin: easily damaged.

RDA 9–14 mg

Herbal sources Alfalfa, celery, horsetail (excellent source), oatstraw tea.

Food sources All stringy fruits and

vegetables, that is, asparagus, artichoke, cabbage, celery, leeks, mango, mushroom, radish, rhubarb, spinach, squash, strawberry, tomato, turnip, sunflower seeds.

It should be easy to maintain enough silicon in the diet. However if you still cut the strings off celery, beans and rhubarb or buy mangoes that are not stringy, you may be missing out on some good dietary sources of this nutrient.

SODIUM: Na

Sodium is an essential nutrient in our diet that maintains blood pressure and is necessary for the transmission of impulses in nerve and muscle tissue. It also plays an important role in our fluid and electrolyte balance.

Deficiency It is extremely rare to develop a deficiency in sodium because our nutritional needs are so small and this mineral is so widespread in our food.

The following symptoms may occur during excessive exercise, from certain diuretics or if you have been burnt: headache, low blood pressure, tachycardia (racing heart), weakness, nausea, diarrhoea, severe muscle cramp, mental confusion.

RDA There is no recommended dietary allowance for sodium in Australia, however it is generally considered that we need 200–300 mg each day.

One level teaspoon of sodium chloride (salt) yields 2000 mg of sodium. One slice of bread contains approximately 150 mg.

Herbal sources Alfalfa, celery, clivers, fennel, kelp, meadowsweet, shepherds purse, stinging nettle, willow.

Food sources Capsicum, cheese, lentils, liver, olives, peas, salmon, sardines, soy sauce, tuna.

SULPHUR

Sulphur is an element that occurs widely in nature. It is called the 'beauty mineral' because it keeps our hair glossy and our skin clear and youthful. It has a number of functions in the body and is a component of many different substances that are necessary for overall health and maintenance.

Sulphur requirements are met when protein intake is adequate.

Herbal sources Broom tops, eyebright, fennel, garlic, horseradish, meadowsweet, mullein, plantain, shepherds purse.

Food sources Cabbage, cauliflower, chestnuts, figs, okra, onions, oranges, potato, watercress.

VANADIUM

This is a trace mineral that inhibits cholesterol build-up on arterial walls. It should always be taken in a natural form.

Herbal sources Kelp.

Food sources Corn, linseed, rye, seafood, soy beans.

ZINC: Zn

Zinc is a trace mineral that is responsible for tissue regeneration, cell multiplication, proper growth and sexual maturity. It is involved in protein digestion, the regulation of insulin and our bodies' numerous enzyme systems. Zinc has a role in regulating the immune system and it speeds wound healing. Our sensory functions are maintained by zinc and it is crucial for proper brain development. Zinc is synergistic with vitamin A and it is concentrated mainly in our eyes, skin, hair and nails.

Deficiency Severe deficiencies of zinc are rare today, however low-grade

273

deficiencies commonly occur. Women must be sure to include zinc-rich foods in their daily diet, especially during pregnancy to prevent birth defects. Older women can be susceptible to deficiency due to impaired absorption and poor dietary habits. A high calcium intake can interfere with zinc absorption.

The first sign of a zinc deficiency is often loss of taste and smell. Other signs are:

Digestive: loss of appetite.
Hair: dull, lifeless; alopecia (hair loss).
Mood: depression; general moodiness.
Nails: white spots on fingernails.
Reproductive: sterility; impotence (in males); delayed sexual maturation.
Skin: dermatitis; gum diseases; slow wound healing (may also be protein deficiency); stretch marks.
General: dementia; learning disorders; poor immunity; inability to concentrate; poor memory; sleep problems.
RDA 15 mg. Pregnancy: 20 mg.

Remember that zinc is a trace mineral and these minerals are found in very low amounts in our bodies. While it is important to avoid and correct deficiencies, we must also be careful with supplements not to take more than we need. Research shows that we absorb more zinc when dietary levels are also low. Taking high doses of zinc usually leads to poor absorption and a high excretion.

Food sources Beef, Brazil nuts, liver, peanuts, pecan nuts, pine nuts, pumpkin seeds, oysters, shellfish, skim milk, sunflower seeds, turkey, wheat germ, wholegrains, yeast.

I have included this information on individual nutrients as a reference and general guide to their sources so that you can benefit from nutritional medicine. Try to keep this information in perspective and always look to the food sources as your self-help approach to achieving good health.

If you suspect that you are ill because of a possible deficiency and you feel you would like some advice about nutritional therapy, see a qualified health practitioner who has studied nutrition. They will carry out a proper health and dietary assessment and provide you with a treatment regime according to your individual needs.

In Conclusion

WOMEN'S *Health in Women's Hands* grew from my desire to share information and to encourage women to have faith in their ability to heal themselves and others. Traditionally women have been healers, not only as midwives, herbalists and nurses but also in our role as mothers and carers. We have developed healing skills over a long time and the importance of these skills is becoming increasingly recognised and valued in our society today.

We must maintain control over our health and broaden our outlook regarding health options. The process of marketing pharmaceuticals to women, for example, must be challenged. We should learn from the mistakes of the past, some of which have affected thousands of women and continue to do so. I have seen many older women who are dependent on tranquillisers that were inappropriately prescribed for them at menopause. Drugs such as Valium, Serepax, Librium and Tranxene can have side effects that include anxiety, disorientation, nervousness, forgetfulness and confusion. Women who take these drugs become afraid to come off them; they are highly addictive and women worry that they will not be able to cope without them.

Who can forget Thalidomide, the morning sickness drug that caused terrible birth defects. It is still being prescribed by doctors as a treatment for leprosy to fertile women in some Third World countries.

Thousands of mothers were given a drug to prevent miscarriage called Diethylstilbestrol (DES). This was a synthetic oestrogen prescribed during the 1940s through to the 1960s when the first cases of vaginal cancer in teenage girls began to appear. These women were exposed to this dangerous drug while they were inside their mother's womb. The women who took the drug had an increased risk of breast cancer and their daughters were at risk of vaginal and cervical cancer, miscarriage, reproductive and genital abnormalities. It is not known how many young women have been affected. Is it possible that this is one of the reasons why there are such high levels of breast and cervical cancers today?

Then there was the Dalkon shield and problems with breast implants. Also, some women have developed, or have a possible risk of developing, the deadly Creutzfeldt-Jakob Disease (CJD) because they were administered contaminated growth hormone, and an increasing number of women are developing hepatitis C from surgical procedures.

I despair when I think of the women who come to see me who have had hysterectomies and oophorectomies, some as young as eighteen years, who are now having to deal with osteoporosis, infertility and hormonal imbalances. It is tragic to discover that many of these women had this invasive surgery performed unnecessarily because they had heavy or painful periods. This seemed to be more common during the 1970s and early '80s. The long-term effects for some have been devastating. Permanent sterility, premature ageing, emotional instability and osteoporosis is a high price to pay for a cure.

A growing majority of women today are fed up with taking pills. Very few women are embracing hormone therapy and there is a return to natural family planning techniques. Women of all generations are questioning a medical system that supports a pharmaceutical industry and encourages drug dependency.

There are other systems of medicine that incorporate a wholistic approach to healing and include safe and effective ways to achieve good health and wellbeing. Nature has provided us with an abundance of substances, without harmful side effects, that we have used effectively to heal our bodies for centuries. There is an increasing shift toward these more natural forms of medicine, with many traditional therapies experiencing a renewed popularity. I hope this book has demystified some of these therapies and their role in women's health care today.

On a personal level, I have spent a lot of time planning, thinking, researching and writing this book and although the project is finished for now, my gathering of women's health information is ongoing. I invite readers to share their healing experiences with me because their contributions and suggestions are valuable for the continuation and upgrading of this publication in the future.

Resources

Australian Natural Therapists
Association Ltd
PO Box A964, Sydney South
NSW 2000
Ph (02) 283 2234
Fax (02) 267 4260
Freecall 1800 817 577

Australian Traditional Medicine Society
PO Box 1027, Meadowbank
NSW 2114
Ph (02) 808 2825
Fax (02) 809 7570

Crisis Line, Northern Territory
Freecall 1800 019 116

Dawn House Women's Shelter
Northern Territory
Ph 089 451 388

Family Planning Australia Inc
PO Box 26, Deakin West
ACT 2600
Ph (06) 285 1244
Family Planning has branches in every
state.

HIV Information Line and Referral
Service
150 Albion Street, Surry Hills
NSW 2010
Ph (02) 332 4000
For deaf and hearing impaired
(TTY) (02) 332 4268
NSW Freecall 1800 451 600
Australia Freecall 1800 011 180

Mudjin–Gal.Aboriginal Corporation
231 Abercrombie Street, Chippendale
New South Wales
Ph (02) 319 2613
Fax (02) 319 0643

National Herbalists Association of
Australia
PO Box 61, Broadway
NSW 2007
Ph (02) 211 6437
Fax (02) 211 6452

NSW Women's Information and
Referral Service (WIRS)
Ph (02) 334 1160
Freecall 1800 817 227

TTY Freecall 1800 673 304

Office of the Status of Women
Tasmania
(for referral and information)
Ph (002) 33 2208
Freecall 1800 001 377

Women's Infolink, Queensland
Ph (07) 229 1264
Freecall 1800 177 577
TTY (07) 221 3343

Women's Information and Referral
Centre
ACT
Ph (06) 205 1075

Women's Information and Referral
Exchange
Victoria
Ph (03) 654 6844
Freecall and TTY 1800 136 570

Women's Information Service
Western Australia
Ph (09) 264 1900
Freecall and TTY 1800 100 9174

Women's Information Switchboard
South Australia
Ph (08) 223 1244
Freecall 1800 188 158
TTY (08) 232 1453

Further Reading

Balaskas, Janet, *Active Birth*, Allen & Unwin Pty Ltd, Sydney, 1983

Balaskas, Janet, *The Active Birth Partners Handbook*, Sidgwick & Jackson, London, 1984

Beckham, Nancy, *Menopause: A Positive Approach Using Natural Therapies*, Penguin Books Ltd, Melbourne, 1995

Bremness, Lesley, *Herbs*, HarperCollins, Australia, 1994

Coelho, Paulo, *The Alchemist: A Fable about Following Your Dream*, HarperCollins, San Francisco, 1993

Cooper, Deborah and Cabot, Sandra, *The Body Shaping Diet*, Women's Health Advisory Service, Sydney, 1993

Greer, Germaine, *The Change: Women, Ageing and the Menopause*, Penguin Books Ltd, Melbourne, 1991

Hay, Louise L., *You Can Heal Your Life*, Specialist Publications, Sydney, 1984

Kenton, Suzannah and Kenton, Leslie, *Endless Energy: For Women on the Move*, Random House Australia Pty Ltd, Sydney, 1993

Lockie, Andrew and Geddes, Nicola, *The Women's Guide to Homoeopathy*, Hamish Hamilton Ltd, London, 1992

Parvati, Jeannine, *Hygieia: A Woman's Herbal*, Freestone Collective; Pan, USA, 1978

Somer, Elizabeth, *Nutrition for Women: The Complete Guide*, Bookman Press, Melbourne, 1993

Watts, Quentin, *Wake Up to Yourself: The Wisdom of Dreaming*, ABC Books, Sydney, 1995

Wolf, Naomi, *The Beauty Myth: How Images of Beauty are used Against Women*, Random House Pty Ltd, Sydney, 1990

Valins, Linda, *The Feminine Principle*, Penguin Books Ltd, Melbourne, 1993

Index

Also available from Random House Australia

Spirited Women
Petrea King

Spirited Women addresses the many practical as well as emotional issues faced by women of diverse backgrounds as they journey with the experience of breast cancer. *Spirited Women* is based on the experiences of hundreds of women who talk frankly and bravely about how breast cancer has changed their priorities, affected their self-esteem, their sexuality and their relationships, and has provided unexpected opportunities for growth.

This book offers guidelines for dealing with the diagnosis, choosing a doctor and treatment plan, minimising the effects of chemotherapy and radiotherapy, using food to support recovery, communicating effectively with partners and families and on how to find peace.

Gentle, honest, informative and moving, *Spirited Women* is an essential book for anyone whose life has been touched by breast cancer.

Petrea King is a naturopath, counsellor and meditation teacher who, since her recovery from leukaemia in 1983 has specialised in working with people with life-threatening illnesses. Petrea lives in Bundanoon, NSW where she runs residential programs for women with breast cancer and others affected by life-threatening illnesses.

Australian RRP: $19.95

The Body Bible
Pamela Allardice

Smooth, caress and nourish your body with products from Nature's bountiful storehouse. What better way to care for your body than with fresh, natural products you have lovingly created yourself. *The Body Bible* contains more than 250 recipes featuring a wonderful array of ingredients so you can nurture and pamper yourself from top to toe.

Cherish your skin with lavender beauty water, luxuriate in a bath scented with sweet rose oil or soothe tired muscles using lime flower massage oil. Cleansers, moisturisers, lotions, oils, masks and powders can all be made simply and inexpensively using the recipes in this book.

And you need look no further than the kitchen for many of the ingredients.

This is an essential guide to total body care that shows you how to nurture and beautify the body from within as well as without. Rejuvenate and invigorate your whole being with a selection of tonics and teas. Maintain a glowing vitality by eating the right foods and taking the right vitamins.

With many helpful hints and pointers along the way for dealing with complaints and problem areas, and an A–Z of plants and herbs for health and beauty, *The Body Bible* is one book you can't afford to have far from your side.

Australian RRP: $19.95

Jobs for the Girls
Caro Llewellyn and Skye Rogers

Motivated by a desire to share their own experiences and discover how other women succeed, Caro Llewellyn and Skye Rogers have compiled this fascinating collection of interviews with 24 women from around Australia who run their own businesses.

With engaging frankness, each of the women talk in detail about their experiences, from the moment they decided to take the plunge through to where they are today. Recurring themes include the challenge of balancing work and family life, securing financial support, working in a partnership, and coping with the everyday crises that inevitably occur.

From dog washing to whale watching, through opera singing, jewellery making, magazine publishing, fashion, building construction, real estate, childcare and a whole host of others, each of these women know well the challenges and joys of self-determination.

If you are one of the many Australian women considering a business of your own and you want information or inspiration, or if you just want to dream about the possibilities, then this book is for you!

A refreshing, practical and inspirational book for anyone considering a business of their own.

Australian RRP: $19.95

Different Kids
Sue Dengate

Do teachers, friends, and family members say that your child is lazy and untidy, easily bored and just needs a firm hand? Is restless and can't sit still, or goes beserk after eating junk food? Has trouble making friends and could do better if they tried?

All these things are typical of children with Attention Deficit Disorder (ADD) and this book is the story of how one mother turned detective to help her child.

Hundreds of parents of ADD children have talked to Sue Dengate in her role as coordinator of a large ADD support group. This book recounts her story, a fascinating and moving account of a mother determined to find answers. Investigating the latest research, she finds an astonishingly successful solution which helps not only her own family but many others as well. It will inspire and challenge others on the same search.

Australian RRP: $17.95